Table of Contents

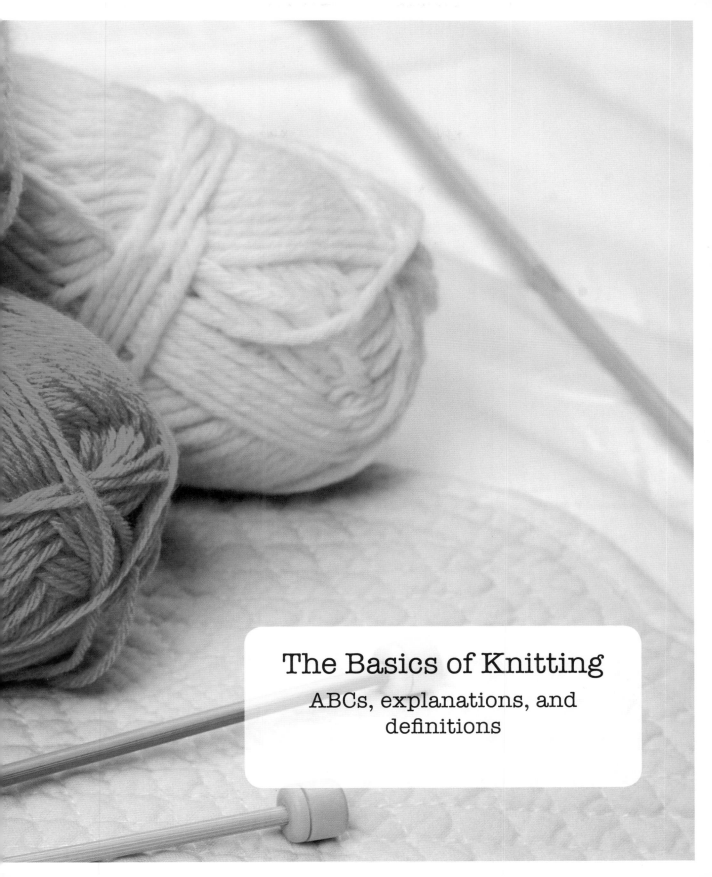

The Basics of Knitting

ABCs, explanations, and definitions

Casting on

To begin knitting you need to mount stitches onto your needles, or cast on.

1. Tuck the end of a knitting needle under your arm or secure it somewhere. From your ball of yarn, pull out a length of yarn that is 3 times the width of what you're going to knit.

2. Knot the yarn on the knitting needle: this is your first stitch. Turn the knot so it's beneath the needle. Now you have a length of yarn on each side of the needle, one in your right hand, the other in your left hand. The yarn from the ball of yarn should be in your left hand; the loose end of yarn, in your right hand.

3. Make a large loop around your right index finger.

4. Insert the needle into the loop without letting the yarn slip off your finger.

5. Loop the yarn in your left hand around the needle.

6. Slip the loop on your right index finger over the tip of the needle, and when it is under the needle, take out your finger.

7. Pull gently on the two ends of yarn to form the stitch.

8. Continue making stitches this way until you have created the desired number of stitches. Pull gently on the ends of yarn in the same way with each stitch in order to get an even row of stitches.

Trick:

Once you've cast on, cut the loose end of yarn to a length of about 4 inches to avoid using the wrong end of the yarn when knitting.

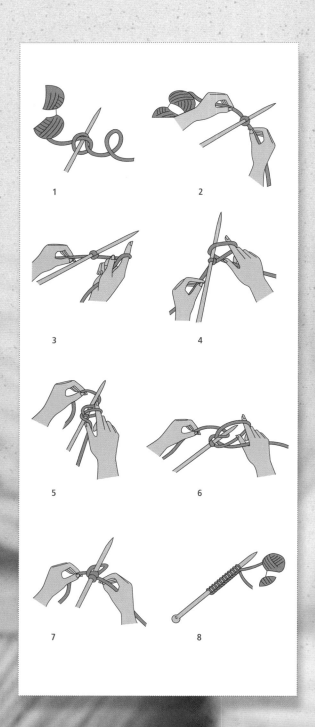

Knit stitch

Now that you know how to cast on, you can learn how to do a knit stitch.

NOTE: In knitting instructions, a knit stitch is abbreviated with a "k." For example, "k1" means "knit 1 stitch."

1. Hold the knitting needle with the row of stitches in your left hand. The loose yarn should be in back of your work. Hold the other knitting needle in your right hand and insert the tip of the right needle into the first stitch on the left needle, going from left to right. The tip of the right needle should cross behind the tip of the left needle.

2. Loop the yarn over the tip of the right needle as shown, going from left to right. Bring the right needle with the yarn back through the stitch.

3. Then carefully pull the first stitch on the left needle off the needle very gently so the rest of the stitches don't come off with it.

4. Now you know how to do a knit stitch.

Purl stitch

NOTE: In knitting instructions, a purl stitch is abbreviated with a "p." For example, "p1" means "purl 1 stitch."

1. Bring the loose yarn in front of your work. Insert the right knitting needle into the first stitch on the left needle, going through the stitch from right to left. The tip of the right needle should cross in front of the left needle.

2. Loop the yarn around the tip of the right knitting needle as shown, going from right to left.

3. Pull the loop to the back through the stitch and move the old stitch towards the tip of the left knitting needle.

4. Let the old stitch come off the left knitting needle and keep the new stitch on the right needle. Now you know how to do a purl stitch.

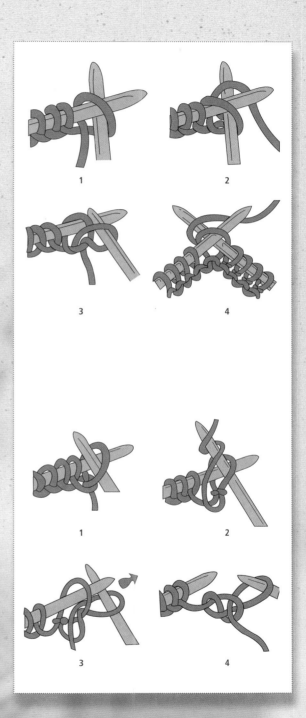

The Basics of Knitting

Changing balls of yarn

While knitting, at some point you will run out of yarn and need to switch to a new ball.

At what point: When you're near the end of the ball and have finished a row of stitches, check to make sure that there is enough yarn left in the ball to knit the next row (approximately 3 times the width of what you are knitting).

If there isn't enough, let the end of the ball of yarn hang down and cut it to about 8 inches in length. Knit the next row with a new skein. That way you will avoid creating a knot in the middle of your knitted piece. The two loose ends of yarn will be sewn into the knitted piece with a yarn or tapestry needle.

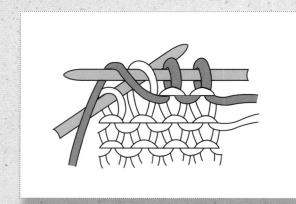

Sewing in the yarn ends

On all work, you must hide the ends of yarn left on the sides of your knitted piece. On the wrong side of your knitted piece, thread a yarn needle with one of the loose yarn ends and sew the loose yarn into an inch or two of stitches. Cut the leftover yarn.

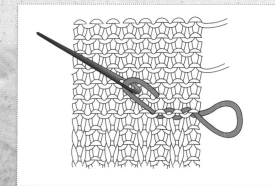

Casting off

To finish your knit piece you must close off the stitches, or cast off.

1. Knit the first two stitches on your left needle.

2. With the tip of your left needle, lift the first stitch on the right needle. Make sure to secure the second stitch in place on the right needle by pulling the yarn end gently with your right hand.

3. Slip the lifted first stitch over the second stitch.

4. Let the lifted stitch slide over and off the right needle. There is only one stitch remaining on the right needle. Knit the next stitch on the left needle. Now there are again two stitches on the right needle. Repeat the same procedure, starting with the directions in Step 2.

5. To cast off all the stitches, repeat until the last stitch remains on the right needle. Cut the yarn and slip it through this stitch, then pull it off the needle.

Trick:

Knit very loosely when you are casting off, as cast-off stitches are not elastic, and if you knit tightly your work may pucker or be too small at the edge for your intended use.

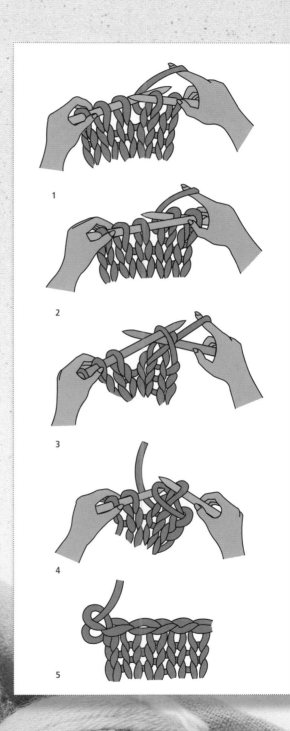

1

2

3

4

5

Tension sample

It is important to knit a tension sample, or gauge swatch, before starting your piece.
This allows you to check whether what you knit (the number of rows and stitches per row needed to get the proper dimensions) coincides with the directions given, depending on the tension of your knitting.
You can adjust your knitting with larger or smaller needles.
When beginning to create knitted clothing, you must make a sample in order to produce the correct size for the pattern you choose.
Therefore, making a tension sample is never a waste of time!
In this manual, we recommend you make samples that are 6" x 6" (15 cm x 15 cm) of each type of stitch used in the pattern, eventually creating a "quilt" of sample squares.

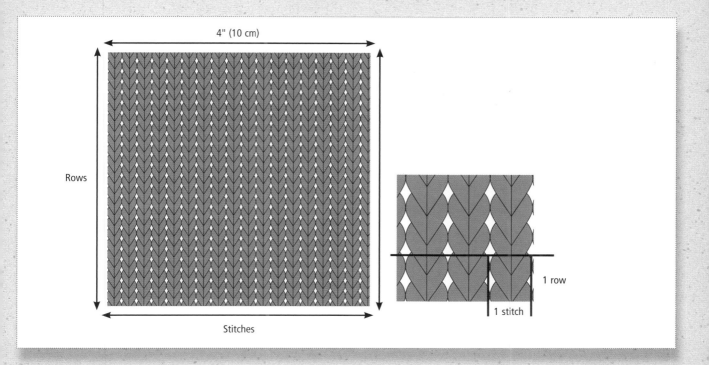

4" (10 cm)

Rows

Stitches

1 row

1 stitch

The sample should conform to the pattern in number of stitches and rows.

How to knit it:
Make a 6" (15 cm) square by casting on half again as many stitches as the number given in the directions for a length of 4" (10 cm). (For knits that have a design, keep in mind the number of stitches needed to knit the entire design.)

How to count stitches:
Using safety pins, mark off a 4" x 4" (10 cm x 10 cm) square in the middle of the sample. Count the number of stitches and rows in that square.

If you have more stitches and rows than indicated by the directions:
This means that the tension of your knitting is tight, so use bigger needles.

If you have fewer stitches and rows than indicated by the directions:
This means that the tension of your knitting is loose, so use smaller needles.

Trick:
We recommend that on the instructions for size-specific patterns, you indicate the size you want to make your piece to avoid mistakes.

Picking up dropped stitches

If you drop a stitch, don't panic! With the help of a crochet hook, you can pick up the dropped stitch and put it back in its proper place.

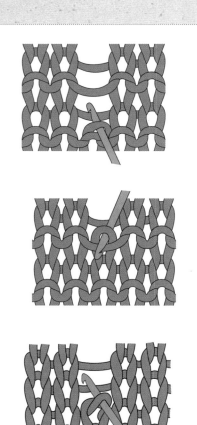

In garter stitch (each row is done in knit stitch)
The dropped stitch is between two rows of the garter stitch.
Insert the crochet hook into the dropped stitch. With the tip of the crochet hook, hook the horizontal yarn just above the dropped stitch.
Now the dropped stitch is at the level of a row of garter stitch.
Reverse the direction of the crochet hook.
Insert the crochet hook into the dropped stitch (that is, the stitch you've just re-made).
With the tip of the crochet hook, hook the horizontal yarn below the dropped stitch.
Pull that yarn through the dropped stitch.
Repeat these two pick-up procedures until you have reached the desired level. Put the picked-up stitch on the left needle and knit it normally.

In a knit row of stockinette stitch (alternate knit one row, purl one row)
Insert the crochet hook into the dropped stitch. With the tip of the crochet hook, hook the horizontal yarn just above the dropped stitch.
Pull the crochet hook towards you and pass the yarn through the stitch on the crochet hook.
Repeat this procedure until you have reached the desired level.
Place the picked-up stitch on the left needle and knit it normally.

Stitch

The foundation of knitting is the loop. Secured by a knot, it forms the first stitch of the work. Stitches are chained to each other from that first row of cast-on stitches. It is the loops themselves that are knit, slipped, increased, crossed, twisted, cast off, etc.

Selvedge stitch

The first stitch and the last stitch of each row are called selvedge stitches. They form the selvedges, or the right and left edges of the knitted piece, which are used to sew parts of the garment together.

Pattern stitch

To avoid confusion, stitches that combine to form a pattern will be identified by the pattern stitch name. This is to be differentiated from the word "stitch" by itself, which signifies each loop of a pattern. A pattern stitch is the configuration, on one or more rows, of groups of stitches worked alternately on the right and wrong sides of the piece, and cast off, knit together, crossed, etc., in such a way as to form a design that is repeated in the work. A pattern stitch is differentiated from the pattern itself, which is the design and style of the garment as given in the directions.

Names of pattern stitches

Pattern stitches are most often named because of how they look and certain motifs that they evoke. Some have very old names that are part of the tradition of knitting.

Families of pattern stitches

Basic patterns or uncommon patterns, full or lacy patterns, smooth patterns or patterns in relief, conservative or spectacular patterns, quick patterns or those requiring patience, patterns you should know by heart or those you discover—they are all the result of a series of stitches repeated row after row using certain techniques. These techniques have guided our choice in presenting the patterned stitches of this collection and in placing them in "family" groups.

Difficulty

The difficulty of a pattern stitch doesn't necessarily depend on the number of rows required for each motif but on the number of rows that are different from each other. It also varies according to the techniques employed and their ease of use. Finally, certain pattern stitches that are easy to execute in straight knitting sections are less simple when it comes to doing them in sections that require increases or decreases in stitches. They should therefore be chosen wisely. Most important of all, the initial tension sample should be knit in order to familiarize yourself with the pattern stitch and gain ease with it.

Right side, wrong side

Some pattern stitches are similar on the right side of the work (the side that will be the right side, or outside, of your finished article) and the wrong side (the wrong side, or inside, of your finished piece) of the work (for example: Garter Stitch, Seed Stitch, Checkerboard Stitch, Fisherman's Rib, etc.), but keep in mind that even if the two sides of a piece look identical, the right edge and left edge may be different. There might be a difference from row to row (for example: the last row of garter stitch is in knit stitch on the right side of the work; on the wrong side of the work, it is purled); or the selvedges might be different (for example: in ribbing, if, besides the stitches on the selvedges, the first and last stitches of the row are double knit on the right side, they will look sunken on the wrong side and will be purled). In fact, most pattern stitches look completely different on the right side than they do on the wrong side, even though the wrong side may sometimes be just as beautiful and even preferable.

The Basics of Knitting

Diagonals

All the diagonals in this book are explained going both toward the right and toward the left. Even though these directions may seem superfluous to experienced knitters, they will undoubtedly be appreciated by less experienced users of this guide. These directions will allow the latter to prepare and easily execute diagonals that mirror each other (for example: the two front pieces of a cardigan; the high or low point of a V-neck; and the front, back, and sleeves of a garment).

Effect

You can create different effects with each pattern stitch, depending on the type of materials used (classic, fluffy, bouclé, lamé, etc.), the thickness of the yarn, and even the color of the yarn. Give your creativity free rein.

Interruption of a row

It is not recommended to interrupt your work in the middle of a row because slight flaws can be created by a slackening of the yarn when you start knitting again. More importantly, beginners risk re-starting the knitting in the wrong direction. If such a break is unavoidable (an unexpected interruption, a phone call), be ready with a marker (a safety pin or an adhesive label) that will allow you to find which side (right or wrong) you were working on.

Be careful: whenever your knitting is interrupted (whether at the end of a row or in the middle), if you're working on a complex pattern stitch that you don't yet know perfectly by heart, make a note of the number of the last row you executed.

Yarn over

To do a yarn over means to pass the yarn over or around the right needle before knitting a stitch. In a knit row, bring the yarn to the front and then pass it over the needle from front to back; in a purl row, loop it around from front to back. A yarn over adds a stitch to the work if it is knit once in the next row; it adds several stitches if you knit into it several times in the next row. It does not add a stitch if compensation is made by decreasing a stitch, whether the decrease is made in a hidden section of the work or by knitting the yarn over together with the next stitch. In any case, the role of a yarn over is decorative, whether it forms an eyelet or, cast off over several stitches, it seems to connect them.

NOTE: In knitting instructions, a yarn over is abbreviated as "yo." For example, "yo1" means "yarn over once." If you see "yo2," "yo3," etc., wrap the yarn around the needle the indicated number of times.

Asterisk

(symbol in the form of a star * or a circle °)
The directions between two asterisks or circles should be repeated the entire length of the row. This section will correspond to the number of stitches necessary for the pattern repeat (see the section entitled "Frame" under "Chart"). Outside these symbols are stitches that are needed for symmetry, seams, selvedges. In some directions the asterisk and circle are replaced by parentheses ( ).

Row

A row is the collection of stitches on a single needle. The first row of the work is the one that comes right after the cast on row of stitches; that is, it is the first row that is knitted. All the odd-numbered rows follow from this first row; these are rows that usually comprise the right side of the work unless some technical or decorative reason exists to start on the wrong side.

Chart

The chart is given in the form of a grid of squares where each square is equivalent to a stitch and each line of squares represents a row. The squares are filled with standard symbols that indicate how to knit the stitches.

In addition, each chart includes the following:

1) Numbering, on the right and on the left, of the rows that comprise the pattern to be repeated;
2) Frame: the frame demarcates, in width and height, the pattern to be repeated by indicating the number of stitches and the number of rows in the pattern. Some frames give displacements—for example, staggered patterns;
3) Under this frame, numbered stitches that comprise the pattern to be repeated;
4) Arrow: the arrow at the first row indicates whether this row is done on the right side of the work (arrow on the right; in this case, which is the most common, the numbering of odd rows is on the right side) or on the wrong side of the work (arrow on the left; in which case the numbering of odd rows is on the left).

Reading

From right to left for each odd row (right side of the work);
From left to right for each even row (wrong side of the work).
If you knit in the round (on circular or double-pointed needles), therefore always knitting on the same side of the work, you should read the grid from right to left for each row.
For an explanation of symbols and abbreviations, see the key beneath each chart, further explained below.

Chart symbols

Each chart is accompanied by a legend: these are the symbols that represent the right side of the work. This allows you to visualize the right side of the work in a precise and visually descriptive way, to use the chart easily to place the stitches, assure symmetry of patterns, and anticipate seam connections.

Abbreviations of unusual or complex stitches are explained in and below the chart legend.

Knit and Purl Stitches

Even the simple combination of these basic stitches can create an infinite number of patterns.

Knit and Purl Stitches

Knit Stockinette Stitch

Using two needles:
Row 1 (right side of work): all knit.
Row 2: all purl.
Keep repeating these 2 rows.

Knitting in the round: Use knit stitch continuously.

 ☐ knit stitch on right side or purl stitch on wrong side

Purled Stockinette Stitch

Using two needles:
Row 1 (right side of work): all purl.
Row 2: all knit.
Keep repeating these 2 rows.

Knitting in the round: Use purl stitch continuously. Or simply use Knit Stockinette Stitch on the wrong side of the work.

 ⊟ purl stitch on right side or knit stitch on wrong side

Garter Stitch

Using two needles:
Knit either always using knit stitch or always using purl stitch. The wrong side of the work is similar to the right side.
Our recommendation: Be careful to count the rows. On both the wrong side and the right side, rows alternate between one row that is indented and one row that appears in relief.

 ☐ knit stitch on right side or purl stitch on wrong side
⊟ purl stitch on right side or knit stitch on wrong side

Seed Stitch

Number of stitches needed for symmetry: multiple of 2 + 1 + 1 selvedge stitch on each end.

Row 1 (right side of work): 1 selvedge stitch, *k1, p1*; repeat from * to *; end with k1, 1 selvedge stitch.

Row 2: same as Row 1.

Keep repeating these 2 rows.

The stitches are thus opposites from row to row. The stitch that appears to be a purl is knitted and the stitch that appears to be a knit is purled.

☐ knit stitch on right side or purl stitch on wrong side
— purl stitch on right side or knit stitch on wrong side

Moss Stitch

Number of stitches needed for symmetry: multiple of 2 + 1 + 1 selvedge stitch on each end.

Row 1 (right side of work): 1 selvedge stitch, *k1, p1*; repeat from * to *; end with k1, 1 selvedge stitch.

Rows 2 and 4: knit each stitch as it appears in previous row (i.e., knit a knit stitch, purl a purl stitch).

Row 3: 1 selvedge stitch, *p1, k1*; repeat from * to *; end with p1, 1 selvedge stitch.

Keep repeating these 4 rows. Thus the stitches are contrasted, or opposites, every other row.

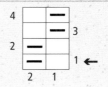

☐ knit stitch on right side or purl stitch on wrong side
— purl stitch on right side or knit stitch on wrong side

Rib Stitch k1, p1

Number of stitches needed for symmetry: multiple of 2 + 1 + 1 selvedge stitch on each end.

Row 1 (right side of work): 1 selvedge stitch, *k1, p1*; repeat from * to *; end with k1, 1 selvedge stitch.

Row 2 and each successive row: knit each stitch as it appears in previous row (i.e., knit a knit stitch, purl a purl stitch).

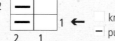

☐ knit stitch on right side or purl stitch on wrong side
— purl stitch on right side or knit stitch on wrong side

19

Knit and Purl Stitches

Rib Stitch k1, p2

Number of stitches needed for symmetry: multiple of 3 + 1 + 1 selvedge stitch on each end.

Row 1 (right side of work): 1 selvedge stitch, *k1, p2*; repeat from * to *; end with k1, 1 selvedge stitch.

Row 2 and each successive row: knit each stitch as it appears in previous row (i.e., knit a knit stitch, purl a purl stitch).

On the wrong side of the work, the ribs appear as *p1, k2*.

Rib Stitch k2, p2

Number of stitches needed for symmetry: multiple of 4 + 2 + 1 selvedge stitch on each end.

Row 1 (right side of work): 1 selvedge stitch, *k2, p2*; repeat from * to *; end with k2, 1 selvedge stitch.

Row 2 and each successive row: knit each stitch as it appears in previous row (i.e., knit a knit stitch, purl a purl stitch).

☐ knit stitch on right side or purl stitch on wrong side

– purl stitch on right side or knit stitch on wrong side

Rib Stitch k3, p2

Number of stitches needed for symmetry: multiple of 5 + 2 + 1 selvedge stitch on each end.

Row 1 (right side of work): 1 selvedge stitch, *k3, p2*; repeat from * to *; end with p2, 1 selvedge stitch.

Row 2 and each successive row: knit each stitch as it appears in previous row (i.e., knit a knit stitch, purl a purl stitch).

On the wrong side of the work, the ribs appear as *k2, p3*.

☐ knit stitch on right side or purl stitch on wrong side

– purl stitch on right side or knit stitch on wrong side

Rib Stitch k5, p1

Number of stitches needed for symmetry: multiple of 6 + 5 + 1 selvedge stitch on each end.

Row 1 (right side of work): 1 selvedge stitch, *k5, p1*; repeat from * to *; end with k5, 1 selvedge stitch.

Row 2 and each successive row: knit each stitch as it appears in previous row (i.e., knit a knit stitch, purl a purl stitch).

On the wrong side of the work, the ribs appear as *p5, k1*.

knit stitch on right side or purl stitch on wrong side
− purl stitch on right side or knit stitch on wrong side

Caterpillar Stitch

Number of stitches needed for symmetry: multiple of 6 + 1 + 1 selvedge stitch on each end.

Rows 1 (right side of work), 3, and 5: 1 selvedge stitch, *k1, p5*; repeat from * to *; end with k1, 1 selvedge stitch.

Row 2 and all even numbered rows: knit each stitch as it appears in previous row (i.e., knit a knit stitch, purl a purl stitch).

Rows 7, 9, and 11: 1 selvedge stitch, *p3, k1, p2*; repeat from * to *; end with p1, 1 selvedge stitch.

Keep repeating these 12 rows.

knit stitch on right side or purl stitch on wrong side
− purl stitch on right side or knit stitch on wrong side

Garter Ribbing k3, p3

Number of stitches needed for symmetry: multiple of 6 + 3 + 1 selvedge stitch on each end.

Row 1 (right side of work): all knit.

Row 2: 1 selvedge stitch, p3, *k3, p3*; repeat from * to *; end with 1 selvedge stitch.

Keep repeating these 2 rows.

knit stitch on right side or purl stitch on wrong side
− purl stitch on right side or knit stitch on wrong side

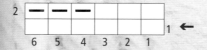

21

Knit and Purl Stitches

Garter Ribbing k2, p2

Number of stitches needed for symmetry: multiple of 4 + 2 + 1 selvedge stitch on each end.

Row 1 (right side of work): all knit.

Row 2: 1 selvedge stitch, p2, *k2, p2*; repeat from * to *; end with 1 selvedge stitch.

Keep repeating these 2 rows.

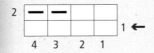

☐ knit stitch on right side or purl stitch on wrong side

— purl stitch on right side or knit stitch on wrong side

Garter Ribbing k1, p2

Number of stitches needed for symmetry: multiple of 3 + 1 + 1 selvedge stitch on each end.

Row 1 (right side of work): all knit.

Row 2: 1 selvedge stitch, p1, *k2, p1*; repeat from * to *; end with 1 selvedge stitch.

Keep repeating these 2 rows.

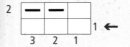

☐ knit stitch on right side or purl stitch on wrong side

— purl stitch on right side or knit stitch on wrong side

Sand Stitch

Number of stitches needed for symmetry: multiple of 2 + 1 + 1 selvedge stitch on each end.

Row 1 (right side of work): all knit.

Row 2: 1 selvedge stitch, p1, *k1, p1*; repeat from * to *; end with 1 selvedge stitch.

Keep repeating these 2 rows.

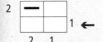

☐ knit stitch on right side or purl stitch on wrong side

— purl stitch on right side or knit stitch on wrong side

Seed Stitch with Ribbing

Number of stitches needed for symmetry: multiple of 5 + 2 + 1 selvedge stitch on each end.
Row 1 (right side of work): 1 selvedge stitch, *k3, p1, k1*; repeat from * to *; end with k2, 1 selvedge stitch.
Row 2: 1 selvedge stitch, p2, *k1, p1, k1 (these 3 stitches will be contrary or opposite stitches—see Seed Stitch on p. 19), p2*; repeat from * to *; end with 1 selvedge stitch.
Keep repeating these 2 rows.

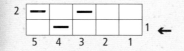

☐ knit stitch on right side or purl stitch on wrong side
− purl stitch on right side or knit stitch on wrong side

Fancy Seed Stitch with Ribbing

Number of stitches needed for symmetry: multiple of 6 + 4 + 1 selvedge stitch on each end.
Row 1 (right side of work): 1 selvedge stitch, *p5, k1*; repeat from * to *; end with p4, 1 selvedge stitch.
Row 2: 1 selvedge stitch, k4, *k1, p1, k4*; repeat from * to *; end with 1 selvedge stitch.
Keep repeating these 2 rows.

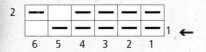

☐ knit stitch on right side or purl stitch on wrong side
− purl stitch on right side or knit stitch on wrong side

False Fisherman Stitch No. 1

Number of stitches needed for symmetry: multiple of 4 + 1 + 1 selvedge stitch on each end.
Row 1 (right side of work): 1 selvedge stitch, *k2, p1, k1*; repeat from * to *; end with k1, 1 selvedge stitch.
Row 2: 1 selvedge stitch, p1, *k3, p1*; repeat from * to *; end with 1 selvedge stitch.
Keep repeating these 2 rows.

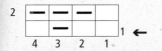

☐ knit stitch on right side or purl stitch on wrong side
− purl stitch on right side or knit stitch on wrong side

False Fisherman Stitch No. 2

Number of stitches needed for symmetry: multiple of 4 + 1 + 1 selvedge stitch on each end.

Row 1 (right side of work): 1 selvedge stitch, *k2, p2*; repeat from * to *; end with k1, 1 selvedge stitch.

Row 2: 1 selvedge stitch, p1, *p1, k2, p1*; repeat from * to *; end with 1 selvedge stitch.

Keep repeating these 2 rows.

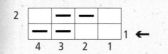

☐ knit stitch on right side or purl stitch on wrong side

— purl stitch on right side or knit stitch on wrong side

Farrow Stitch

Number of stitches needed for symmetry: multiple of 3 + 1 + 1 selvedge stitch on each end.

Row 1 (right side of work): 1 selvedge stitch, *k2, p1*; repeat from * to *; end with k1, 1 selvedge stitch.

Row 2: 1 selvedge stitch, p1, *k2, p1*; repeat from * to *; end with 1 selvedge stitch.

Keep repeating these 2 rows.

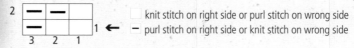

☐ knit stitch on right side or purl stitch on wrong side

— purl stitch on right side or knit stitch on wrong side

Sandy Ribbing

Number of stitches needed for symmetry: multiple of 4 + 1 + 1 selvedge stitch on each end.

Row 1 (right side of work): 1 selvedge stitch, *p1, k3*; repeat from * to *; end with p1, 1 selvedge stitch.

Row 2: 1 selvedge stitch, k1, *p1, k1, p1, k1*; repeat from * to *; end with 1 selvedge stitch.

Keep repeating these 2 rows.

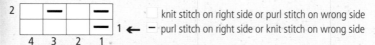

☐ knit stitch on right side or purl stitch on wrong side

— purl stitch on right side or knit stitch on wrong side

Piqué Stitch

Number of stitches needed for symmetry: multiple of 4 + 1 + 1 selvedge stitch on each end.

Rows 1 (right side of work), 3, 5, and 7: all knit.

Rows 2 and 6: all purl.

Row 4: 1 selvedge stitch, k1, *p3, k1*; repeat from * to *; end with 1 selvedge stitch.

Row 8: 1 selvedge stitch, p1, *p1, k1, p2*; repeat from * to *; end with 1 selvedge stitch.

Keep repeating these 8 rows.

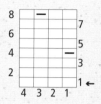

☐ knit stitch on right side or purl stitch on wrong side

— purl stitch on right side or knit stitch on wrong side

Little Raindrop Stitch

Number of stitches needed for symmetry: multiple of 4 + 3 + 1 selvedge stitch on each end.

Row 1 (right side of work): 1 selvedge stitch, *p3, k1*; repeat from * to *; end with p3, 1 selvedge stitch.

Rows 2 and 4: knit each stitch as it appears in previous row (i.e., knit a knit stitch, purl a purl stitch).

Row 3: 1 selvedge stitch, *p1, k1, p2*; repeat from * to *; end with p1, k1, p1, 1 selvedge stitch.

Keep repeating these 4 rows.

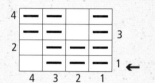

☐ knit stitch on right side or purl stitch on wrong side

— purl stitch on right side or knit stitch on wrong side

Raindrop Stitch

Number of stitches needed for symmetry: multiple of 2 + 1 + 1 selvedge stitch on each end.

Rows 1 (right side of work) and 5: all knit.

Rows 2 and 6: all purl.

Row 3: 1 selvedge stitch, *p1, k1*; repeat from * to *; end with p1, 1 selvedge stitch.

Rows 4 and 8: knit each stitch as it appears in previous row (i.e., knit a knit stitch, purl a purl stitch).

Row 7: 1 selvedge stitch, *k1, p1*; repeat from * to *; end with k1, 1 selvedge stitch.

Keep repeating these 8 rows.

☐ knit stitch on right side or purl stitch on wrong side

— purl stitch on right side or knit stitch on wrong side

Knit and Purl Stitches

Diamond Blister Stitch

Number of stitches needed for symmetry: multiple of 4 + 1 + 1 selvedge stitch on each end.

Rows 1 (right side of work) and 5: 1 selvedge stitch, *k1, p1, k1, p1*; repeat from * to *; end with k1, 1 selvedge stitch.

Row 2 and all even numbered rows: knit each stitch as it appears in previous row (i.e., knit a knit stitch, purl a purl stitch).

Row 3: 1 selvedge stitch, *p1, k3*; repeat from * to *; end with p1, 1 selvedge stitch.

Row 7: 1 selvedge stitch, *k2, p1, k1*; repeat from * to *; end with k1, 1 selvedge stitch.

Keep repeating Rows 1 through 8.

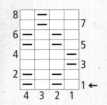

knit stitch on right side or purl stitch on wrong side

− purl stitch on right side or knit stitch on wrong side

Stockinette Stripes

Rows 1 (right side of work), 3, 4, and 6: all knit.
Rows 2 and 5: all purl.
Keep repeating these 6 rows.
Tip: Very elastic, recommended for baby clothes.

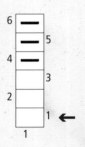

knit stitch on right side or purl stitch on wrong side

− purl stitch on right side or knit stitch on wrong side

Garter Stripes

Rows 1 (right side of work), 3, and 4: all knit.
Row 2: all purl.
Keep repeating these 4 rows.

knit stitch on right side or purl stitch on wrong side

− purl stitch on right side or knit stitch on wrong side

Garter Blocks

Number of stitches needed for symmetry: multiple of 14 + 7 + 1 selvedge stitch on each end.

Rows 1 (right side of work), 2, 3, 5, 6, and 7: all knit.

Row 4: 1 selvedge stitch, k7, *p7, k7*; repeat from * to *; end with 1 selvedge stitch.

Row 8: 1 selvedge stitch, p7, *k7, p7*; repeat from * to *; end with 1 selvedge stitch.

Keep repeating these 8 rows.

☐ knit stitch on right side or purl stitch on wrong side

— purl stitch on right side or knit stitch on wrong side

Checkerboard Stitch k5/p5

Number of stitches needed for symmetry: multiple of 10 + 5 + 1 selvedge stitch on each end.

Row 1 (right side of work): 1 selvedge stitch, *k5, p5*; repeat from * to *; end with k5, 1 selvedge stitch.

Rows 2, 3, 4, 5, 6, 7, 9, 10, 11, 12, 13, and 14: knit each stitch as it appears in previous row (i.e., knit a knit stitch, purl a purl stitch).

Row 8: 1 selvedge stitch, k5, *p5, k5*; repeat from * to *; end with 1 selvedge stitch.

Keep repeating these 14 rows.

A whole family of checked patterns can be created by varying the number of stitches and the number of rows that constitute each check.

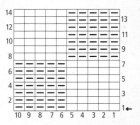

☐ knit stitch on right side or purl stitch on wrong side

— purl stitch on right side or knit stitch on wrong side

Knit and Purl Stitches

Cobblestone Stitch

Number of stitches needed for symmetry: multiple of 18 + 5 + 1 selvedge stitch on each end.

Rows 1 (right side of work), 3, 11, 13, 15, and 23: all knit.

Row 2 and all even numbered rows: knit each stitch as it appears in previous row (i.e., knit a knit stitch, purl a purl stitch).

Rows 5, 7, and 9: 1 selvedge stitch, *k9, p5, k4*; repeat from * to *; end with k5, 1 selvedge stitch.

Rows 17, 19, and 21: 1 selvedge stitch, *p5, k13*; repeat from * to *; end with p5, 1 selvedge stitch.

Keep repeating these 24 rows.

Lines of Rectangles

Number of stitches needed for symmetry: multiple of 12 + 6 + 1 selvedge stitch on each end.

Rows 1 (right side of work) and 3: 1 selvedge stitch, *k6, p6*; repeat from * to *; end with k6, 1 selvedge stitch.

Row 2 and all even numbered rows: knit each stitch as it appears in previous row (i.e., knit a knit stitch, purl a purl stitch).

Rows 5 and 11: all knit.

Rows 7 and 9: 1 selvedge stitch, *p6, k6*; repeat from * to *; end with p6, 1 selvedge stitch.

Keep repeating these 12 rows.

☐   knit stitch on right side or purl stitch on wrong side

–   purl stitch on right side or knit stitch on wrong side

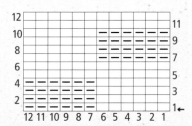

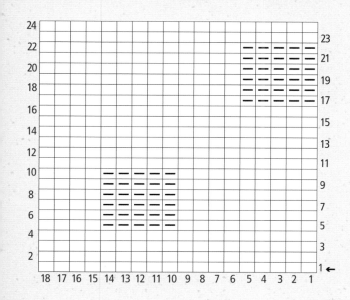

knit stitch on right side or purl stitch on wrong side
− purl stitch on right side or knit stitch on wrong side

Basketweave Stitch

knit stitch on right side or purl stitch on wrong side
− purl stitch on right side or knit stitch on wrong side

Number of stitches needed for symmetry: multiple of 6 + 2 + 1 selvedge stitch on each end.

Rows 1 (right side of work) and 7: all knit.

Rows 2 and 8: all purl.

Rows 3 and 5: 1 selvedge stitch, *k2, p4*; repeat from * to *; end with k2, 1 selvedge stitch.

Rows 4, 6, 10, and 12: knit each stitch as it appears in previous row (i.e., knit a knit stitch, purl a purl stitch).

Rows 9 and 11: 1 selvedge stitch, *p3, k2, p1*; repeat from * to *; end with p2, 1 selvedge stitch.

Keep repeating these 12 rows.

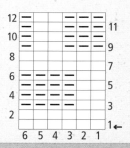

Knit and Purl Stitches

Alternating Ribbing

Number of stitches needed for symmetry and joining: multiple of 6 + 1 selvedge stitch on each end.

Rows 1 (right side of work) and 7: all knit.

Rows 2 and 8: all purl.

Row 3: 1 selvedge stitch, *k2, p2, k2*; repeat from * to *; end with 1 selvedge stitch.

Rows 4, 5, 6, 10, 11, and 12: knit each stitch as it appears in previous row (i.e., knit a knit stitch, purl a purl stitch).

Row 9: 1 selvedge stitch, *k1, p4, k1*; repeat from * to *; end with 1 selvedge stitch.

Keep repeating these 12 rows.

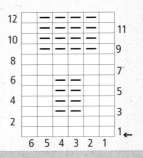

☐ knit stitch on right side or purl stitch on wrong side

− purl stitch on right side or knit stitch on wrong side

Cut Ribbing

Number of stitches needed for symmetry: multiple of 4 + 2 + 1 selvedge stitch on each end.

Row 1 (right side of work): 1 selvedge stitch, *k2, p2*; repeat from * to *; end with k2, 1 selvedge stitch.

Row 2: knit each stitch as it appears in previous row (i.e., knit a knit stitch, purl a purl stitch).

Row 3: all purl.

Row 4: all knit.

Keep repeating these 4 rows.

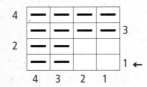

☐ knit stitch on right side or purl stitch on wrong side

− purl stitch on right side or knit stitch on wrong side

Piqué Raised Rows

Number of stitches needed for symmetry and joining: multiple of 12 + 1 selvedge stitch on each end.

Rows 1 (right side of work) and 3: all knit.

Row 2 and all even numbered rows: knit each stitch as it appears in previous row (i.e., knit a knit stitch, purl a purl stitch).

Rows 5 and 7: 1 selvedge stitch, *k3, p6*; repeat from * to *; end with k3 and 1 selvedge stitch.

Keep repeating these 8 rows.

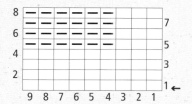

☐ knit stitch on right side or purl stitch on wrong side

− purl stitch on right side or knit stitch on wrong side

Horizontal Caterpillar Stitch

Number of stitches needed for symmetry: multiple of 10 + 4 + 1 selvedge stitch on each end.

Rows 1 (right side of work), 3, 5, and 7: all knit.

Rows 2 and 6: all purl.

Row 4: 1 selvedge stitch, p4, *k6, p4*; repeat from * to *; end with 1 selvedge stitch.

Row 8: 1 selvedge stitch, k4, *k1, p4, k5*; repeat from * to *; end with 1 selvedge stitch.

Keep repeating these 8 rows.

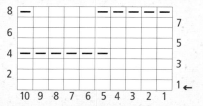

☐ knit stitch on right side or purl stitch on wrong side

− purl stitch on right side or knit stitch on wrong side

Garter Cobblestone Stitch

Number of stitches needed for joining: multiple of 12 + 1 selvedge stitch on each end.

Row 1 (right side of work) and all odd rows: all knit.

Rows 2, 10, 12, 14, 22, and 24: all purl.

Rows 4, 6, and 8: 1 selvedge stitch, *p3, k6, p3*; repeat from * to *; end with 1 selvedge stitch.

Rows 16, 18, and 20: 1 selvedge stitch, *p6, k6*; repeat from * to *; end with 1 selvedge stitch.

Keep repeating these 24 rows.

☐ knit stitch on right side or purl stitch on wrong side
− purl stitch on right side or knit stitch on wrong side

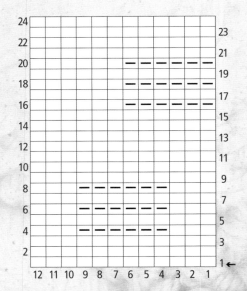

Stockinette and Garter Rectangles

Number of stitches needed for symmetry: multiple of 6 + 3 + 1 selvedge stitch on each end.

Row 1 (right side of work) and all odd rows: all knit.

Rows 2, 4, 6, 8, 10, and 12: 1 selvedge stitch, p3, *k3, p3*; repeat from * to *; end with 1 selvedge stitch.

Rows 14, 16, 18, 20, 22, and 24: 1 selvedge stitch, k3, *p3, k3*; repeat from * to *; end with 1 selvedge stitch.

Keep repeating these 24 rows.

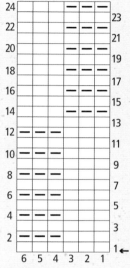

☐ knit stitch on right side or purl stitch on wrong side
— purl stitch on right side or knit stitch on wrong side

Piqué Ribbing (1)

Number of stitches needed for symmetry: multiple of 3 + 2 + 1 selvedge stitch on each end.

Rows 1 (right side of work) and 3: 1 selvedge stitch, *k2, p1*; repeat from * to *; end with k2, 1 selvedge stitch.

Row 2: knit each stitch as it appears in previous row (i.e., knit a knit stitch, purl a purl stitch).

Row 4: all knit.

Keep repeating these 4 rows.

☐ knit stitch on right side or purl stitch on wrong side
— purl stitch on right side or knit stitch on wrong side

Garter Checkerboard Stitch k5/p5

Number of stitches needed for symmetry: multiple of 10 + 5 + 1 selvedge stitch on each end.

Rows 1 (right side of work), 3, 5, and 7: 1 selvedge stitch, *k5, p5*; repeat from * to *; end with k5, 1 selvedge stitch.

Rows 2, 4, and 6: all purl.

Rows 8, 10, 12, and 14: 1 selvedge stitch, k5, *p5, k5*; repeat from * to *; end with 1 selvedge stitch.

Rows 9, 11, and 13: all knit.

Keep repeating these 14 rows.

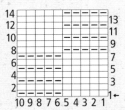

☐ knit stitch on right side or purl stitch on wrong side

— purl stitch on right side or knit stitch on wrong side

Andalusian Stitch

Number of stitches needed for symmetry: multiple of 2 + 1 + 1 selvedge stitch on each end.

Rows 1 (right side of work) and 3: all knit.

Row 2: all purl.

Row 4: 1 selvedge stitch, p1, *k1, p1*; repeat from * to *; end with 1 selvedge stitch.

Keep repeating these 4 rows.

☐ knit stitch on right side or purl stitch on wrong side

— purl stitch on right side or knit stitch on wrong side

Contrasting Andalusian Stitch

Number of stitches needed for symmetry: multiple of 2 + 1 + 1 selvedge stitch on each end.

Rows 1 (right side of work), 3, 5, and 7: all knit.

Rows 2 and 6: all purl.

Row 4: 1 selvedge stitch, p1, *k1, p1*; repeat from * to *; end with 1 selvedge stitch.

Row 8: 1 selvedge stitch, k1, *p1, k1*; repeat from * to *; end with 1 selvedge stitch.

Keep repeating these 8 rows.

☐ knit stitch on right side or purl stitch on wrong side

— purl stitch on right side or knit stitch on wrong side

Grid Stitch

Number of stitches needed for symmetry: multiple of 2 + 1 + 1 selvedge stitch on each end.

Row 1 (right side of work): 1 selvedge stitch, *k1, p1*; repeat from * to *; end with k1, 1 selvedge stitch.

Row 2: knit each stitch as it appears in previous row (i.e., knit a knit stitch, purl a purl stitch).

Rows 3 and 4: all knit.

Keep repeating these 4 rows.

☐ knit stitch on right side or purl stitch on wrong side
— purl stitch on right side or knit stitch on wrong side

Cut Staggered Row Ribbing

Number of stitches needed for symmetry: multiple of 4 + 2 + 1 selvedge stitch on each end.

Row 1 (right side of work): 1 selvedge stitch, *k2, p2*; repeat from * to *; end with k2, 1 selvedge stitch.

Rows 2 and 6: knit each stitch as it appears in previous row (i.e., knit a knit stitch, purl a purl stitch).

Rows 3, 4, 7, and 8: all knit.

Row 5: 1 selvedge stitch, *p2, k2*; repeat from * to *; end with p2, 1 selvedge stitch.

Keep repeating these 8 rows.

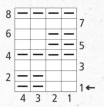

☐ knit stitch on right side or purl stitch on wrong side
— purl stitch on right side or knit stitch on wrong side

Piqué Ribbing (2)

Number of stitches needed for symmetry: multiple of 5 + 2 + 1 selvedge stitch on each end.

Rows 1 (right side of work) and 3: 1 selvedge stitch, *k2, p3*; repeat from * to *; end with k2, 1 selvedge stitch.

Row 2: knit each stitch as it appears in previous row (i.e., knit a knit stitch, purl a purl stitch).

Row 4: all knit.

Keep repeating these 4 rows.

☐ knit stitch on right side or purl stitch on wrong side
— purl stitch on right side or knit stitch on wrong side

Knit and Purl Stitches

Seed Checkerboard Stitch k6/p6

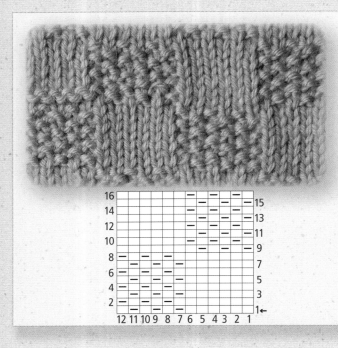

Number of stitches needed for symmetry: multiple of 12 + 6 + 1 selvedge stitch on each end.

Rows 1 (right side of work), 3, 5, and 7: 1 selvedge stitch, *k6, °p1, k1°; repeat from ° to ° another 2 times*; repeat from * to *; end with k6, 1 selvedge stitch.

Rows 2, 4, 6, and 8: 1 selvedge stitch, p6, *°k1, p1°; repeat from ° to ° another 2 times, p6*; repeat from * to *; end with 1 selvedge stitch.

Rows 9, 11, 13, and 15: 1 selvedge stitch, *°p1, k1°; repeat from ° to ° another 2 times, k6*; repeat from * to *; end with °p1, k1°; repeat from ° to ° another 2 times, 1 selvedge stitch.

Rows 10, 12, 14, and 16: 1 selvedge stitch, k1, p1, k1, p1, k1, p1, *p6, °k1, p1°; repeat from ° to ° another 2 times*; repeat from * to *; end with 1 selvedge stitch.

Keep repeating these 16 rows.

☐ knit stitch on right side or purl stitch on wrong side
— purl stitch on right side or knit stitch on wrong side

Tiles

Number of stitches needed for symmetry: multiple of 5 + 4 + 1 selvedge stitch on each end.

Rows 1 (right side of work), 3, 5, and 6: all knit.

Rows 2 and 4: 1 selvedge stitch, p4, *k1, p4*; repeat from * to *; end with 1 selvedge stitch.

Keep repeating these 6 rows.

☐ knit stitch on right side or purl stitch on wrong side
— purl stitch on right side or knit stitch on wrong side

Diagonals 1 (to the left)

Number of stitches needed for joining: multiple of 6 + 1 selvedge stitch on each end.

Row 1 (right side of work): 1 selvedge stitch, *p1, k5*; repeat from * to *; end with 1 selvedge stitch.

Row 2 and all even numbered rows: knit each stitch as it appears in previous row (i.e., knit a knit stitch, purl a purl stitch).

Row 3: 1 selvedge stitch, *k1, p1, k4*; repeat from * to *; end with 1 selvedge stitch.

Row 5: 1 selvedge stitch, *k2, p1, k3*; repeat from * to *; end with 1 selvedge stitch.

Row 7: 1 selvedge stitch, *k3, p1, k2*; repeat from * to *; end with 1 selvedge stitch.

Row 9: 1 selvedge stitch, *k4, p1, k1*; repeat from * to *; end with 1 selvedge stitch.

Row 11: 1 selvedge stitch, *k5, p1*; repeat from * to *; end with 1 selvedge stitch.

Keep repeating Rows 1 to 12. Shift one stitch to the left, on the right side of the work, every two rows.

☐ knit stitch on right side or purl stitch on wrong side

— purl stitch on right side or knit stitch on wrong side

Diagonals 1 (to the right)

Number of stitches needed for joining: multiple of 6 + 1 selvedge stitch on each end.

Row 1 (right side of work): 1 selvedge stitch, *k5, p1*; repeat from * to *; end with 1 selvedge stitch.

Row 2 and all even numbered rows: knit each stitch as it appears in previous row (i.e., knit a knit stitch, purl a purl stitch).

Row 3: 1 selvedge stitch, *k4, p1, k1*; repeat from * to *; end with 1 selvedge stitch.

Row 5: 1 selvedge stitch, *k3, p1, k2*; repeat from * to *; end with 1 selvedge stitch.

Row 7: 1 selvedge stitch, *k2, p1, k3*; repeat from * to *; end with 1 selvedge stitch.

Row 9: 1 selvedge stitch, *k1, p1, k4*; repeat from * to *; end with 1 selvedge stitch.

Row 11: 1 selvedge stitch, *p1, k5*; repeat from * to *; end with 1 selvedge stitch.

Keep repeating Rows 1 to 12. Shift one stitch to the right, on the right side of the work, every two rows.

☐ knit stitch on right side or purl stitch on wrong side

— purl stitch on right side or knit stitch on wrong side

Knit and Purl Stitches

Diagonals 2 (to the left)

Number of stitches needed for joining: multiple of 6 + 1 selvedge stitch on each end.

Row 1 (right side of work): 1 selvedge stitch, *p3, k3*; repeat from * to *; end with 1 selvedge stitch.

Row 2 and all even numbered rows: knit each stitch as it appears in previous row (i.e., knit a knit stitch, purl a purl stitch).

Row 3: 1 selvedge stitch, *k1, p3, k2*; repeat from * to *; end with 1 selvedge stitch.

Row 5: 1 selvedge stitch, *k2, p3, k1*; repeat from * to *; end with 1 selvedge stitch.

Row 7: 1 selvedge stitch, *k3, p3*; repeat from * to *; end with 1 selvedge stitch.

Row 9: 1 selvedge stitch, *p1, k3, p2*; repeat from * to *; end with 1 selvedge stitch.

Row 11: 1 selvedge stitch, *p2, k3, p1*; repeat from * to *; end with 1 selvedge stitch.

Keep repeating Rows 1 to 12. Shift one stitch to the left, on the right side of the work, every two rows.

Diagonals 2 (to the right)

Number of stitches needed for joining: multiple of 6 + 1 selvedge stitch on each end.

Row 1 (right side of work): 1 selvedge stitch, *k3, p3*; repeat from * to *; end with 1 selvedge stitch.

Row 2 and all even numbered rows: knit each stitch as it appears in previous row (i.e., knit a knit stitch, purl a purl stitch).

Row 3: 1 selvedge stitch, *k2, p3, k1*; repeat from * to *; end with 1 selvedge stitch.

Row 5: 1 selvedge stitch, *k1, p3, k2*; repeat from * to *; end with 1 selvedge stitch.

Row 7: 1 selvedge stitch, *p3, k3*; repeat from * to *; end with 1 selvedge stitch.

Row 9: 1 selvedge stitch, *p2, k3, p1*; repeat from * to *; end with 1 selvedge stitch.

Row 11: 1 selvedge stitch, *p1, k3, p2*; repeat from * to *; end with 1 selvedge stitch.

Keep repeating Rows 1 to 12. Shift one stitch to the right, on the right side of the work, every two rows.

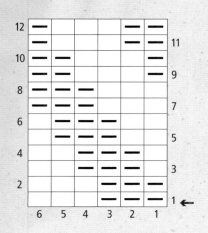

Diagonals 3 (to the left)

Number of stitches needed for joining: multiple of 4 + 1 selvedge stitch on each end.

Row 1 (right side of work): 1 selvedge stitch, *p2, k2*; repeat from * to *; end with 1 selvedge stitch.

Row 2 and all even numbered rows: knit each stitch as it appears in previous row (i.e., knit a knit stitch, purl a purl stitch).

Row 3: 1 selvedge stitch, *k1, p2, k1*; repeat from * to *; end with 1 selvedge stitch.

Row 5: 1 selvedge stitch, *k2, p2*; repeat from * to *; end with 1 selvedge stitch.

Row 7: 1 selvedge stitch, *p1, k2, p1*; repeat from * to *; end with 1 selvedge stitch.

Keep repeating Rows 1 to 8. Shift one stitch to the left, on the right side of the work, every two rows.

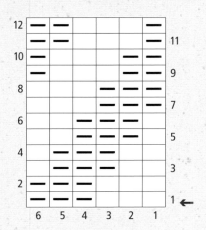

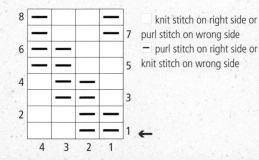

Knit and Purl Stitches

Diagonals 3 (to the right)

Number of stitches needed for joining: multiple of 4 + 1 selvedge stitch on each end.

Row 1 (right side of work): 1 selvedge stitch, *k2, p2*; repeat from * to *; end with 1 selvedge stitch.

Row 2 and all even numbered rows: knit each stitch as it appears in previous row (i.e., knit a knit stitch, purl a purl stitch).

Row 3: 1 selvedge stitch, *k1, p2, k1*; repeat from * to *; end with 1 selvedge stitch.

Row 5: 1 selvedge stitch, *p2, k2*; repeat from * to *; end with 1 selvedge stitch.

Row 7: 1 selvedge stitch, *p1, k2, p1*; repeat from * to *; end with 1 selvedge stitch.

Keep repeating Rows 1 to 8. Shift one stitch to the right, on the right side of the work, every two rows.

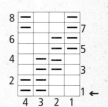

☐ knit stitch on right side or purl stitch on wrong side

— purl stitch on right side or knit stitch on wrong side

Diagonals 4 (to the left)

Number of stitches needed for joining: multiple of 6 + 1 selvedge stitch on each end.

Row 1 (right side of work): 1 selvedge stitch, *p2, k4*; repeat from * to *; end with 1 selvedge stitch.

Rows 2, 3, 4, 6, 7, 8, 10, 11, and 12: knit each stitch as it appears in previous row (i.e., knit a knit stitch, purl a purl stitch).

Row 5: 1 selvedge stitch, *k2, p2, k2*; repeat from * to *; end with 1 selvedge stitch.

Row 9: 1 selvedge stitch, *k4, p2*; repeat from * to *; end with 1 selvedge stitch.

Keep repeating these 12 rows. Shift two stitches to the left, on the right side of the work, every four rows.

On the wrong side of the work, diagonals slant to right *p4, k2*.

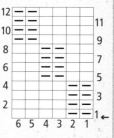

☐ knit stitch on right side or purl stitch on wrong side

— purl stitch on right side or knit stitch on wrong side

Diagonals 4 (to the right)

Number of stitches needed for joining:
multiple of 6 + 1 selvedge stitch on each end.
Row 1 (right side of work): 1 selvedge
stitch, *k4, p2*; repeat from * to *; end with
1 selvedge stitch.
Rows 2, 3, 4, 6, 7, 8, 10, 11, and 12: knit
each stitch as it appears in previous row (i.e.,
knit a knit stitch, purl a purl stitch).
Row 5: 1 selvedge stitch, *k2, p2, k2*; repeat
from * to *; end with 1 selvedge stitch.
Row 9: 1 selvedge stitch, *p2, k4*; repeat
from * to *; end with 1 selvedge stitch.
**Keep repeating these 12 rows. Shift two
stitches to the right, on the right side of
the work, every four rows.**

**On the wrong side of the work,
diagonals slant to left *p4, k2*.**

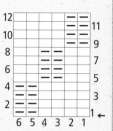

☐ knit stitch on right
side or purl stitch on
wrong side

▬ purl stitch on right
side or knit stitch on
wrong side

Diagonals 5 (to the left)

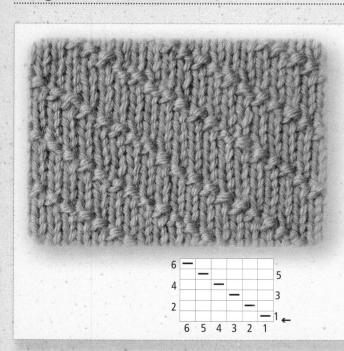

Number of stitches needed for joining: multiple of 6 + 1 selvedge stitch
on each end.
Row 1 (right side of work): 1 selvedge stitch, *p1, k5*; repeat
from * to *; end with 1 selvedge stitch.
Row 2: 1 selvedge stitch, *p4, k1, p1*; repeat from * to *; end with 1
selvedge stitch.
Row 3: 1 selvedge stitch, *k2, p1, k3*; repeat from * to *; end with 1
selvedge stitch.
Row 4: 1 selvedge stitch, *p2, k1, p3*; repeat from * to *; end with 1
selvedge stitch.
Row 5: 1 selvedge stitch, *k4, p1, k1*; repeat from * to *; end with 1
selvedge stitch.
Row 6: 1 selvedge stitch, *k1, p5*; repeat from * to *; end with 1
selvedge stitch.
**Keep repeating these 6 rows. Shift one stitch to the left, on
the right side of the work, in each row.**

☐ knit stitch on right side or purl stitch on wrong side
▬ purl stitch on right side or knit stitch on wrong side

Knit and Purl Stitches

Diagonals 5 (to the right)

Number of stitches needed for joining: multiple of 6 + 1 selvedge stitch on each end.

Row 1 (right side of work): 1 selvedge stitch, *k5, p1*; repeat from * to *; end with 1 selvedge stitch.

Row 2: 1 selvedge stitch, *p1, k1, p4*; repeat from * to *; end with 1 selvedge stitch.

Row 3: 1 selvedge stitch, *k3, p1, k2*; repeat from * to *; end with 1 selvedge stitch.

Row 4: 1 selvedge stitch, *p3, k1, p2*; repeat from * to *; end with 1 selvedge stitch.

Row 5: 1 selvedge stitch, *k1, p1, k4*; repeat from * to *; end with 1 selvedge stitch.

Row 6: 1 selvedge stitch, *p5, k1*; repeat from * to *; end with 1 selvedge stitch.

Keep repeating these 6 rows. Shift one stitch to the right, on the right side of the work, in each row.

☐ knit stitch on right side or purl stitch on wrong side

– purl stitch on right side or knit stitch on wrong side

Triangles

Number of stitches needed for symmetry: multiple of 14 + 1 + 1 selvedge stitch on each end.

Row 1 (right side of work): 1 selvedge stitch, *p1, k13*; repeat from * to *; end with p1, 1 selvedge stitch.

Row 2: 1 selvedge stitch, k1, *k1, p11, k2*; repeat from * to *; end with 1 selvedge stitch.

Row 3: 1 selvedge stitch, *p3, k9, p2*; repeat from * to *; end with p1, 1 selvedge stitch.

Row 4: 1 selvedge stitch, k1, *k3, p7, k4*; repeat from * to *; end with 1 selvedge stitch.

Row 5: 1 selvedge stitch, *p5, k5, p4*; repeat from * to *; end with p1, 1 selvedge stitch.

Row 6: 1 selvedge stitch, k1, *k5, p3, k6*; repeat from * to *; end with 1 selvedge stitch.

Row 7: 1 selvedge stitch, *p7, k1, p6*; repeat from * to *; end with p1, 1 selvedge stitch.

Row 8: 1 selvedge stitch, p1, *p6, k1, p7*; repeat from * to *; end with 1 selvedge stitch.

Row 9: 1 selvedge stitch, *k6, p3, k5*; repeat from * to *; end with k1, 1 selvedge stitch.

Row 10: 1 selvedge stitch, p1, *p4, k5, p5*; repeat from * to *; end with 1 selvedge stitch.

Row 11: 1 selvedge stitch, *k4, p7, k3*; repeat from * to *; end with k1, 1 selvedge stitch.

Row 12: 1 selvedge stitch, p1, *p2, k9, p3*; repeat from * to *; end with 1 selvedge stitch.

Row 13: 1 selvedge stitch, *k2, p11, k1*; repeat from * to *; end with k1, 1 selvedge stitch.

Row 14: 1 selvedge stitch, p1, *k13, p1*; repeat from * to *; end with 1 selvedge stitch.

Keep repeating these 14 rows.

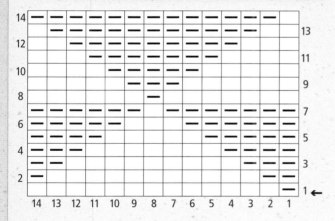

- ☐ knit stitch on right side or purl stitch on wrong side
- — purl stitch on right side or knit stitch on wrong side

Knit and Purl Stitches

Diagonal Lozenges

Number of stitches needed for joining: multiple of 12 + 1 selvedge stitch on each end.

Rows 1 (right side of work) and 8: 1 selvedge stitch, *p6, k6*; repeat from * to *; end with 1 selvedge stitch.

Row 2: 1 selvedge stitch, *p5, k6, p1*; repeat from * to *; end with 1 selvedge stitch.

Row 3: 1 selvedge stitch, *k2, p6, k4*; repeat from * to *; end with 1 selvedge stitch.

Row 4: 1 selvedge stitch, *p3, k6, p3*; repeat from * to *; end with 1 selvedge stitch.

Row 5: 1 selvedge stitch, *k4, p6, k2*; repeat from * to *; end with 1 selvedge stitch.

Row 6: 1 selvedge stitch, *p1, k6, p5*; repeat from * to *; end with 1 selvedge stitch.

Rows 7 and 14: 1 selvedge stitch, *k6, p6*; repeat from * to *; end with 1 selvedge stitch.

Row 9: 1 selvedge stitch, *k1, p6, k5*; repeat from * to *; end with 1 selvedge stitch.

Cut Diagonals

Number of stitches needed for joining: multiple of 8 + 1 selvedge stitch on each end.

Rows 1 (right side of work) and 8: 1 selvedge stitch, *p4, k4*; repeat from * to *; end with 1 selvedge stitch.

Rows 2 and 9: 1 selvedge stitch, *p3, k4, p1*; repeat from * to *; end with 1 selvedge stitch.

Rows 3 and 10: 1 selvedge stitch, *k2, p4, k2*; repeat from * to *; end with 1 selvedge stitch.

Rows 4 and 11: 1 selvedge stitch, *p1, k4, p3*; repeat from * to *; end with 1 selvedge stitch.

Rows 5 and 12: 1 selvedge stitch, *k4, p4*; repeat from * to *; end with 1 selvedge stitch.

Row 6: 1 selvedge stitch, *k3, p4, k1*; repeat from * to *; end with 1 selvedge stitch.

Row 7: 1 selvedge stitch, *k1, p4, k3*; repeat from * to *; end with 1 selvedge stitch.

Keep repeating these 12 rows.

Row 10: 1 selvedge stitch, *p4, k6, p2*; repeat from * to *; end with 1 selvedge stitch.

Row 11: 1 selvedge stitch, *k3, p6, k3*; repeat from * to *; end with 1 selvedge stitch.

Row 12: 1 selvedge stitch, *p2, k6, p4*; repeat from * to *; end with 1 selvedge stitch.

Row 13: 1 selvedge stitch, *k5, p6, k1*; repeat from * to *; end with 1 selvedge stitch.

Keep repeating these 14 rows.

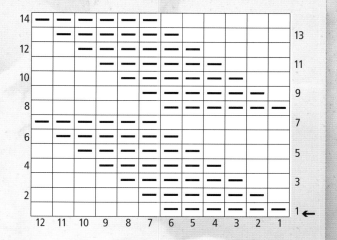

☐ knit stitch on right side or purl stitch on wrong side
– purl stitch on right side or knit stitch on wrong side

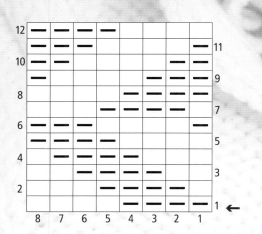

☐ knit stitch on right side or purl stitch on wrong side
– purl stitch on right side or knit stitch on wrong side

Knit and Purl Stitches

Piqué Leaves

Number of stitches needed for joining: multiple of 10 + 1 selvedge stitch on each end.

Rows 1 (right side of work), 3, 4, and 16: all purl.

Row 2: all knit.

Row 5: 1 selvedge stitch, *p5, k5*; repeat from * to *; end with 1 selvedge stitch.

Row 6: 1 selvedge stitch, *k1, p5, k4*; repeat from * to *; end with 1 selvedge stitch.

Row 7: 1 selvedge stitch, *p3, k5, p2*; repeat from * to *; end with 1 selvedge stitch.

Row 8: 1 selvedge stitch, *k3, p5, k2*; repeat from * to *; end with 1 selvedge stitch.

Row 9: 1 selvedge stitch, *p1, k5, p4*; repeat from * to *; end with 1 selvedge stitch.

Row 10: all knit.

Row 11: 1 selvedge stitch, *k1, p5, k4*; repeat from * to *; end with 1 selvedge stitch.

Row 12: 1 selvedge stitch, *p3, k5, p2*; repeat from * to *; end with 1 selvedge stitch.

Diamond Brocade Stitch

Number of stitches needed for symmetry: multiple of 8 + 1 + 1 selvedge stitch on each end.

Row 1 (right side of work): 1 selvedge stitch, *p1, k7*; repeat from * to *; end with p1, 1 selvedge stitch.

Rows 2 and 8: 1 selvedge stitch, p1, *k1, p5, k1, p1*; repeat from * to *; end with 1 selvedge stitch.

Rows 3 and 7: 1 selvedge stitch, *k2, p1, k3, p1, k1*; repeat from * to *; end with k1, 1 selvedge stitch.

Rows 4 and 6: 1 selvedge stitch, p1, *p2, k1, p1, k1, p3*; repeat from * to *; end with 1 selvedge stitch.

Row 5: 1 selvedge stitch, *k4, p1, k3*; repeat from * to *; end with k1, 1 selvedge stitch.

Keep repeating these 8 rows.

□ knit stitch on right side or purl stitch on wrong side

– purl stitch on right side or knit stitch on wrong side

Row 13: 1 selvedge stitch, *k3, p5, k2*; repeat from * to *; end with 1 selvedge stitch.

Row 14: 1 selvedge stitch, *p1, k5, p4*; repeat from * to *; end with 1 selvedge stitch.

Row 15: 1 selvedge stitch, *k5, p5*; repeat from * to *; end with 1 selvedge stitch.

Keep repeating these 16 rows.

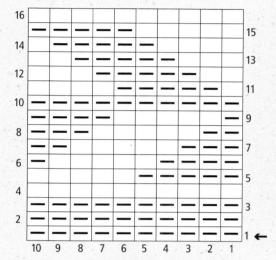

☐ knit stitch on right side or purl stitch on wrong side
– purl stitch on right side or knit stitch on wrong side

Diamonds (1)

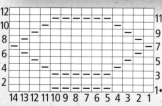

☐ knit stitch on right side or purl stitch on wrong side
– purl stitch on right side or knit stitch on wrong side

Number of stitches needed for symmetry and joining: multiple of 14 + 1 selvedge stitch on each end.

Rows 1 (right side of work), 3, and 11: 1 selvedge stitch, *k4, p6, k4*; repeat from * to *; end with 1 selvedge stitch.

Rows 2 and 12: all purl.

Rows 4 and 10: 1 selvedge stitch, *p3, k1, p6, k1, p3*; repeat from * to *; end with 1 selvedge stitch.

Rows 5 and 9: 1 selvedge stitch, *k2, p1, k8, p1, k2*; repeat from * to *; end with 1 selvedge stitch.

Rows 6 and 8: 1 selvedge stitch, *p1, k1, p10, k1, p1*; repeat from * to *; end with 1 selvedge stitch.

Row 7: 1 selvedge stitch, *p1, k12, p1*; repeat from * to *; end with 1 selvedge stitch.

Keep repeating these 12 rows.

Knit and Purl Stitches

Lozenges and Garter Ribbing

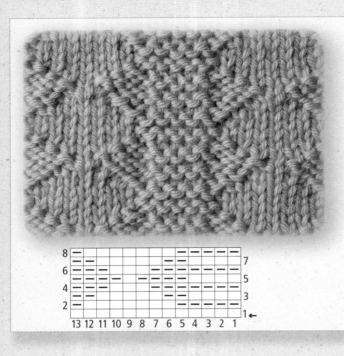

Number of stitches needed for symmetry: multiple of 13 + 4 + 1 selvedge stitch on each end.

Row 1 (right side of work): all knit.

Rows 2 and 8: 1 selvedge stitch, k4, *k1, p7, k5*; repeat from * to *; end with 1 selvedge stitch.

Rows 3 and 7: 1 selvedge stitch, *k4, p2, k5, p2*; repeat from * to *; end with k4, 1 selvedge stitch.

Rows 4 and 6: 1 selvedge stitch, k4, *k3, p3, k7*; repeat from * to *; end with 1 selvedge stitch.

Row 5: 1 selvedge stitch, *k4, p4, k1, p4*; repeat from * to *; end with k4, 1 selvedge stitch.

Keep repeating these 8 rows.

☐   knit stitch on right side or purl stitch on wrong side

−   purl stitch on right side or knit stitch on wrong side

Diamonds (2)

Number of stitches needed for symmetry: multiple of 16 + 1 + 1 selvedge stitch on each end.

Row 1 (right side of work): 1 selvedge stitch, *k1, p15*; repeat from * to *; end with k1, 1 selvedge stitch.

Rows 2 and 18: 1 selvedge stitch, p1, *p1, k13, p2*; repeat from * to *; end with 1 selvedge stitch.

Rows 3 and 17: 1 selvedge stitch, *p1, k2, p11, k2*; repeat from * to *; end with p1, 1 selvedge stitch.

Rows 4 and 16: 1 selvedge stitch, k1, *k1, p2, k9, p2, k2*; repeat from * to *; end with 1 selvedge stitch.

Rows 5 and 15: 1 selvedge stitch, *k1, p2, k2, p7, k2, p2*; repeat from * to *; end with k1, 1 selvedge stitch.

Rows 6 and 14: 1 selvedge stitch, k1, *p1, k2, p2, k5, p2, k2, p1, k1*; repeat from * to *; end with 1 selvedge stitch.

Rows 7 and 13: 1 selvedge stitch, *k1, p1, k1, p2, k2, p3, k2, p2, k1, p1*; repeat from * to *; end with k1, 1 selvedge stitch.

Rows 8 and 12: 1 selvedge stitch, k1, *p1, k1, p1, k2, p2, k1, p2, k2, p1, k1, p1, k1*; repeat from * to *; end with 1 selvedge stitch.

Rows 9 and 11: 1 selvedge stitch, *k1, p1, k1, p1, k1, p2, k3, p2, k1, p1, k1, p1*; repeat from * to *; end with k1, 1 selvedge stitch.

Row 10: 1 selvedge stitch, k1, *p1, k1, p1, k1, p1, k2, p1, k2, p1, k1, p1, k1, p1, k1*; repeat from * to *; end with 1 selvedge stitch.

Keep repeating these 18 rows.

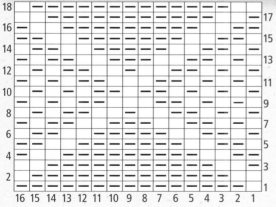

☐ knit stitch on right side or purl stitch on wrong side
— purl stitch on right side or knit stitch on wrong side

Knit and Purl Stitches

Diamonds (3)

Number of stitches needed for symmetry: multiple of 28 + 1 + 1 selvedge stitch on each end.

Row 1 (right side of work): 1 selvedge stitch, *k1, p2, k1, p2, k3, p11, k3, p2, k1, p2*; repeat from * to *; end with k1, 1 selvedge stitch.

Rows 2 and 16: 1 selvedge stitch, k1, *p1, k2, p1, k2, p3, k9, p3, k2, p1, k2, p1, k1*; repeat from * to *; end with 1 selvedge stitch.

Rows 3 and 15: 1 selvedge stitch, *p2, k1, p2, k1, p2, k3, p7, k3, p2, k1, p2, k1, p1*; repeat from * to *; end with p1, 1 selvedge stitch.

Rows 4 and 14: 1 selvedge stitch, p1, *k2, p1, k2, p1, k2, p3, k5, p3, k2, p1, k2, p1, k2, p1*; repeat from * to *; end with 1 selvedge stitch.

Rows 5 and 13: 1 selvedge stitch, *k2, p2, k1, p2, k1, p2, k3, p3, k3, p2, k1, p2, k1, p2, k1*; repeat from * to *; end with k1, 1 selvedge stitch.

Rows 6 and 12: 1 selvedge stitch, p1, *p2, k2, p1, k2, p1, k2, p3, k1, p3, k2, p1, k2, p1, k2, p3*; repeat from * to *; end with 1 selvedge stitch.

Rows 7 and 11: 1 selvedge stitch, *k4, p2, k1, p2, k1, p2, k5, p2, k1, p2, k1, p2, k3*; repeat from * to *; end with k1, 1 selvedge stitch.

Rows 8 and 10: 1 selvedge stitch, p1, *p4, k2, p1, k2, p1, k2, p3, k2, p1, k2, p1, k2, p5*; repeat from * to *; end with 1 selvedge stitch.

Row 9: 1 selvedge stitch, *k6, p2, k1, p2, k1, p2, k1, p2, k1, p2, k5*; repeat from * to *; end with k1, 1 selvedge stitch.

Keep repeating these 16 rows.

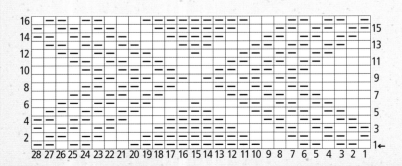

☐ knit stitch on right side or purl stitch on wrong side

— purl stitch on right side or knit stitch on wrong side

Lozenges and Moss Stitch

Number of stitches needed for symmetry: multiple of 16 + 5 + 1 selvedge stitch on each end.

Row 1 (right side of work): 1 selvedge stitch, *p5, k1, p1, k1, p1, k3, p1, k1, p1, k1*; repeat from * to *; end with p5, 1 selvedge stitch.

Row 2 and all even numbered rows: knit each stitch as it appears in previous row (i.e., knit a knit stitch, purl a purl stitch).

Rows 3 and 19: 1 selvedge stitch, *p6, k1, p1, k5, p1, k1, p1*; repeat from * to *; end with p5, 1 selvedge stitch.

Rows 5 and 17: 1 selvedge stitch, *p5, k1, p1, k3, p1, k3, p1, k1*; repeat from * to *; end with p5, 1 selvedge stitch.

Rows 7 and 15: 1 selvedge stitch, *p6, k3, p1, k1, p1, k3, p1*; repeat from * to *; end with p5, 1 selvedge stitch.

Rows 9 and 13: 1 selvedge stitch, *p5, k3, p1, k1, p1, k1, p1, k3*; repeat from * to *; end with p5, 1 selvedge stitch.

Row 11: 1 selvedge stitch, *p5, k2, p1, k1, p1, k1, p1, k1, p1, k2*; repeat from * to *; end with p5, 1 selvedge stitch.

Keep repeating Rows 1 to 20.

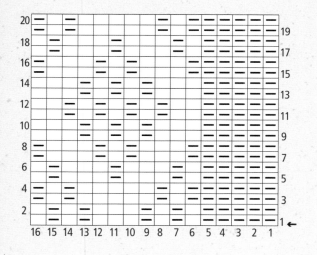

☐ knit stitch on right side or purl stitch on wrong side
— purl stitch on right side or knit stitch on wrong side

Lozenges in Relief

Number of stitches needed for joining: multiple of 8 + 1 selvedge stitch on each end.

Rows 1 (right side of work) and 15: 1 selvedge stitch, *p1, k1, p1, k1, p1, k1, p1, k1*; repeat from * to *; end with 1 selvedge stitch.

Row 2 and all even numbered rows: knit each stitch as it appears in previous row (i.e., knit a knit stitch, purl a purl stitch).

Row 3: 1 selvedge stitch, *k1, p1, k2, p2, k1, p1*; repeat from * to *; end with 1 selvedge stitch.

Row 5: 1 selvedge stitch, *p1, k3, p3, k1*; repeat from * to *; end with 1 selvedge stitch.

Row 7: 1 selvedge stitch, *k4, p4*; repeat from * to *; end with 1 selvedge stitch.

Row 9: 1 selvedge stitch, *k3, p1, k1, p3*; repeat from * to *; end with 1 selvedge stitch.

Row 11: 1 selvedge stitch, *k2, p1, k1, p1, k1, p2*; repeat from * to *; end with 1 selvedge stitch.

Rows 13 and 27: 1 selvedge stitch, *k1, p1, k1, p1, k1, p1, k1, p1*; repeat from * to *; end with 1 selvedge stitch.

Mosaic Stitch

Number of stitches needed for symmetry: multiple of 20 + 1 selvedge stitch on each end.

Rows 1 (right side of work), 5, and 9: 1 selvedge stitch, *k1, °p2, k2° (4 times), p2, k1*; repeat from * to *; end with 1 selvedge stitch.

Row 2 and all even numbered rows: knit each stitch as it appears in previous row (i.e., knit a knit stitch, purl a purl stitch).

Rows 3, 7, 13, and 17: 1 selvedge stitch, *k1, p2, k4, p2, k2, p2, k4, p2, k1*; repeat from * to *; end with 1 selvedge stitch.

Rows 11, 15, and 19: 1 selvedge stitch, *p1, °k2, p2° (4 times), k2, p1*; repeat from * to *; end with 1 selvedge stitch.

Keep repeating these 20 rows.

Row 17: 1 selvedge stitch, *p2, k1, p1, k1, p1, k2*; repeat from * to *; end with 1 selvedge stitch.

Row 19: 1 selvedge stitch, *p3, k1, p1, k3*; repeat from * to *; end with 1 selvedge stitch.

Row 21: 1 selvedge stitch, *p4, k4*; repeat from * to *; end with 1 selvedge stitch.

Row 23: 1 selvedge stitch, *k1, p3, k3, p1*; repeat from * to *; end with 1 selvedge stitch.

Row 25: 1 selvedge stitch, *p1, k1, p2, k2, p1, k1*; repeat from * to *; end with 1 selvedge stitch.

Keep repeating these 28 rows.

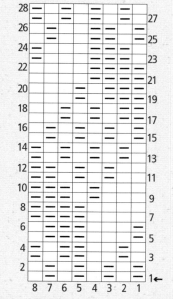

▢ knit stitch on right side or purl stitch on wrong side

▬ purl stitch on right side or knit stitch on wrong side

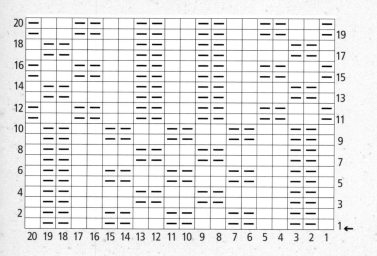

▢ knit stitch on right side or purl stitch on wrong side

▬ purl stitch on right side or knit stitch on wrong side

Twisted Rib k1/p1 (on right and wrong side of the work)

Number of stitches needed for symmetry: multiple of 2 + 1 + 1 selvedge stitch on each end.

Knitting/purling through the back of the loop, or k tbl/p tbl: For a knit stitch, insert the right needle into the back of the loop (behind the work) instead of the front, and knit as usual; for a purl stitch, insert the right needle into the back of the loop, slide it in front of the left needle, and purl as usual. This creates a twisted stitch.

Row 1 (right side of work): 1 selvedge stitch, *k1 tbl, p1 tbl*; repeat from * to *; end with k1 tbl, 1 selvedge stitch.

Row 2: 1 selvedge stitch, p1 tbl, *k1 tbl, p1 tbl*; repeat from * to *; end with 1 selvedge stitch.

Keep repeating these 2 rows.

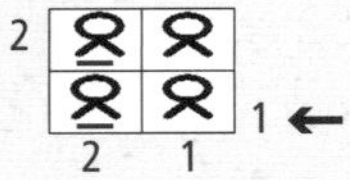

k tbl: knit through the back of the loop on right side, creating a twisted stitch, or purl through the back of the loop on wrong side

p tbl: purl through the back of the loop on right side, creating a twisted stitch, or knit through the back of the loop on wrong side

Stable Garter Stitch

Knit any number of stitches.

Knitting/purling through the back of the loop, or k tbl/p tbl: For a knit stitch, insert the right needle into the back of the loop (behind the work) instead of the front, and knit as usual; for a purl stitch, insert the right needle into the back of the loop, slide it in front of the left needle, and purl as usual. This creates a twisted stitch.

Row 1: all knit through the back of the loop.

Row 2: all knit through the back of the loop.

Keep repeating these 2 rows.

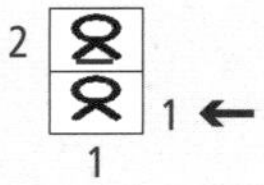

k tbl: knit through the back of the loop on right side, creating a twisted stitch, or purl through the back of the loop on wrong side

p tbl: purl through the back of the loop on right side, creating a twisted stitch, or knit through the back of the loop on wrong side

Twisted Jersey

Knit any number of stitches.

Knitting/purling through the back of the loop, or k tbl/p tbl: For a knit stitch, insert the right needle into the back of the loop (behind the work) instead of the front, and knit as usual; for a purl stitch, insert the right needle into the back of the loop, slide it in front of the left needle, and purl as usual. This creates a twisted stitch.

Row 1 (right side of work): all knit through the back of the loop.

Row 2: all purl through the back of the loop.

Keep repeating these 2 rows.

⅄ k tbl: knit through the back of the loop on right side, creating a twisted stitch, or purl through the back of the loop on wrong side

Cable Stitches

Crossed stitches and cabling techniques can achieve a multitude of forms and effects.

Cable Stitches

Small Cables (right cross)

Number of stitches needed for symmetry: multiple of 5 + 3 + 1 selvedge stitch at each end.

Row 1 (right side of work): 1 selvedge stitch, *p3, k2*; repeat from * to *; end with p3, 1 selvedge stitch.

Rows 2 and 4: knit each stitch as it appears in previous row (i.e., knit a knit stitch, purl a purl stitch).

Row 3: 1 selvedge stitch, *p3, knit 2 right cross stitches (knit the second stitch on the left needle first, passing the right needle in front of the first stitch, then knit the first stitch)*; repeat from * to *; end with p3, 1 selvedge stitch.

Keep repeating these 4 rows.

- ☐ knit stitch on right side or purl stitch on wrong side
- − purl stitch on right side or knit stitch on wrong side
- ✕ 2 right cross stitches: knit the second stitch on the left needle first, passing the right needle in front of the first stitch, then knit the first stitch

Small Cables (left cross)

Number of stitches needed for symmetry: multiple of 5 + 3 + 1 selvedge stitch at each end.

Row 1 (right side of work): 1 selvedge stitch, *p3, k2*; repeat from * to *; end with p3, 1 selvedge stitch.

Rows 2 and 4: knit each stitch as it appears in previous row (i.e., knit a knit stitch, purl a purl stitch).

Row 3: 1 selvedge stitch, *p3, knit 2 left cross stitches (knit the second stitch on the left needle first, passing the right needle behind the first stitch, then knit the first stitch)*; repeat from * to *; end with p3, 1 selvedge stitch.

Keep repeating these 4 rows.

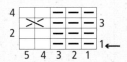

- ☐ knit stitch on right side or purl stitch on wrong side
- − purl stitch on right side or knit stitch on wrong side
- ✕ 2 left cross stitches: knit the second stitch on the left needle first, passing the right needle behind the first stitch, then knit the first stitch

Small Fancy Cable

Number of stitches needed for symmetry and joining: multiple of 7 + 1 selvedge stitch at each end.

Row 1 (right side of work): 1 selvedge stitch, *p2, k3, p2*; repeat from * to *; end with 1 selvedge stitch.

Rows 2 and 4: 1 selvedge stitch, *k2, p3, k2*; repeat from * to *; end with 1 selvedge stitch.

Row 3: 1 selvedge stitch, *p2, sl 1 kwise wyib, k2, yo1, psso, p2*; repeat from * to *; end with 1 selvedge stitch.

Keep repeating these 4 rows.

☐ knit stitch on right side or purl stitch on wrong side

— purl stitch on right side or knit stitch on wrong side

O̅I̅I̅V̅ sl 1 kwise wyib, k2, yo1, psso: slip 1 knitwise with yarn in back, k2, yo1, pass slipped stitch over stitches/yarn overs and off the needle

4-Stitch Cables (right cross)

Number of stitches needed for symmetry: multiple of 7 + 3 + 1 selvedge stitch at each end.

Row 1 (right side of work): 1 selvedge stitch, *p3, k4*; repeat from * to *; end with p3, 1 selvedge stitch.

Rows 2, 3, 4, and 6: knit each stitch as it appears in previous row (i.e., knit a knit stitch, purl a purl stitch).

Row 5: 1 selvedge stitch, *p3, knit 4 right cross stitches (2 and 2: sl 2 on a cable needle behind work, k2 from left needle, then k2 from cable needle)*; repeat from * to *; end with p3, 1 selvedge stitch.

Keep repeating these 6 rows.

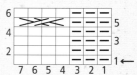

☐ knit stitch on right side or purl stitch on wrong side

— purl stitch on right side or knit stitch on wrong side

⤫ 4 right cross stitches: sl 2 on a cable needle behind work, k2 from left needle, then k2 from cable needle

sl: slip stitch from one needle to another without knitting it

Cable Stitches

4-Stitch Cables (left cross)

Number of stitches needed for symmetry and joining: multiple of 6 + 2 + 1 selvedge stitch at each end.

Row 1 (right side of work): 1 selvedge stitch, *p2, k4*; repeat from * to *; end with p2 and 1 selvedge stitch.

Rows 2, 3, 4, and 6: knit each stitch as it appears in previous row (i.e., knit a knit stitch, purl a purl stitch).

Row 5: 1 selvedge stitch, *p2, knit 4 left cross stitches (2 and 2: sl 2 on a cable needle in front of work, k2 from left needle, then k2 from cable needle)*; repeat from * to *; end with p2 and 1 selvedge stitch.

Keep repeating these 6 rows.

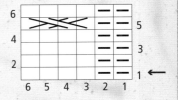

◻ knit stitch on right side or purl stitch on wrong side

− purl stitch on right side or knit stitch on wrong side

⧓ 4 left cross stitches: sl 2 on a cable needle in front of work, k2 from left needle, then k2 from cable needle

sl: slip stitch from one needle to another without knitting it

Mixed Cable (garter and stockinette)

The directions for this pattern consist of 16 stitches on a background of knit stockinette stitch.

Rows 1 (right side of work), 3, 5, 9, 11, 13, 15, 17, 21, and 23: p4, k8, p4.

Rows 2, 4, 6, 20, 22, and 24: k8, p4, k4.

Rows 7 and 19: p4, knit 8 left cross stitches (4 and 4: sl 4 on a cable needle in front of work, k4 from left needle, then k4 from cable needle), p4.

Rows 8, 10, 12, 14, 16, and 18: k4, p4, k8.

Keep repeating these 24 rows.

12-Stitch Cable

The directions for this pattern consist of 12 stitches on a background of purled stockinette stitch.

Rows 1 (right side of work) and 5: k12.

Row 2 and all even numbered rows: knit each stitch as it appears in previous row (i.e., knit a knit stitch, purl a purl stitch).

Row 3: knit 6 right cross stitches (3 and 3: sl 3 on a cable needle behind work, k3 from left needle, then k3 from cable needle), knit 6 left cross stitches (3 and 3: sl 3 on a cable needle in front of work, k3 from left needle, then k3 from cable needle).

Keep repeating these 6 rows.

☐ knit stitch on right side or purl stitch on wrong side

⤬ 6 left cross stitches: sl 3 on a cable needle in front of work, k3 from left needle, then k3 from cable needle

⤬ 6 right cross stitches: sl 3 on a cable needle behind work, k3 from left needle, then k3 from cable needle

sl: slip stitch from one needle to another without knitting it

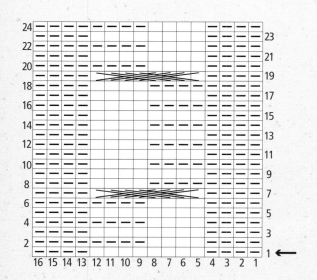

☐ knit stitch on right side or purl stitch on wrong side

− purl stitch on right side or knit stitch on wrong side

⤬ 8 left cross stitches: sl 4 on a cable needle in front of work, k4 from left needle, then k4 from cable needle

sl: slip stitch from one needle to another without knitting it

Cable Stitches

Threaded Cable

Number of stitches needed for symmetry: multiple of 17 + 5 + 1 selvedge stitch at each end.

Rows 1 (right side of work), 3, 7, and 9: 1 selvedge stitch, *p5, k12*, repeat from * to *; end with p5, 1 selvedge stitch.

Rows 2, 4, 6, and 8: knit each stitch as it appears in previous row (i.e., knit a knit stitch, purl a purl stitch).

Row 5: 1 selvedge stitch, *p5, knit 12 left cross stitches (6 and 6: sl 6 on a cable needle in front of work, k6 from left needle, then k6 from cable needle)*; repeat from * to *; end with p5, 1 selvedge stitch.

Row 10: 1 selvedge stitch, k5, *p3, purl 6 left cross stitches (3 and 3: sl 3 on a cable needle in front of work, p3 from left needle, then p3 from cable needle), p3, k5*; repeat from * to *; end with 1 selvedge stitch.

Keep repeating these 10 rows.

6-Stitch Braid

Number of stitches needed for symmetry and joining: multiple of 8 + 1 selvedge stitch at each end.

Row 1 (right side of work): 1 selvedge stitch, *p1, k6, p1*; repeat from * to *; end with 1 selvedge stitch.

Rows 2, 4, and 6: knit each stitch as it appears in previous row (i.e., knit a knit stitch, purl a purl stitch).

Row 3: 1 selvedge stitch, *p1, knit 4 right cross stitches (2 and 2: sl 2 on a cable needle behind work, k2 from left needle, then k2 from cable needle), k2, p1*; repeat from * to *; end with 1 selvedge stitch.

Row 5: 1 selvedge stitch, *p1, k2, knit 4 left cross stitches (2 and 2: sl 2 on a cable needle in front of work, k2 from left needle, then k2 from cable needle), p1*; repeat from * to *; end with 1 selvedge stitch.

Keep repeating the 4 rows from Row 3 through Row 6.

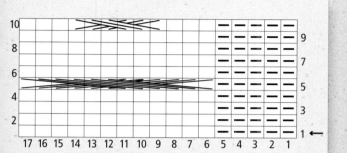

knit stitch on right side or purl stitch on wrong side
− purl stitch on right side or knit stitch on wrong side

6 left cross stitches: sl 3 on a cable needle in front of work, p3 from left needle, then p3 from cable needle

12 left cross stitches: sl 6 on a cable needle in front of work, k6 from left needle, then k6 from cable needle
sl: slip stitch from one needle to another without knitting it

8-Stitch Braid

The directions for this pattern consist of 12 stitches on a background of purled stockinette stitch.

RIGHT CABLE:
Rows 1 and 5: k12.
Row 2 and all even numbered rows: knit each stitch as it appears in previous row (i.e., knit a knit stitch, purl a purl stitch).
Row 3: k4, knit 8 right cross stitches (4 and 4: sl 4 on a cable needle behind work, k4 from left needle, then k4 from cable needle).
Row 7: knit 8 left cross stitches (4 and 4: sl 4 on a cable needle in front of work, k4 from left needle, then k4 from cable needle), k4.
Keep repeating these 8 rows.

LEFT CABLE:
Rows 1 and 5: k12.
Row 2 and all even numbered rows: knit each stitch as it appears in previous row (i.e., knit a knit stitch, purl a purl stitch).
Row 3: k4, knit 8 left cross stitches (4 and 4: sl 4 on a cable needle in front of work, k4 from left needle, then k4 from cable needle).
Row 7: knit 8 right cross stitches (4 and 4: sl 4 on a cable needle behind work, k4 from left needle, then k4 from cable needle), k4.
Keep repeating these 8 rows.

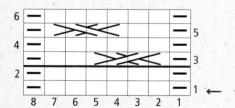

knit stitch on right side or purl stitch on wrong side
− purl stitch on right side or knit stitch on wrong side

4 right cross stitches: sl 2 on a cable needle behind work, k2 from left needle, then k2 from cable needle

4 left cross stitches: sl 2 on a cable needle in front of work, k2 from left needle, then k2 from cable needle
sl: slip stitch from one needle to another without knitting it

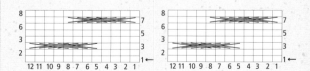

knit stitch on right side or purl stitch on wrong side

8 left cross stitches: sl 4 on a cable needle in front of work, k4 from left needle, then k4 stitches from cable needle

8 right cross stitches: sl 4 on a cable needle behind work, k4 from left needle, then k4 from cable needle
sl: slip stitch from one needle to another without knitting it

Cable Stitches

Ribs and Cables

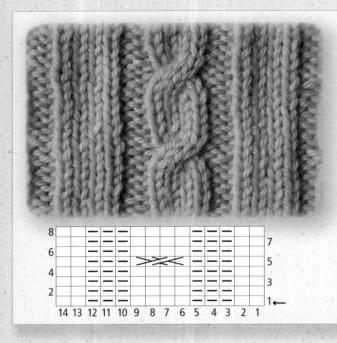

Number of stitches needed for symmetry and joining: multiple of 14 + 1 selvedge stitch at each end.

Rows 1 (right side of work), 3, and 7: 1 selvedge stitch, *k2, p3, k4, p3, k2*, repeat from * to *; end with 1 selvedge stitch.
Row 2 and all even numbered rows: knit each stitch as it appears in previous row (i.e., knit a knit stitch, purl a purl stitch).
Row 5: 1 selvedge stitch, *k2, p3, knit 4 right cross stitches (2 and 2: sl 2 on a cable needle behind work, k2 from left needle, then k2 from cable needle), p3, k2*; repeat from * to *; end with 1 selvedge stitch.

Keep repeating these 8 rows.

☐ knit stitch on right side or purl stitch on wrong side
– purl stitch on right side or knit stitch on wrong side
⟩⟨ 4 right cross stitches: sl 2 on a cable needle behind work, k2 from left needle, then k2 from cable needle
sl: slip stitch from one needle to another without knitting it

Cable Ribbing (1)

The directions for this pattern stitch consist of 8 stitches on a background of purled stockinette stitch.

Rows 1 (right side of work), 3, 7, 9, 11, 13, 15, and 17: k3, p2, k3.
Row 2 and all even numbered rows: knit the stitches as they appear (knit a knit, purl a purl).
Row 5: 8 left cross stitches (k3, p2, k3: sl 3 on a cable needle placed in front of your work, sl 2 on a second cable needle placed behind your work, k3 from left needle, p2 from second cable needle, then k3 from first cable needle).
Keep repeating these 18 rows.

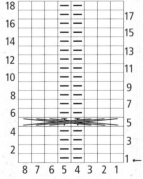

☐ knit stitch on right side or purl stitch on wrong side
– purl stitch on right side or knit stitch on wrong side
⟩⟨ 8 left cross stitches: sl 3 on a cable needle in front of work, sl 2 on a second cable needle behind work, k3 from left needle, p2 from second cable needle, then k3 from first cable needle
sl: slip stitch from one needle to another without knitting it

Cable Ribbing (2)

The directions for this pattern stitch consist of 24 stitches on a background of knit stockinette stitch.

Rows 1 (right side of work), 3, 5, 9, 11, and 13: p3, *k3, p2*; repeat from * to * 3 times; k3, p3.

Row 2 and all even numbered rows: knit the stitches as they appear (knit a knit, purl a purl).

Row 7: p3, 8 right cross stitches (k3, p2, k3: sl 5 on a cable needle behind work, k3 from left needle, then p2 and k3 from cable needle), p2, 8 left cross stitches (sl 3 on a cable needle in front of work, sl 2 on a second cable needle behind work, k3 from left needle, p2 from second cable needle, then k3 from first cable needle), p3.

Keep repeating these 14 rows.

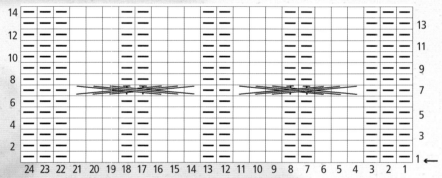

☐ knit stitch on right side or purl stitch on wrong side

― purl stitch on right side or knit stitch on wrong side

⟋⟍ 8 left cross stitches: sl 3 on a cable needle in front of work, sl 2 on a second cable needle behind work, k3 from left needle, p2 from second cable needle, then k3 from first cable needle

⟍⟋ 8 right cross stitches: sl 5 on a cable needle behind work, k3 from left needle, then p2 and k3 from cable needle

sl: slip stitch from one needle to another without knitting it

Cabled Chains

Number of stitches needed for symmetry and joining: multiple of 18 + 1 selvedge stitch at each end.

Rows 1 (right side of work), 5, and 7: 1 selvedge stitch, *k2, p4, k6, p4, k2*; repeat from * to *; end with 1 selvedge stitch.

Row 2 and all even numbered rows: knit each stitch as it appears in previous row (i.e., knit a knit stitch, purl a purl stitch).

Rows 3 and 9: 1 selvedge stitch, *k2, p4, knit 6 right cross stitches (3 and 3: sl 3 on a cable needle behind work, k3 from left needle, then k3 from cable needle), p4, k2*; repeat from * to *; end with 1 selvedge stitch.

Row 11: 1 selvedge stitch, *k2, p3, 4 right cross stitches (p1, k3: sl 1 on a cable needle behind work, k3 from left needle, then p1 from cable needle), 4 left cross stitches (k3, p1: sl 3 on a cable needle in front of work, p1 from left needle, then k3 from cable needle), p3, k2*; repeat from * to *; end with 1 selvedge stitch.

Rows 13, 15, 17, 19, 21, and 23: knit each stitch as it appears in previous row (i.e., knit a knit stitch, purl a purl stitch).

Cabled Ribbing (3)

The directions for this pattern consist of 6 stitches on a background of purled stockinette stitch.

Rows 1 (right side of work), 5, 7, 11, 13, 15, 17, and 19: k6.

Row 2 and all even numbered rows: knit each stitch as it appears in previous row (i.e., knit a knit stitch, purl a purl stitch).

Rows 3 and 9: knit 6 left cross stitches (3 and 3: sl 3 on a cable needle in front of work, k3 from left needle, then k3 from cable needle).

Keep repeating these 20 rows.

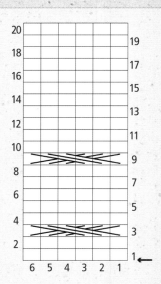

☐ knit stitch on right side or purl stitch on wrong side

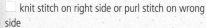 6 left cross stitches: sl 3 on a cable needle in front of work, k3 from left needle, then k3 from cable needle

sl: slip stitch from one needle to another without knitting it

Row 25: 1 selvedge stitch, *k2, p3, 4 left cross stitches (k3, p1), 4 right cross stitches (p1, k3), p3, k2*; repeat from * to *; end with 1 selvedge stitch.
Keep repeating the 24 rows from Row 3 to Row 26.

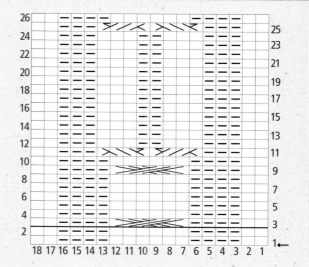

☐ knit stitch on right side or purl stitch on wrong side
– purl stitch on right side or knit stitch on wrong side
⟩⟨ 4 left cross stitches: sl 3 on a cable needle in front of work, p1 from left needle, then k3 from cable needle
⟩⟨ 4 right cross stitches: sl 1 on a cable needle behind work, k3 from left needle, then p1 from cable needle
⟩⟩⟨⟨ 6 right cross stitches: sl 3 on a cable needle behind work, k3 from left needle, then k3 from cable needle
sl: slip stitch from one needle to another without knitting it

Cut Striped Ribbing

Number of stitches needed for symmetry and joining: multiple of 7 + 1 selvedge stitch at each end.
Row 1 (right side of work): 1 selvedge stitch, *p1, 2 left cross stitches (knit the second stitch on the left needle first, passing the right needle behind the first stitch, then knit the first stitch), k3, p1*; repeat from * to *; end with 1 selvedge stitch.
Rows 2, 4, 6, and 8: knit each stitch as it appears in previous row (i.e., knit a knit stitch, purl a purl stitch).
Row 3: 1 selvedge stitch, *p1, k1, 2 left cross stitches, k2, p1*; repeat from * to *; end with 1 selvedge stitch.
Row 5: 1 selvedge stitch, *p1, k2, 2 left cross stitches, k1, p1*; repeat from * to *; end with 1 selvedge stitch.
Row 7: 1 selvedge stitch, *p1, k3, 2 left cross stitches, p1*; repeat from * to *; end with 1 selvedge stitch.
Keep repeating these 8 rows.

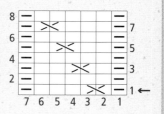

☐ knit stitch on right side or purl stitch on wrong side
– purl stitch on right side or knit stitch on wrong side
⟩⟨ 2 left cross stitches: knit the second stitch on the left needle first, passing the right needle behind the first stitch, then knit the first stitch

6-Stitch Reverse Caduceus

Number of stitches needed for symmetry: multiple of 20 + 1 selvedge stitch at each end.

Rows 1 (right side of work), 3, 5, 9, 11, and 13: 1 selvedge stitch, *p2, k6, p4, k6, p2*; repeat from * to *; end with 1 selvedge stitch.

Row 2 and all even numbered rows: knit each stitch as it appears in previous row (i.e., knit a knit stitch, purl a purl stitch).

Row 7: 1 selvedge stitch, *p2, knit 6 right cross stitches (3 and 3: sl 3 on a cable needle behind work, k3 from left needle, then k3 from cable needle), p4, knit 6 left cross stitches (3 and 3: sl 3 on a cable needle in front of work, k3 from left needle, then k3 from cable needle), p2*; repeat from * to *; end with 1 selvedge stitch.

Row 15: 1 selvedge stitch, *p2, knit 6 left cross stitches (3 and 3), p4, knit 6 right cross stitches (3 and 3), p2*; repeat from * to *; end with 1 selvedge stitch.

Keep repeating these 16 rows.

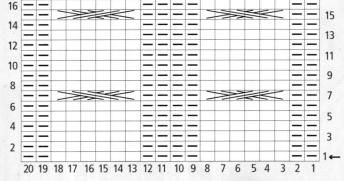

☐ knit stitch on right side or purl stitch on wrong side

— purl stitch on right side or knit stitch on wrong side

⟩⟩⟩⟨ 6 left cross stitches: sl 3 on a cable needle in front of work, k3 from left needle, then k3 from cable needle

⟩⟩⟩⟨ 6 right cross stitches: sl 3 on a cable needle behind work, k3 from left needle, then k3 from cable needle

sl: slip stitch from one needle to another without knitting it

6-Stitch Caduceus

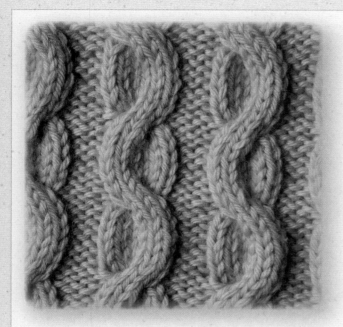

Number of stitches needed for symmetry and joining: multiple of 10 + 1 selvedge stitch at each end.

Rows 1 (right side of work), 3, 5, 9, 11, and 13: 1 selvedge stitch, *p2, k6, p2*; repeat from * to *; end with 1 selvedge stitch.

Row 2 and all even numbered rows: knit each stitch as it appears in previous row (i.e., knit a knit stitch, purl a purl stitch).

Row 7: 1 selvedge stitch, *p2, knit 6 left cross stitches (3 and 3: sl 3 on a cable needle in front of work, k3 from left needle, then k3 from cable needle), p2*; repeat from * to *; end with 1 selvedge stitch.

Row 15: 1 selvedge stitch, *p2, knit 6 right cross stitches (3 and 3: sl 3 on a cable needle behind work, k3 from left needle, then k3 from cable needle), p2*; repeat from * to *; end with 1 selvedge stitch.

Keep repeating these 16 rows.

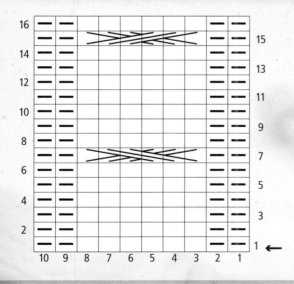

knit stitch on right side or purl stitch on wrong side

− purl stitch on right side or knit stitch on wrong side

6 left cross stitches: sl 3 on a cable needle in front of work, k3 from left needle, then k3 from cable needle

6 right cross stitches: sl 3 on a cable needle behind work, k3 from left needle, then k3 from cable needle

sl: slip stitch from one needle to another without knitting it

Caduceus Cable

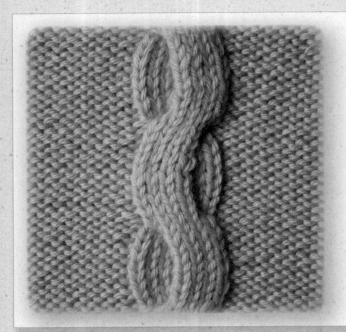

The directions for this pattern consist of 10 stitches on a background of purled stockinette stitch.

Rows 1 (right side of work), 5, 7, 9, 11, 15, 17, and 19: k10.

Row 2 and all even numbered rows: knit each stitch as it appears in previous row (i.e., knit a knit stitch, purl a purl stitch).

Row 3: knit 10 left cross stitches (5 and 5: sl 5 on a cable needle in front of work, k5 from left needle, then k5 from cable needle).

Row 13: knit 10 right cross stitches (5 and 5: sl 5 on a cable needle behind work, k5 from left needle, then k5 from cable needle).

Keep repeating these 20 rows.

6-Stitch Fancy Cables

The directions for this pattern consist of 9 stitches on a background of purled stockinette stitch.

Rows 1 (right side of work), 5, 7, 11, 15, and 17: k9.

Row 2 and all even numbered rows: knit each stitch as it appears in previous row (i.e., knit a knit stitch, purl a purl stitch).

Rows 3 and 9: k3, knit 6 left cross stitches (3 and 3: sl 3 on a cable needle in front of work, k3 from left needle, then k3 from cable needle).

Rows 13 and 19: 6 right cross stitches (3 and 3: sl 3 on a cable needle behind work, k3 from left needle, then k3 from cable needle), k3.

Keep repeating these 20 rows.

knit stitch on right side or purl stitch on wrong side

− purl stitch on right side or knit stitch on wrong side

10 left cross stitches: sl 5 on a cable needle in front of work, k5 from left needle, then k5 from cable needle

10 right cross stitches: sl 5 on a cable needle behind work, k5 from left needle, then k5 from cable needle

sl: slip stitch from one needle to another without knitting it

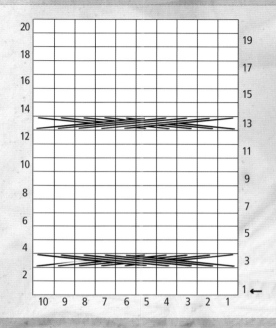

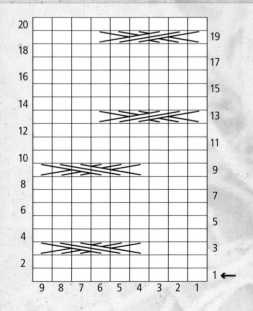

knit stitch on right side or purl stitch on wrong side

6 left cross stitches: sl 3 on a cable needle in front of work, k3 from left needle, then k3 from cable needle

6 right cross stitches: sl 3 on a cable needle behind work, k3 from left needle, then k3 from cable needle

sl: slip stitch from one needle to another without knitting it

Braided Cables

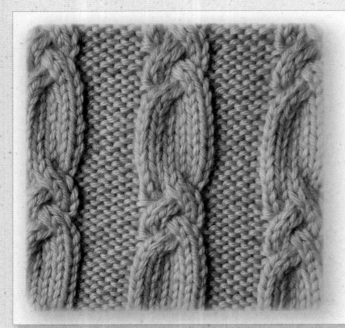

Number of stitches needed for symmetry and joining: multiple of 12 + 1 selvedge stitch at each end.

Rows 1 (right side of work), 3, 13, and 15: 1 selvedge stitch, *p3, k6, p3*; repeat from * to *; end with 1 selvedge stitch.

Row 2 and all even numbered rows: knit each stitch as it appears in previous row (i.e., knit a knit stitch, purl a purl stitch).

Rows 5 and 9: 1 selvedge stitch, *p3, k2, knit 4 right cross stitches (2 and 2: sl 2 on a cable needle behind work, k2 from left needle, then k2 from cable needle), p3*; repeat from * to *; end with 1 selvedge stitch.

Rows 7 and 11: 1 selvedge stitch, *p3, knit 4 left cross stitches (2 and 2: sl 2 on a cable needle in front of work, k2 from left needle, then k2 from cable needle), k2, p3*; repeat from * to *; end with 1 selvedge stitch.

Keep repeating these 16 rows.

Layered Cable

The directions for this pattern consist of 14 stitches on a background of purled stockinette stitch.

Rows 1 (right side of work), 3, 5, 7, 13, 15, and 17: k3, p1, k6, p1, k3.

Row 2 and all even numbered rows: knit each stitch as it appears in previous row (i.e., knit a knit stitch, purl a purl stitch).

Row 9: 7 left cross stitches (k3, p1, k3: sl 3 on a cable needle in front of work, sl 1 on a second cable needle behind work, k3 from left needle, p1 from second cable needle, then k3 from first cable needle), 7 right cross stitches (k3, p1, k3: sl 4 on a cable needle behind work, k3 from left needle, sl fourth stitch on cable needle back to left needle, purl it while passing it behind the 3 stitches on cable needle, then k3 from cable needle).

Rows 11 and 19: k3, p1, knit 6 right cross stitches (3 and 3: sl 3 on a cable needle behind work, k3 from left needle, then k3 from cable needle), p1, k3.

Keep repeating these 20 rows.

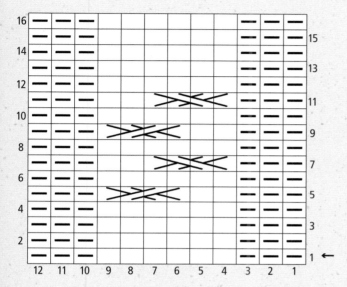

☐ knit stitch on right side or purl stitch on wrong side

— purl stitch on right side or knit stitch on wrong side

⟩⟨ 4 left cross stitches: sl 2 on a cable needle in front of work, k2 from left needle, then k2 from cable needle

⟩⟨ 4 right cross stitches: sl 2 on a cable needle behind work, k2 from left needle, then k2 from cable needle

sl: slip stitch from one needle to another without knitting it

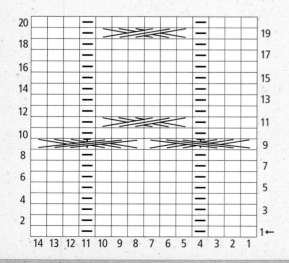

☐ knit stitch on right side or purl stitch on wrong side

— purl stitch on right side or knit stitch on wrong side

⟩⟨ 7 right cross stitches: sl 4 on a cable needle behind work, k3 from left needle, sl fourth stitch on cable needle back to left needle, purl it while passing it behind the 3 stitches on cable needle, then k3 from cable needle

⟩⟨ 7 left cross stitches: sl 3 on a cable needle in front of work, sl 1 on a second cable needle behind work, k3 from left needle, p1 from second cable needle, then k3 from first cable needle

⟩⟨ 6 right cross stitches: sl 3 on a cable needle behind work, k3 from left needle, then k3 from cable needle

sl: slip stitch from one needle to another without knitting it

8-Stitch Double Cables (interlocked inward)

Number of stitches needed for symmetry and joining: multiple of 12 + 1 selvedge stitch at each end.

Row 1 (right side of work): 1 selvedge stitch, *p2, k8, p2*; repeat from * to *; end with 1 selvedge stitch.

Rows 2, 3, 4, and 6: knit each stitch as it appears in previous row (i.e., knit a knit stitch, purl a purl stitch).

Row 5: 1 selvedge stitch, *p2, knit 4 left cross stitches (2 and 2: sl 2 on a cable needle in front of work, k2 from left needle, then k2 from cable needle), knit 4 right cross stitches (2 and 2: sl 2 on a cable needle behind work, k2 from left needle, then k2 from cable needle), p2*; repeat from * to *; end with 1 selvedge stitch.

Keep repeating these 6 rows.

8-Stitch Double Cables (interlocked outward)

Number of stitches needed for symmetry and joining: multiple of 12 + 1 selvedge stitch at each end.

Row 1 (right side of work): 1 selvedge stitch, *p2, k8, p2*; repeat from * to *; end with 1 selvedge stitch.

Rows 2, 3, 4, and 6: knit each stitch as it appears in previous row (i.e., knit a knit stitch, purl a purl stitch).

Row 5: 1 selvedge stitch, *p2, knit 4 right cross stitches (2 and 2: sl 2 on a cable needle behind work, k2 from left needle, then k2 from cable needle), knit 4 left cross stitches (2 and 2: sl 2 on a cable needle in front of work, k2 from left needle, then k2 from cable needle), p2*; repeat from * to *; end with 1 selvedge stitch.

Keep repeating these 6 rows.

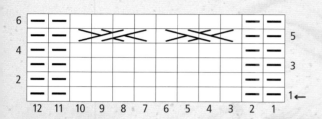

knit stitch on right side or purl stitch on wrong side

− purl stitch on right side or knit stitch on wrong side

4 left cross stitches: sl 2 on a cable needle in front of work, k2 from left needle, then k2 from cable needle

4 right cross stitches: sl 2 on a cable needle behind work, k2 from left needle, then k2 from cable needle

sl: slip stitch from one needle to another without knitting it

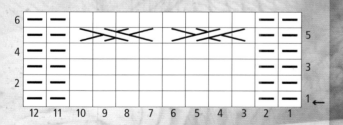

knit stitch on right side or purl stitch on wrong side

− purl stitch on right side or knit stitch on wrong side

4 left cross stitches: sl 2 on a cable needle in front of work, k2 from left needle, then k2 from cable needle

4 right cross stitches: sl 2 on a cable needle behind work, k2 from left needle, then k2 from cable needle

sl: slip stitch from one needle to another without knitting it

Chain Cables

Number of stitches needed for symmetry and joining: multiple of 11 + 3 + 1 selvedge stitch at each end.

Row 1 (right side of work): 1 selvedge stitch, *p3, k8*; repeat from * to *; end with p3, 1 selvedge stitch.

Row 2 and all even numbered rows: knit each stitch as it appears in previous row (i.e., knit a knit stitch, purl a purl stitch).

Row 3: 1 selvedge stitch, *p3, 4 left cross stitches (k2, p2: sl 2 on a cable needle in front of work, p2 from left needle, then k2 from cable needle), 4 right cross stitches (p2, k2: sl 2 on a cable needle behind work, k2 from left needle, then p2 from cable needle)*; repeat from * to *; end with p3, 1 selvedge stitch.

Row 5: 1 selvedge stitch, *p5, k4, p2*; repeat from * to *; end with p3, 1 selvedge stitch.

Row 7: 1 selvedge stitch, *p3, knit 4 right cross stitches (2 and 2: sl 2 stitches on a cable needle behind work, k2 from left needle, then k2 from cable needle), knit 4 left cross stitches (2 and 2: sl 2 on a cable needle in front of work, k2 from left needle, then k2 from cable needle)*; repeat from * to *; end with p3, 1 selvedge stitch.

Keep repeating these 8 rows.

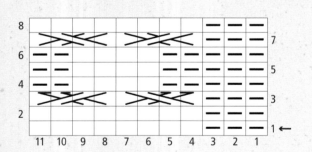

☐ knit stitch on right side or purl stitch on wrong side

— purl stitch on right side or knit stitch on wrong side

>✕< 4 left cross stitches: sl 2 on a cable needle in front of work, p2 from left needle, then k2 from cable needle

>✕< 4 right cross stitches: sl 2 on a cable needle behind work, k2 from left needle, then p2 from cable needle

>✕< 4 left cross stitches: sl 2 on a cable needle in front of work, k2 from left needle, then k2 from cable needle

>✕< 4 right cross stitches: sl 2 stitches on a cable needle behind work, k2 from left needle, then k2 from cable needle

sl: slip stitch from one needle to another without knitting it

Blister Stitch (1)

Number of stitches needed for symmetry and joining: multiple of 8 + 1 selvedge stitch at each end.

Rows 1 (right side of work) and 5: all knit.

Row 2 and all even numbered rows: knit each stitch as it appears in previous row (i.e., knit a knit stitch, purl a purl stitch).

Row 3: 1 selvedge stitch, *knit 4 right cross stitches (2 and 2: sl 2 on a cable needle behind work, k2 from left needle, then k2 from cable needle), knit 4 left cross stitches (2 and 2: sl 2 on a cable needle in front of work, k2 from left needle, then k2 from cable needle)*; repeat from * to *; end with 1 selvedge stitch.

Row 7: 1 selvedge stitch, *knit 4 left cross stitches (2 and 2), knit 4 right cross stitches (2 and 2)*; repeat from * to *; end with 1 selvedge stitch.

Keep repeating Rows 1 through 8.

☐ knit stitch on right side or purl stitch on wrong side

⟩⟩⟨ 4 left cross stitches: sl 2 on a cable needle in front of work, k2 from left needle, then k2 from cable needle

⟩⟨⟨ 4 right cross stitches: sl 2 on a cable needle behind work, k2 from left needle, then k2 from cable needle
sl: slip stitch from one needle to another without knitting it

Blister Stitch (2)

Number of stitches needed for symmetry and joining: multiple of 6 + 1 selvedge stitch at each end.

Rows 1 (right side of work) and 5: all knit.

Row 2 and all even numbered rows: all purl.

Row 3: 1 selvedge stitch, *knit 3 right cross stitches (1 and 2: sl 1 on a cable needle behind work, k2 from left needle, then k1 from cable needle), knit 3 left cross stitches (2 and 1: sl 2 on a cable needle in front of work, k1 from left needle, then k2 from cable needle)*; repeat from * to *; end with 1 selvedge stitch.

Row 7: 1 selvedge stitch, *knit 3 left cross stitches (2 and 1), knit 3 right cross stitches (1 and 2)*; repeat from * to *; end with 1 selvedge stitch.

Keep repeating Rows 1 through 8.

☐ knit stitch on right side or purl stitch on wrong side

⟩⟨ 3 left cross stitches: sl 2 on a cable needle in front of work, k1 from left needle, then k2 from cable needle

⟩⟨ 3 right cross stitches: sl 1 on a cable needle behind work, k2 from left needle, then k1 from cable needle
sl: slip stitch from one needle to another without knitting it

Cable Stitches

Honeycomb Stitch (1)

Number of stitches needed for symmetry and joining: multiple of 4 + 1 selvedge stitch at each end.

Row 1 (right side of work): 1 selvedge stitch, *knit 2 right cross stitches (knit the second stitch on the left needle first, passing the right needle in front of the first stitch, then knit the first stitch), knit 2 left cross stitches (knit the second stitch on the left needle first, passing the right needle behind the first stitch, then knit the first stitch)*; repeat from * to *; end with 1 selvedge stitch.

Rows 2 and 4: all purl.

Row 3: 1 selvedge stitch, *knit 2 left cross stitches, knit 2 right cross stitches*; repeat from * to *; end with 1 selvedge stitch.

Keep repeating Rows 1 through 4.

☐ knit stitch on right side or purl stitch on wrong side

✕ 2 left cross stitches: knit the second stitch on the left needle first, passing the right needle behind the first stitch, then knit the first stitch

✕ 2 right cross stitches: knit the second stitch on the left needle first, passing the right needle in front of the first stitch, then knit the first stitch

sl: slip stitch from one needle to another without knitting it

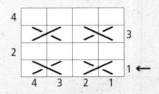

Honeycomb Stitch (2)

Number of stitches needed for symmetry and joining: multiple of 4 + 1 selvedge stitch at each end.

Row 1 (right side of work): 1 selvedge stitch, *knit 2 right cross stitches (knit the second stitch on the left needle first, passing the right needle in front of the first stitch, then knit the first stitch), knit 2 left cross stitches (knit the second stitch on the left needle first, passing the right needle behind the first stitch, then knit the first stitch)*; repeat from * to *; end with 1 selvedge stitch.

Row 2 and all even numbered rows: all purl.

Rows 3 and 7: all knit.

Row 5: 1 selvedge stitch, *knit 2 left cross stitches, knit 2 right cross stitches*; repeat from * to *; end with 1 selvedge stitch.

Keep repeating Rows 1 through 8.

☐ knit stitch on right side or purl stitch on wrong side

✕ 2 left cross stitches: knit the second stitch on the left needle first, passing the right needle behind the first stitch, then knit the first stitch

✕ 2 right cross stitches: knit the second stitch on the left needle first, passing the right needle in front of the first stitch, then knit the first stitch

sl: slip stitch from one needle to another without knitting it

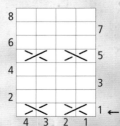

12-Stitch Chain Cables

The directions for this pattern consist of 12 stitches on a background of purled stockinette stitch.

Rows 1 (right side of work), 5, 7, and 11: k12.

Row 2 and all even numbered rows: knit each stitch as it appears in previous row (i.e., knit a knit stitch, purl a purl stitch).

Row 3: knit 6 right cross stitches (3 and 3: sl 3 on a cable needle behind work, k3 from left needle, then k3 from cable needle), knit 6 left cross stitches (3 and 3: sl 3 on a cable needle in front of work, k3 from left needle, then k3 from cable needle).

Row 9: knit 6 left cross stitches (3 and 3), knit 6 right cross stitches (3 and 3).

Keep repeating these 12 rows.

☐ knit stitch on right side or purl stitch on wrong side

▷▷◁ 6 left cross stitches: sl 3 on a cable needle in front of work, k3 from left needle, then k3 from cable needle

▷▷◁ 6 right cross stitches: sl 3 on a cable needle behind work, k3 from left needle, then k3 from cable needle

sl: slip stitch from one needle to another without knitting it

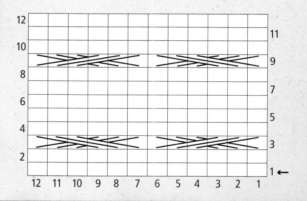

Link Cable

The directions for this pattern consist of 10 stitches on a background of purled stockinette stitch.

Rows 1 (right side of work) and 5: p1, k8, p1.

Row 2 and all even numbered rows: knit each stitch as it appears in previous row (i.e., knit a knit stitch, purl a purl stitch).

Row 3: p1, knit 4 right cross stitches (2 and 2: sl 2 on a cable needle behind work, k2 from left needle, then k2 from cable needle), knit 4 left cross stitches (2 and 2: sl 2 on a cable needle in front of work, k2 from left needle, then k2 from cable needle), p1.

Row 7: p1, 4 right cross stitches (p2, k2: sl 2 on a cable needle behind work, k2 from left needle, then p2 from cable needle), 4 left cross stitches (k2, p2: sl 2 on a cable needle in front of work, p2 from left needle, then k2 from cable needle), p1.

Row 9: 3 right cross stitches (p1, k2: sl 1 on a cable needle behind work, k2 from left needle, then p1 from cable needle), p4, 3 left cross stitches (k2, p1: sl 2 on a cable needle in front of work, p1 from left needle, then k2 from cable needle).

Row 11: k2, p6, k2.

Row 13: 3 left cross stitches (k2, p1), p4, 3 right cross stitches (p1, k2).

Row 15: p1, knit 4 left cross stitches (2 and 2), knit 4 right cross stitches (2 and 2), p1.

Keep repeating these 16 rows.

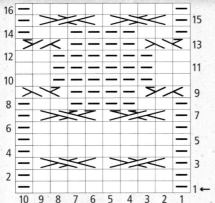

| | knit stitch on right side or purl stitch on wrong side |
| - | purl stitch on right side or knit stitch on wrong side |

>\< 3 left cross stitches: sl 2 on a cable needle in front of work, p1 from left needle, then k2 from cable needle

>\< 3 right cross stitches: sl 1 on a cable needle behind work, k2 from left needle, then p1 from cable needle

>\< 4 left cross stitches: sl 2 on a cable needle in front of work, k2 from left needle, then k2 from cable needle

>\< 4 right cross stitches: sl 2 on a cable needle behind work, k2 from left needle, then k2 from cable needle

>\< 4 left cross stitches: sl 2 on a cable needle in front of work, p2 from left needle, then k2 from cable needle

>\< 4 right cross stitches: sl 2 stitches on a cable needle behind work, k2 from left needle, then p2 from cable needle

sl: slip stitch from one needle to another without knitting it

Crowns

The directions for this pattern consist of 18 stitches on a background of purled stockinette stitch.

Rows 1 (right side of work) and 3: p3, k4, *p1, k1*; repeat from * to * 2 times, p1, k3, p3.

Rows 2 and 4: k3, p4, *k1, p1*; repeat from * to * 2 times, k1, p3, k3.

Row 5: p3, 6 right cross stitches (k3, p1, k1, p1: sl 3 on a cable needle behind work, p1, k1, p1 from left needle, then k3 from cable needle), 6 left cross stitches (p1, k1, p1, k3: sl 3 on a cable needle in front of work, k3 from left needle, then p1, k1, p1 from cable needle), p3.

Rows 6, 8, 10, 12, and 14: k4, p1, k1, p6, k1, p1, k4.

Rows 7, 9, 11, and 13: p3, k1, p1, k8, p1, k1, p3.

Row 15: p3, 6 left cross stitches (k1, p1, k1, k3: sl 3 on a cable needle in front of work, k3 from left needle, then p1, k1, p1 from cable needle), 6 right cross stitches (k3, k1, p1, k1: sl 3 on a cable needle behind work, k1, p1, k1 from left needle, then k3 from cable needle), p3.

Rows 16, 18, 20, 22, and 24: k3, p4, *k1, p1*; repeat from * to * 2 times, k1, p3, k3.

Rows 17, 19, 21, and 23: p3, k4, *p1, k1*; repeat from * to * 2 times, p1, k3, p3.

Keep repeating these 24 rows.

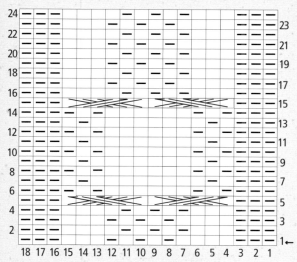

☐ knit stitch on right side or purl stitch on wrong side
– purl stitch on right side or knit stitch on wrong side
6 left cross stitches: sl 3 on a cable needle in front of work, k3 from left needle, then p1, k1, p1 from cable needle

6 right cross stitches: sl 3 on a cable needle behind work, p1, k1, p1 from left needle, then k3 from cable needle
6 right cross stitches: sl 3 on a cable needle behind work, k1, p1, k1 from left needle, then k3 from cable needle
sl: slip stitch from one needle to another without knitting it

Cable Stitches

Fancy Links

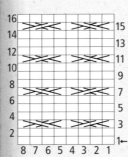

The directions for this pattern consist of 8 stitches on a background of purled stockinette stitch.

Rows 1 (right side of work), 5, 9, and 13: k8.

Row 2 and all even numbered rows: knit each stitch as it appears in previous row (i.e., knit a knit stitch, purl a purl stitch).

Rows 3 and 7: knit 4 right cross stitches (2 and 2: sl 2 on a cable needle behind work, k2 from left needle, then k2 from cable needle), knit 4 left cross stitches (2 and 2: sl 2 on a cable needle in front of work, k2 from left needle, then k2 from cable needle).

Rows 11 and 15: knit 4 left cross stitches (2 and 2), knit 4 right cross stitches (2 and 2).

Keep repeating these 16 rows.

☐ knit stitch on right side or purl stitch on wrong side

✕ 4 left cross stitches: sl 2 on a cable needle in front of work, k2 from left needle, then k2 from cable needle

✕ 4 right cross stitches: sl 2 on a cable needle behind work, k2 from left needle, then k2 from cable needle

sl: slip stitch from one needle to another without knitting it

Chain

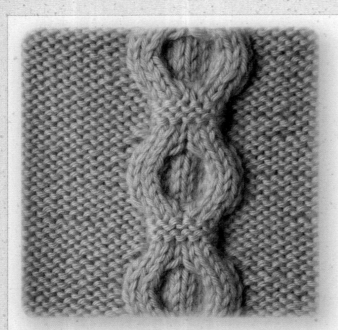

The directions for this pattern consist of 12 stitches on a background of purled stockinette stitch.

Rows 1 (right side of work), 6, 8, and 10: all purl.

Rows 2, 7, and 9: all knit.

Row 3: p3, k6, p3.

Rows 4 and 12: k3, p6, k3.

Row 5: 6 right cross stitches (3 and 3: sl 3 on a cable needle behind work, k3 from left needle, then k3 from cable needle), knit 6 left cross stitches (3 and 3: sl 3 on a cable needle in front of work, k3 from left needle, then k3 from cable needle).

Row 11: 6 left cross stitches (k3, p3: sl 3 stitches on a cable needle in front of work, p3 from left needle, then k3 from cable needle), 6 right cross stitches (p3, k3: sl 3 on a cable needle behind work, k3 from left needle, then p3 from cable needle).

Keep repeating these 12 rows.

Fancy Cable

Note: Uses 2 cable needles. Number of stitches needed for symmetry: multiple of 12 + 3 + 1 selvedge stitch at each end.

Row 1 (right side of work): 1 selvedge stitch, *p3, k9*; repeat from * to *; end with p3, 1 selvedge stitch.

Rows 2, 3, 4, 5, 6, 7, 8, 10, 11, 12, 13, 14, 15, and 16: knit each stitch as it appears in previous row (i.e., knit a knit stitch, purl a purl stitch).

Row 9: 1 selvedge stitch, *p3, knit 9 right cross stitches with the center stitches in front of your work (3 + 3 + 3: sl 3 on a cable needle behind work, sl 3 on a second cable needle in front of work, k3 from left needle, k3 from second cable needle, k3 from first cable needle)*; repeat from * to *; end with p3, 1 selvedge stitch.

Keep repeating these 16 rows.

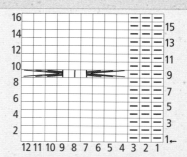

☐ knit stitch on right side or purl stitch on wrong side

— purl stitch on right side or knit stitch on wrong side

9 right cross stitches with the center stitches in front of your work: sl 3 on a cable needle behind work, sl 3 on a second cable needle in front of work, k3 from left needle, k3 from second cable needle, k3 from first cable needle

sl: slip stitch from one needle to another without knitting it

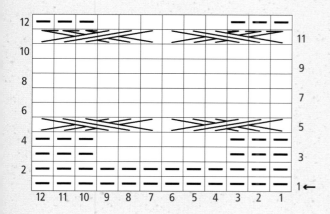

☐ knit stitch on right side or purl stitch on wrong side

— purl stitch on right side or knit stitch on wrong side

6 left cross stitches: sl 3 on a cable needle in front of work, k3 from left needle, then k3 from cable needle

6 right cross stitches: sl 3 on a cable needle behind work, k3 from left needle, then k3 from cable needle

6 left cross stitches: sl 3 stitches on a cable needle in front of work, p3 from left needle, then k3 from cable needle

6 right cross stitches: sl 3 on a cable needle behind work, k3 from left needle, then p3 from cable needle

sl: slip stitch from one needle to another without knitting it

Cable Stitches

Fancy Large Cable

The directions for this pattern consist of 8 stitches on a background of purled stockinette stitch.

Rows 1 (right side of work), 3, 9, and 11: k2, p1, k2, p1, k2.

Row 2 and all even numbered rows: knit each stitch as it appears in previous row (i.e., knit a knit stitch, purl a purl stitch).

Row 5: all knit.

Row 7: knit 8 left cross stitches with the center stitches in front of your work (3 + 2 + 3: sl 5 on a cable needle in front of work, k3 from left needle, sl the fifth and fourth stitches on the cable needle back to the left needle, knit these 2 stitches while passing them behind the 3 stitches on the cable needle, then k3 from cable needle).

Rows 13 and 15: k2, p4, k2.

Keep repeating these 16 rows.

Seed Motif

Number of stitches needed for symmetry: multiple of 18 + 10 + 1 selvedge stitch at each end.

Rows 1 (right side of work), 5, 9, and 13: all knit.

Row 2 and all even numbered rows: knit each stitch as it appears in previous row (i.e., knit a knit stitch, purl a purl stitch).

Row 3: 1 selvedge stitch, *k1, knit 4 right cross stitches (2 and 2: sl 2 on a cable needle behind work, k2 from left needle, then k2 from cable needle), knit 4 left cross stitches (2 and 2: sl 2 on a cable needle in front of work, k2 from left needle, then k2 from cable needle), k9*; repeat from * to *; end with k1, knit 4 right cross stitches (2 and 2), knit 4 left cross stitches (2 and 2), k1, 1 selvedge stitch.

Row 7: 1 selvedge stitch, *k1, knit 4 left cross stitches (2 and 2), knit 4 right cross stitches (2 and 2), k9*; repeat from * to *; end with k1, knit 4 left cross stitches (2 and 2), knit 4 right cross stitches (2 and 2), k1, 1 selvedge stitch.

Row 11: 1 selvedge stitch, *k10, knit 4 right cross stitches (2 and 2), knit 4 left cross stitches (2 and 2)*; repeat from * to *; end with k10, 1 selvedge stitch.

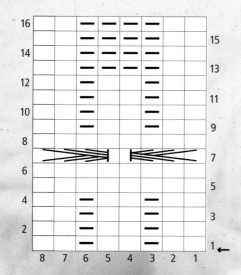

– purl stitch on right side or knit stitch on wrong side

8 left cross stitches with the center stitches in front of your work: sl 5 on a cable needle in front of work, k3 from left needle, sl the fifth and fourth stitches on the cable needle back to the left needle, knit these 2 stitches while passing them behind the 3 stitches on the cable needle, then k3 from cable needle

sl: slip stitch from one needle to another without knitting it

Row 15: 1 selvedge stitch, *k10, knit 4 left cross stitches (2 and 2), knit 4 right cross stitches (2 and 2)*; repeat from * to *; end with k10, 1 selvedge stitch.

Keep repeating these 16 rows.

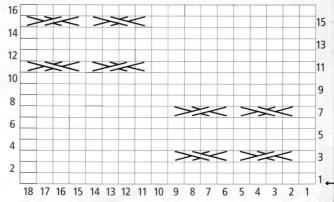

knit stitch on right side or purl stitch on wrong side

4 left cross stitches: sl 2 on a cable needle in front of work, k2 from left needle, then k2 from cable needle

4 right cross stitches: sl 2 on a cable needle behind work, k2 from left needle, then k2 from cable needle

sl: slip stitch from one needle to another without knitting it

Seeds and Cables

Number of stitches needed for symmetry: multiple of 16 + 8 + 1 selvedge stitch at each end.

Rows 1 (right side of work) and 9: 1 selvedge stitch, *k2, knit 4 right cross stitches (2 and 2: sl 2 on a cable needle behind work, k2 from left needle, then k2 from cable needle), k4, knit 4 right cross stitches (2 and 2), k2*; repeat from * to *; end with k2, knit 4 right cross stitches (2 and 2), k2, 1 selvedge stitch.

Rows 2, 4, 5, 6, 8, 10, 12, 13, 14, and 16: knit each stitch as it appears in previous row (i.e., knit a knit stitch, purl a purl stitch).

Row 3: 1 selvedge stitch, *knit 4 right cross stitches (2 and 2), knit 4 left cross stitches (2 and 2: sl 2 on a cable needle in front of work, k2 from left needle, then k2 from cable needle), k8*; repeat from * to *; end with knit 4 right cross stitches (2 and 2), knit 4 left cross stitches (2 and 2), 1 selvedge stitch.

Row 7: 1 selvedge stitch, *knit 4 left cross stitches (2 and 2), knit 4 right cross stitches (2 and 2), k8*; repeat from * to *; end with knit 4 left cross stitches (2 and 2), knit 4 right cross stitches (2 and 2), 1 selvedge stitch.

Row 11: 1 selvedge stitch, *k8, knit 4 right cross stitches (2 and 2), knit 4 left cross stitches (2 and 2)*; repeat from * to *; end with k8, 1 selvedge stitch.

Row 15: 1 selvedge stitch, *k8, knit 4 left cross stitches (2 and 2), knit 4 right cross stitches (2 and 2)*; repeat from * to *; end with k8, 1 selvedge stitch.

Keep repeating these 16 rows.

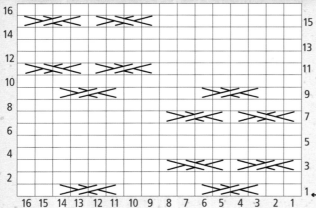

☐ knit stitch on right side or purl stitch on wrong side

✕ 4 left cross stitches: sl 2 on a cable needle in front of work, k2 from left needle, then k2 from cable needle

✕ 4 right cross stitches: sl 2 on a cable needle behind work, k2 from left needle, then k2 from cable needle

sl: slip stitch from one needle to another without knitting it

Large Cable in Relief

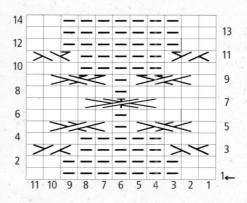

knit stitch on right side or purl stitch on wrong side

− purl stitch on right side or knit stitch on wrong side

⤡ 3 left cross stitches: sl 2 on a cable needle in front of work, k1 from left needle, then k2 from cable needle

⤢ 3 right cross stitches: sl 1 on a cable needle behind work, k2 from left needle, then k1 from cable needle

⤡ 3 left cross stitches: sl 2 on a cable needle in front of work, p1 from left needle, then k2 from cable needle

⤢ 3 right cross stitches: sl 1 on a cable needle behind work, k2 from left needle, then p1 from cable needle

⤡ 4 left cross stitches: sl 2 on a cable needle in front of work, k2 from left needle, then k2 from cable needle

⤢ 4 right cross stitches: sl 2 on a cable needle behind work, k2 from left needle, then k2 from cable needle

⤡ 4 left cross stitches: sl 2 stitches on a cable needle in front of work, p2 from left needle, then k2 from cable needle

⤢ 4 right cross stitches: sl 2 on a cable needle behind work, k2 from left needle, then p2 from cable needle

⤢ 5 right cross stitches: sl 3 on a cable needle behind work, k2 from left needle, sl the third stitch on the cable needle back to the left needle, knit it while passing it behind the 2 stitches on the cable needle, then k2 from cable needle

sl: slip stitch from one needle to another without knitting it

The directions for this pattern consist of 11 stitches on a background of knit stockinette stitch.

Rows 1 (right side of work) and 13: k2, p7, k2.

Row 2 and all even numbered rows: knit each stitch as it appears in previous row (i.e., knit a knit stitch, purl a purl stitch).

Row 3: knit 3 left cross stitches (2 and 1: sl 2 on a cable needle in front of work, k1 from left needle, then k2 from cable needle), p5, knit 3 right cross stitches (1 and 2: sl 1 on a cable needle behind work, k2 from left needle, then k1 from cable needle).

Row 5: k1, knit 4 left cross stitches (2 and 2: sl 2 on a cable needle in front of work, k2 from left needle, then k2 from cable needle), p1, knit 4 right cross stitches (2 and 2: sl 2 on a cable needle behind work, k2 from left needle, then k2 from cable needle), k1.

Row 7: k3, 5 right cross stitches (k2, p1, k2: sl 3 on a cable needle behind work, k2 from left needle, sl the third stitch on the cable needle back to the left needle, knit it while passing it behind the 2 stitches on the cable needle, then k2 from cable needle), k3.

Row 9: k1, 4 right cross stitches (p2, k2: sl 2 on a cable needle behind work, k2 from left needle, then p2 from cable needle), p1, 4 left cross stitches (k2, p2: sl 2 stitches on a cable needle in front of work, p2 from left needle, then k2 from cable needle), k1.

Row 11: 3 right cross stitches (p1, k2: sl 1 on a cable needle behind work, k2 from left needle, then p1 from cable needle), p5, 3 left cross stitches (k2, p1: sl 2 on a cable needle in front of work, p1 from left needle, then k2 from cable needle).

Keep repeating these 14 rows.

Cable Stitches

Shadow Cable

Number of stitches needed for symmetry: multiple of 12 + 6 + 1 selvedge stitch at each end.

Rows 1 (right side of work) and 5: all knit.

Row 2 and all even numbered rows: all purl.

Row 3: 1 selvedge stitch, *knit 6 left cross stitches (3 and 3: sl 3 on a cable needle in front of work, k3 from left needle, then k3 from cable needle), k6*; repeat from * to *; end with 6 knit left cross stitches (3 and 3), 1 selvedge stitch.

Row 7: 1 selvedge stitch, *k6, knit 6 right cross stitches (3 and 3: sl 3 on a cable needle behind work, k3 from left needle, then k3 from cable needle)*; repeat from * to *; end with k6, 1 selvedge stitch.

Keep repeating Rows 1 through 8.

☐ knit stitch on right side or purl stitch on wrong side

⋙⋘ 6 left cross stitches: sl 3 on a cable needle in front of work, k3 from left needle, then k3 from cable needle

⋙⋘ 6 right cross stitches: sl 3 on a cable needle behind work, k3 from left needle, then k3 from cable needle

sl: slip stitch from one needle to another without knitting it

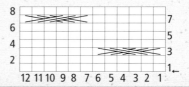

Cable Lozenges (1)

The directions for this pattern consist of 12 stitches on a background of knit stockinette stitch.

Rows 1 (right side of work) and 5: all knit.

Row 2 and all even numbered rows: all purl.

Row 3: knit 4 right cross stitches (2 and 2: sl 2 on a cable needle behind work, k2 from left needle, then k2 from cable needle), k4, knit 4 left cross stitches (2 and 2: sl 2 on a cable needle in front of work, k2 from left needle, then k2 from cable needle).

Row 7: k2, knit 4 left cross stitches (2 and 2), knit 4 right cross stitches (2 and 2), k2.

Keep repeating these 8 rows.

☐ knit stitch on right side or purl stitch on wrong side

⋊⋉ 4 left cross stitches: sl 2 on a cable needle in front of work, k2 from left needle, then k2 from cable needle

⋊⋉ 4 right cross stitches: sl 2 on a cable needle behind work, k2 from left needle, then k2 from cable needle

sl: slip stitch from one needle to another without knitting it

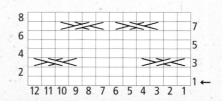

Cable Waves

Number of stitches needed for symmetry: multiple of 7 + 1 + 1 selvedge stitch at each end.

Rows 1 (right side of work) and 5: all knit.

Row 2 and all even numbered rows: all purl.

Row 3: 1 selvedge stitch, *k1, knit 4 right cross stitches (2 and 2: sl 2 on a cable needle behind work, k2 from left needle, then k2 from cable needle), k2*; repeat from * to *; end with k1, 1 selvedge stitch.

Row 7: 1 selvedge stitch, *k3, knit 4 left cross stitches (2 and 2: sl 2 on a cable needle in front of work, k2 from left needle, then k2 from cable needle)*; repeat from * to *; end with k1, 1 selvedge stitch.

Keep repeating Rows 1 through 8.

☐ knit stitch on right side or purl stitch on wrong side

⟩⟨ 4 left cross stitches: sl 2 on a cable needle in front of work, k2 from left needle, then k2 from cable needle

⟩⟨ 4 right cross stitches: sl 2 on a cable needle behind work, k2 from left needle, then k2 from cable needle

sl: slip stitch from one needle to another without knitting it

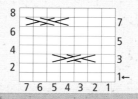

Cable Lozenges (2)

Number of stitches needed for symmetry and joining: multiple of 12 + 1 selvedge stitch at each end.

Rows 1 (right side of work) and 5: all knit.

Row 2 and all even numbered rows: all purl.

Row 3: 1 selvedge stitch, *knit 4 right cross stitches (2 and 2: sl 2 on a cable needle behind work, k2 from left needle, then k2 from cable needle), k4, knit 4 left cross stitches (2 and 2: sl 2 on a cable needle in front of work, k2 from left needle, then k2 from cable needle)*; repeat from * to *; end with 1 selvedge stitch.

Row 7: 1 selvedge stitch, *k2, knit 4 left cross stitches (2 and 2), knit 4 right cross stitches (2 and 2), k2*; repeat from * to *; end with 1 selvedge stitch.

Keep repeating Rows 1 through 8.

☐ knit stitch on right side or purl stitch on wrong side

⟩⟨ 4 left cross stitches: sl 2 on a cable needle in front of work, k2 from left needle, then k2 from cable needle

⟩⟨ 4 right cross stitches: sl 2 on a cable needle behind work, k2 from left needle, then k2 from cable needle

sl: slip stitch from one needle to another without knitting it

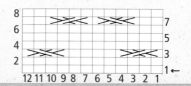

Cable Stitches

Left-Bias Cables (3 stitches)

Number of stitches needed for symmetry and joining: multiple of 8 + 3 + 1 selvedge stitch at each end.

Row 1 (right side of work): 1 selvedge stitch, p3, *4 left cross stitches (k3, p1: sl 3 on a cable needle in front of work, p1 from left needle, then k3 from cable needle), p4*; repeat from * to *; end with 1 selvedge stitch.

Row 2 and all even numbered rows: knit each stitch as it appears in previous row (i.e., knit a knit stitch, purl a purl stitch).

Row 3: 1 selvedge stitch, p3, *p1, 4 left cross stitches (k3, p1), p3*; repeat from * to *; end with 1 selvedge stitch.

Row 5: 1 selvedge stitch, p3, *p2, 4 left cross stitches (k3, p1), p2*; repeat from * to *; end with 1 selvedge stitch.

Row 7: 1 selvedge stitch, p3, *p3, 4 left cross stitches (k3, p1), p1*; repeat from * to *; end with 1 selvedge stitch.

Row 9: 1 selvedge stitch, p3, *p4, 4 left cross stitches (k3, p1)*; repeat from * to *; end with 1 selvedge stitch.

Row 11: 1 selvedge stitch, *4 left cross stitches (k3, p1), p4*; repeat from * to *; end with p3, 1 selvedge stitch.

Right-Bias Cables (3 stitches)

Number of stitches needed for symmetry and joining: multiple of 8 + 3 + 1 selvedge stitch at each end.

Row 1 (right side of work): 1 selvedge stitch, *p4, 4 right cross stitches (p1, k3: sl 1 on a cable needle behind work, k3 from left needle, then p1 from cable needle)*; repeat from * to *; end with p3, 1 selvedge stitch.

Row 2 and all even numbered rows: knit each stitch as it appears in previous row (i.e., knit a knit stitch, purl a purl stitch).

Row 3: 1 selvedge stitch, *p3, 4 right cross stitches (p1, k3), p1*; repeat from * to *; end with p3, 1 selvedge stitch.

Row 5: 1 selvedge stitch, *p2, 4 right cross stitches (p1, k3), p2*; repeat from * to *; end with p3, 1 selvedge stitch.

Row 7: 1 selvedge stitch, *p1, 4 right cross stitches (p1, k3), p3*; repeat from * to *; end with p3, 1 selvedge stitch.

Row 9: 1 selvedge stitch, *4 right cross stitches (p1, k3), p4*; repeat from * to *; end with p3, 1 selvedge stitch.

Row 11: 1 selvedge stitch, p3, *p4, 4 right cross stitches (p1, k3)*; repeat from * to *; end with 1 selvedge stitch.

Row 13: 1 selvedge stitch, *p1, 4 left cross stitches (k3, p1), p3*; repeat from * to *; end with p3, 1 selvedge stitch.
Row 15: 1 selvedge stitch, *p2, 4 left cross stitches (k3, p1), p2*; repeat from * to *; end with p3, 1 selvedge stitch.
Keep repeating these 16 rows.

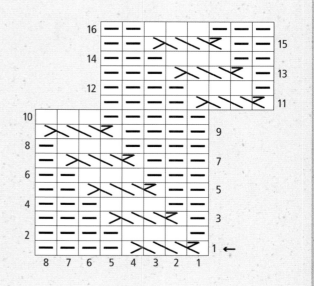

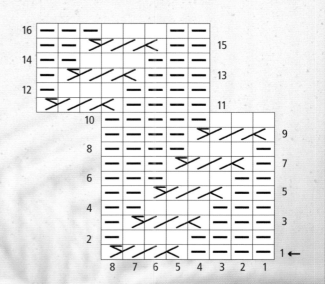 purl stitch on right side or knit stitch on wrong side
 4 left cross stitches: sl 3 on a cable needle in front of work, p1 from left needle, then k3 from cable needle
sl: slip stitch from one needle to another without knitting it

Row 13: 1 selvedge stitch, p3, *p3, 4 right cross stitches (p1, k3), p1*; repeat from * to *; end with 1 selvedge stitch.
Row 15: 1 selvedge stitch, p3, *p2, 4 right cross stitches (p1, k3), p2*; repeat from * to *; end with 1 selvedge stitch.
Keep repeating these 16 rows.

purl stitch on right side or knit stitch on wrong side
4 right cross stitches: sl 1 on a cable needle behind work, k3 from left needle, then p1 from cable needle
sl: slip stitch from one needle to another without knitting it

Diamonds in Relief

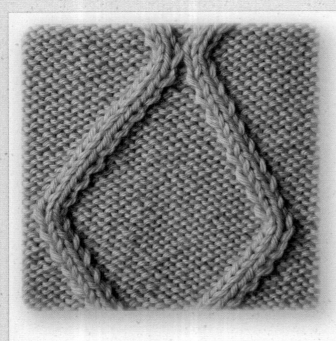

knit stitch on right side or purl stitch on wrong side

− purl stitch on right side or knit stitch on wrong side

⟩⟨ 3 left cross stitches: sl 2 on a cable needle in front of work, p1 from left needle, then k2 from cable needle

⟩⟨ 3 right cross stitches: sl 1 on a cable needle behind work, k2 from left needle, then p1 from cable needle

sl: slip stitch from one needle to another without knitting it

The directions for this pattern consist of 22 stitches on a background of purled stockinette stitch.

Row 1 (right side of work): p8, 3 right cross stitches (p1, k2: sl 1 on a cable needle behind work, k2 from left needle, then p1 from cable needle), 3 left cross stitches (k2, p1: sl 2 on a cable needle in front of work, p1 from left needle, then k2 from cable needle), p8.

Row 2 and all even numbered rows: knit each stitch as it appears in previous row (i.e., knit a knit stitch, purl a purl stitch).

Row 3: p7, 3 right cross stitches (p1, k2), p2, 3 left cross stitches (k2, p1), p7.

Row 5: p6, 3 right cross stitches (p1, k2), p4, 3 left cross stitches (k2, p1), p6.

Row 7: p5, 3 right cross stitches (p1, k2), p6, 3 left cross stitches (k2, p1), p5.

Row 9: p4, 3 right cross stitches (p1, k2), p8, 3 left cross stitches (k2, p1), p4.

Row 11: p3, 3 right cross stitches (p1, k2), k10, 3 left cross stitches (k2, p1), p3.

Row 13: p2, 3 right cross stitches (p1, k2), p12, 3 left cross stitches (k2, p1), p2.

Row 15: p1, 3 right cross stitches (p1, k2), p14, 3 left cross stitches (k2, p1), p1.

Row 17: 3 right cross stitches (p1, k2), p16, 3 left cross stitches (k2, p1).

Row 19: 3 left cross stitches (k2, p1), p16, 3 right cross stitches (p1, k2).

Row 21: p1, 3 left cross stitches (k2, p1), p14, 3 right cross stitches (p1, k2), p1.

Row 23: p2, 3 left cross stitches (k2, p1), p12, 3 right cross stitches (p1, k2), p2.

Row 25: p3, 3 left cross stitches (k2, p1), k10, 3 right cross stitches (p1, k2), p3.

Row 27: p4, 3 left cross stitches (k2, p1), p8, 3 right cross stitches (p1, k2), p4.

Row 29: p5, 3 left cross stitches (k2, p1), p6, 3 right cross stitches (p1, k2), p5.

Row 31: p6, 3 left cross stitches (k2, p1), p4, 3 right cross stitches (p1, k2), p6.

Row 33: p7, 3 left cross stitches (k2, p1), p2, 3 right cross stitches (p1, k2), p7.

Row 35: p8, 3 left cross stitches (k2, p1), 3 right cross stitches (p1, k2), p8.

Keep repeating these 36 rows.

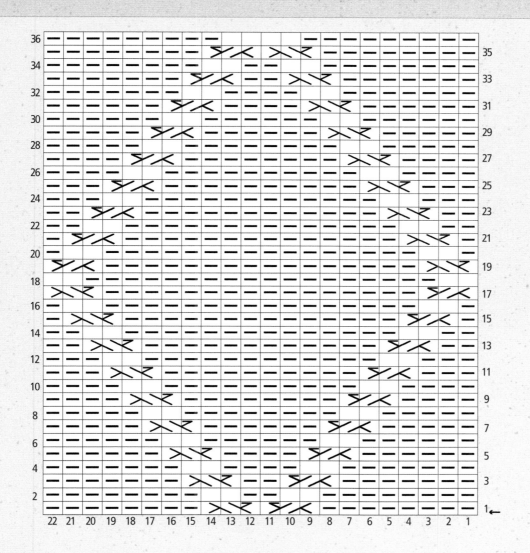

Diamonds and Cables

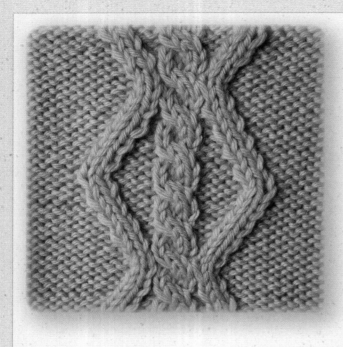

The directions for this pattern consist of 18 stitches on a background of purled stockinette stitch.

Row 1 (right side of work): p5, k8, p5.

Row 2 and all even numbered rows: knit each stitch as it appears in previous row (i.e., knit a knit stitch, purl a purl stitch).

Row 3: p4, 3 right cross stitches (p1, k2: sl 1 on a cable needle behind work, k2 from left needle, then p1 from cable needle), knit 4 left cross stitches (2 and 2: sl 2 on a cable needle in front of work, k2 from left needle, then k2 from cable needle), 3 left cross stitches (k2, p1: sl 2 on a cable needle in front of work, p1 from left needle, then k2 from cable needle), p4.

Row 5: p3, 3 right cross stitches (p1, k2), p1, k4, p1, 3 left cross stitches (k2, p1), p3.

Row 7: p2, 3 right cross stitches (p1, k2), p2, knit 4 left cross stitches (2 and 2), p2, 3 left cross stitches (k2, p1), p2.

Row 9: p1, 3 right cross stitches (p1, k2), p3, k4, p3, 3 left cross stitches (k2, p1), p1.

Row 11: 3 right cross stitches (p1, k2), p4, knit 4 left cross stitches (2 and 2), p4, 3 left cross stitches (k2, p1).

Row 13: 3 left cross stitches (k2, p1), p4, k4, p4, 3 right cross stitches (p1, k2).

Row 15: p1, 3 left cross stitches (k2, p1), p3, knit 4 left cross stitches (2 and 2), p3, 3 right cross stitches (p1, k2), p1.

Row 17: p2, 3 left cross stitches (k2, p1), p2, k4, p2, 3 right cross stitches (p1, k2), p2.

Row 19: p3, 3 left cross stitches (k2, p1), p1, knit 4 left cross stitches (2 and 2), p1, 3 right cross stitches (p1, k2), p3.

Row 21: p4, 3 left cross stitches (k2, p1), k4, 3 right cross stitches (p1, k2), p4.

Keep repeating Rows 3 through 22.

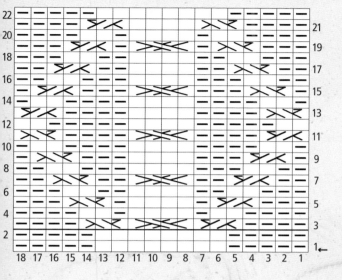

knit stitch on right side or purl stitch on wrong side

− purl stitch on right side or knit stitch on wrong side

⟩⟨ 3 left cross stitches: sl 2 on a cable needle in front of work, p1 from left needle, then k2 from cable needle

⟩⟨ 3 right cross stitches: sl 1 on a cable needle behind work, k2 from left needle, then p1 from cable needle

⟩⟨ 4 left cross stitches: sl 2 on a cable needle in front of work, k2 from left needle, then k2 from cable needle

sl: slip stitch from one needle to another without knitting it

Cable Lattice (1)

Number of stitches needed for symmetry: multiple of 12 + 1 selvedge stitch at each end.

Note: The directions for this pattern consist of a minimum of 26 stitches.

Row 1 (right side of work): 1 selvedge stitch, *k2, p8, k2*; repeat from * to *; end with 1 selvedge stitch.

Row 2 and all even numbered rows: knit each stitch as it appears in previous row (i.e., knit a knit stitch, purl a purl stitch).

Row 3: 1 selvedge stitch, *3 left cross stitches (k2, p1: sl 2 on a cable needle in front of work, p1 from left needle, then k2 from cable needle), p6, 3 right cross stitches (p1, k2: sl 1 on a cable needle behind work, k2 from left needle, then p1 from cable needle)*; repeat from * to *; end with 1 selvedge stitch.

Row 5: 1 selvedge stitch, *p1, 3 left cross stitches (k2, p1), p4, 3 right cross stitches (p1, k2), p1*; repeat from * to *; end with 1 selvedge stitch.

Row 7: 1 selvedge stitch, *p2, 3 left cross stitches (k2, p1), p2, 3 right cross stitches (p1, k2), p2*; repeat from * to *; end with 1 selvedge stitch.

Row 9: 1 selvedge stitch, *p3, 3 left cross stitches (k2, p1), 3 right cross stitches (p1, k2), p3*; repeat from * to *; end with 1 selvedge stitch.

Row 11: 1 selvedge stitch, *p4, knit 4 left cross stitches (2 and 2: sl 2 on a cable needle in front of work, k2 from left needle, then k2 from cable needle), p4*; repeat from * to *; end with 1 selvedge stitch.

Row 13: 1 selvedge stitch, p3, 3 right cross stitches (p1, k2); *3 left cross stitches (k2, p1), p6, 3 right cross stitches (p1, k2)*; repeat from * to *; end with 3 left cross stitches (k2, p1), p3, 1 selvedge stitch.

Row 15: 1 selvedge stitch, p2, 3 right cross stitches (p1, k2), p1; *p1, 3 left cross stitches (k2, p1), p4, 3 right cross stitches (p1, k2), p1*; repeat from * to *; end with p1, 3 left cross stitches (k2, p1), p2, 1 selvedge stitch.

Row 17: 1 selvedge stitch, p1, 3 right cross stitches (p1, k2), p2; *p2, 3 left cross stitches (k2, p1), p2, 3 right cross stitches (p1, k2), p2*; repeat from * to *; end with p2, 3 left cross stitches (k2, p1), p1, 1 selvedge stitch.

Row 19: 1 selvedge stitch, 3 right cross stitches (p1, k2), p3; *p3, 3 left cross stitches (k2, p1), 3 right cross stitches (p1, k2), p3*; repeat from * to *; end with p3, 3 left cross stitches (k2, p1), 1 selvedge stitch.

Row 21: 1 selvedge stitch, k2, p4; *p4, knit 4 left cross stitches (2 and 2), p4*; repeat from * to *; end with p4, k2, 1 selvedge stitch.

Keep repeating Rows 3 through 22.

knit stitch on right side or purl stitch on wrong side

− purl stitch on right side or knit stitch on wrong side

3 left cross stitches: sl 2 on a cable needle in front of work, p1 from left needle, then k2 from cable needle

3 right cross stitches: sl 1 on a cable needle behind work, k2 from left needle, then p1 from cable needle

4 left cross stitches: sl 2 on a cable needle in front of work, k2 from left needle, then k2 from cable needle

sl: slip stitch from one needle to another without knitting it

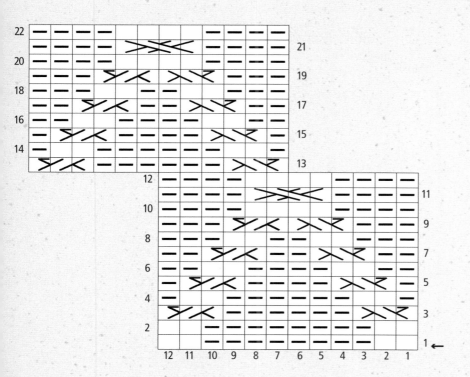

Cable Lattice (2)

Number of stitches needed for symmetry: multiple of 12 + 1 selvedge stitch at each end.

Row 1 (right side of work): 1 selvedge stitch, *p2, 4 right cross stitches (p2, k2: sl 2 on a cable needle behind work, k2 from left needle, then p2 from cable needle), 4 left cross stitches (k2, p2: sl 2 on a cable needle in front of work, p2 from left needle, then k2 from cable needle), p2*; repeat from * to *; end with 1 selvedge stitch.

Row 2 and all even numbered rows: knit each stitch as it appears in previous row (i.e., knit a knit stitch, purl a purl stitch).

Row 3: 1 selvedge stitch, *4 right cross stitches (p2, k2), p4, 4 left cross stitches (k2, p2)*; repeat from * to *; end with 1 selvedge stitch.

Row 5: 1 selvedge stitch, k2, *p8, knit 4 right cross stitches (2 and 2: sl 2 on a cable needle behind work, k2 from left needle, then k2 from cable needle)*; repeat from * to *; end with p8, k2, 1 selvedge stitch.

Row 7: 1 selvedge stitch, *4 left cross stitches (k2, p2), p4, 4 right cross stitches (p2, k2)*; repeat from * to *; end with 1 selvedge stitch.

Row 9: 1 selvedge stitch, *p2, 4 left cross stitches (k2, p2), 4 right cross stitches (p2, k2), p2*; repeat from * to *; end with 1 selvedge stitch.

Row 11: 1 selvedge stitch, *p4, knit 4 left cross stitches (2 and 2: sl 2 on a cable needle in front of work, k2 from left needle, then k2 from cable needle), p4*; repeat from * to *; end with 1 selvedge stitch.

Keep repeating Rows 1 through 12.

☐ knit stitch on right side or purl stitch on wrong side

– purl stitch on right side or knit stitch on wrong side

4 left cross stitches: sl 2 on a cable needle in front of work, p2 from left needle, then k2 from cable needle

4 right cross stitches: sl 2 on a cable needle behind work, k2 from left needle, then p2 from cable needle

4 left cross stitches: sl 2 on a cable needle in front of work, k2 from left needle, then k2 from cable needle

4 right cross stitches: sl 2 on a cable needle behind work, k2 from left needle, then k2 from cable needle

sl: slip stitch from one needle to another without knitting it

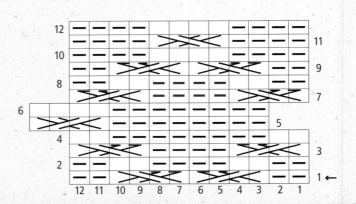

Double Lattice Stitch

The directions for this pattern consist of 28 stitches.

Row 1 (right side of work): p2, *k2, p8, k2*; repeat from * to *; end with p2.

Row 2 and all even numbered rows: knit each stitch as it appears in previous row (i.e., knit a knit stitch, purl a purl stitch).

Row 3: p2, k2, p8, knit 4 right cross stitches (2 and 2: sl 2 on a cable needle behind work, k2 from left needle, then k2 from cable needle), p8, k2, p2.

Row 5: p2, *4 left cross stitches (k2, p2: sl 2 on a cable needle in front of work, p2 from left needle, then k2 from cable needle), p4, 4 right cross stitches (p2, k2: sl 2 on cable needle behind work, k2 from left needle, then p2 from cable needle)*; repeat from * to *; end with p2.

Row 7: p4, *4 left cross stitches (k2, p2), 4 right cross stitches (p2, k2), p4*; repeat from * to *.

Row 9: p6, knit 4 right cross stitches (2 and 2), p8, knit 4 right cross stitches (2 and 2), p6.

Row 11: p4, *4 right cross stitches (p2, k2), 4 left cross stitches (k2, p2), p4*; repeat from * to *.

Row 13: p2, *4 right cross stitches (p2, k2), p4, 4 left cross stitches (k2, p2)*; repeat from * to *; end with p2.

Keep repeating Rows 3 through 14.

☐ knit stitch on right side or purl stitch on wrong side

– purl stitch on right side or knit stitch on wrong side

⧓ 4 right cross stitches: sl 2 on a cable needle behind work, k2 from left needle, then k2 from cable needle

⧓ 4 left cross stitches: sl 2 on a cable needle in front of work, p2 from left needle, then k2 from cable needle

⧓ 4 right cross stitches: sl 2 on cable needle behind work, k2 from left needle, then p2 from cable needle

sl: slip stitch from one needle to another without knitting it

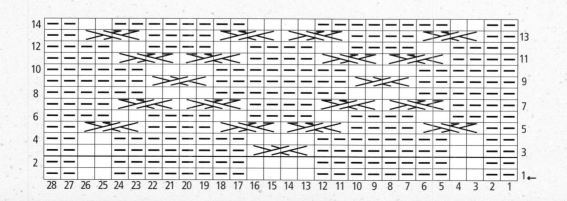

Diamonds, Ribbing, and Garter

knit stitch on right side or purl stitch on wrong side

− purl stitch on right side or knit stitch on wrong side

⟍⟋ 4 left cross stitches: sl 3 on a cable needle in front of work, k1 from left needle, then k3 from cable needle

⟋⟍ 4 right cross stitches: sl 1 on a cable needle behind work, k3 from left needle, then k1 from cable needle

⟍⟋ 4 left cross stitches: sl 3 on a cable needle in front of work, p1 from left needle, then k3 from cable needle

⟋⟍ 4 right cross stitches: sl 1 on a cable needle behind work, k3 from left needle, then p1 from cable needle

⟩⟩⟩ 6 right cross stitches: sl 3 on a cable needle behind work, k3 from left needle, then k3 from cable needle

⟩⟩⟩ 7 right cross stitches: sl 4 on a cable needle behind work, k3 from left needle, sl the fourth stitch on the cable needle back to the left needle, purl it while passing it behind the 3 stitches on the cable needle, then k3 from cable needle

sl: slip stitch from one needle to another without knitting it

Number of stitches needed for symmetry: multiple of 17 + 1 selvedge stitch at each end.

Row 1 (right side of work): 1 selvedge stitch, *k4, knit 4 right cross stitches (1 and 3: sl 1 on a cable needle behind work, k3 from left needle, then k1 from cable needle), p1, knit 4 left cross stitches (3 and 1: sl 3 on a cable needle in front of work, k1 from left needle, then k3 from cable needle), k4*; repeat from * to *; end with 1 selvedge stitch.

Rows 2 and 20: 1 selvedge stitch, *k4, p4, k1, p4, k4*; repeat from * to *; end with 1 selvedge stitch.

Row 3: 1 selvedge stitch, *k3, 4 right cross stitches (p1, k3: sl 1 on a cable needle behind work, k3 from left needle, then p1 from cable needle), k1, p1, k1, 4 left cross stitches (k3, p1: sl 3 on a cable needle in front of work, p1 from left needle, then k3 from cable needle), k3*; repeat from * to *; end with 1 selvedge stitch.

Rows 4 and 18: 1 selvedge stitch, *k3, p3, °k1, p1°; repeat from ° to ° 2 times, k1, p3, k3*; repeat from * to *; end with 1 selvedge stitch.

Row 5: 1 selvedge stitch, *k2, knit 4 right cross stitches (1 and 3), °p1, k1°; repeat from ° to ° 2 times, p1, knit 4 left cross stitches (3 and 1), k2*; repeat from * to *; end with 1 selvedge stitch.

Rows 6 and 16: 1 selvedge stitch, *k2, p4, °k1, p1°; repeat from ° to ° 2 times, k1, p4, k2*; repeat from * to *; end with 1 selvedge stitch.

Row 7: 1 selvedge stitch, *k1, 4 right cross stitches (p1, k3), °k1, p1°; repeat from ° to ° 3 times, k1, 4 left cross stitches (k3, p1), k1*; repeat from * to *; end with 1 selvedge stitch.

Rows 8 and 14: 1 selvedge stitch, *k1, p3, °k1, p1°; repeat from ° to ° 4 times, k1, p3, k1*; repeat from * to *; end with 1 selvedge stitch.

Row 9: 1 selvedge stitch, *knit 4 right cross stitches (1 and 3), °p1, k1°; repeat from ° to ° 4 times, p1, knit 4 left cross stitches (3 and 1)*; repeat from * to *; end with 1 selvedge stitch.

Rows 10 and 12: knit each stitch as it appears in previous row (i.e., knit a knit stitch, purl a purl stitch).

Row 11: 1 selvedge stitch, k4, *°p1, k1°; repeat from ° to ° 5 times, knit 6 right cross stitches (3 and 3: sl 3 on a cable needle behind work, k3 from left needle, then k3 from cable needle), k1*; repeat from * to *; end with °p1, k1°; repeat from ° to ° 4 times, p1, k4, 1 selvedge stitch.

Row 13: 1 selvedge stitch, *knit 4 left cross stitches (3 and 1), °p1, k1°; repeat from ° to ° 4 times, p1, knit 4 right cross stitches (1 and 3)*; repeat from * to *; end with 1 selvedge stitch.

Row 15: 1 selvedge stitch, *k1, knit 4 left cross stitches (3 and 1), °k1, p1°; repeat from ° to ° 3 times, k1, knit 4 right cross stitches (1 and 3), k1*; repeat from * to *; end with 1 selvedge stitch.

Row 17: 1 selvedge stitch, *k2, knit 4 left cross stitches (3 and 1), °p1, k1°; repeat from ° to ° 2 times, p1, knit 4 right cross stitches (1 and 3), k2*; repeat from * to *; end with 1 selvedge stitch.

Row 19: 1 selvedge stitch, *k3, knit 4 left cross stitches (3 and 1), k1, p1, k1, knit 4 right cross stitches (1 and 3), k3*; repeat from * to *; end with 1 selvedge stitch.

Row 21: 1 selvedge stitch, *k4, knit 4 left cross stitches (3 and 1), p1, knit 4 right cross stitches (1 and 3), k4*; repeat from * to *; end with 1 selvedge stitch.

Rows 22 and 24: 1 selvedge stitch, *k5, p3, k1, p3, k5*; repeat from * to *; end with 1 selvedge stitch.

Row 23: 1 selvedge stitch, *k5, 7 right cross stitches (k3, p1, k3: sl 4 on a cable needle behind work, k3 from left needle, sl the fourth stitch on the cable needle back to the left needle, purl it while passing it behind the 3 stitches on the cable needle, then k3 from cable needle), k5*; repeat from * to *; end with 1 selvedge stitch.

Keep repeating Rows 1 through 24.

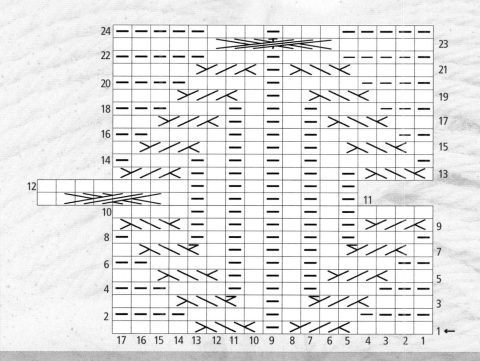

Attached Lozenges

Number of stitches needed for symmetry: multiple of 10 + 1 selvedge stitch at each end.

Row 1 (right side of work): 1 selvedge stitch, *k2, p6, k2*; repeat from * to *; end with 1 selvedge stitch.

Rows 2, 4, 6, 8, 10, 14, 16, 18, and 20: knit each stitch as it appears in previous row (i.e., knit a knit stitch, purl a purl stitch).

Row 3: 1 selvedge stitch, *3 left cross stitches (k2, p1: sl 2 on a cable needle in front of work, p1 from left needle, then k2 from cable needle), p4, 3 right cross stitches (p1, k2: sl 1 on a cable needle behind work, k2 from left needle, then p1 from cable needle)*; repeat from * to *; end with 1 selvedge stitch.

Row 5: 1 selvedge stitch, *p1, 3 left cross stitches (k2, p1), p2, 3 right cross stitches (p1, k2), p1*; repeat from * to *; end with 1 selvedge stitch.

Row 7: 1 selvedge stitch, *p2, 3 left cross stitches (k2, p1), 3 right cross stitches (p1, k2), p2*; repeat from * to *; end with 1 selvedge stitch.

Rows 9, 11, 19, and 21: all purl.

Row 12: 1 selvedge stitch, *k3, p4, k3*; repeat from * to *; end with 1 selvedge stitch.

Row 13: 1 selvedge stitch, *p2, 3 right cross stitches (p1, k2), 3 left cross stitches (k2, p1), p2*; repeat from * to *; end with 1 selvedge stitch.

Row 15: 1 selvedge stitch, *p1, 3 right cross stitches (p1, k2), p2, 3 left cross stitches (k2, p1), p1*; repeat from * to *; end with 1 selvedge stitch.

Row 17: 1 selvedge stitch, *3 right cross stitches (p1, k2), p4, 3 left cross stitches (k2, p1)*; repeat from * to *; end with 1 selvedge stitch.

Row 22: 1 selvedge stitch, *p2, k6, p2*; repeat from * to *; end with 1 selvedge stitch.

Keep repeating Rows 3 through 22.

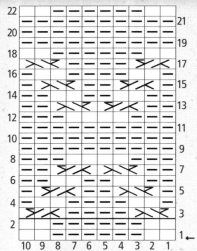

☐ knit stitch on right side or purl stitch on wrong side

− purl stitch on right side or knit stitch on wrong side

╲╱ 3 left cross stitches: sl 2 on a cable needle in front of work, p1 from left needle, then k2 from cable needle

╱╲ 3 right cross stitches: sl 1 on a cable needle behind work, k2 from left needle, then p1 from cable needle

sl: slip stitch from one needle to another without knitting it

Basketweave Stitch

Number of stitches needed for symmetry: multiple of 2 + 1 selvedge stitch at each end.

Row 1 (right side of work): 1 selvedge stitch, *knit 2 left cross stitches (knit the second stitch on the left needle first, passing the right needle behind the first stitch, then knit the first stitch)*; repeat from * to *; end with 1 selvedge stitch.

Row 2: 1 selvedge stitch, p1, *purl 2 right cross stitches (purl the second stitch on the left needle first, passing the right needle in front of the first stitch, then purl the first stitch)*; repeat from * to *; end with p1, 1 selvedge stitch.

Keep repeating these 2 rows.

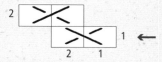

✕ 2 left cross stitches: knit the second stitch on the left needle first, passing the right needle behind the first stitch, then knit the first stitch

✕ 2 right cross stitches: knit the second stitch on the left needle first, passing the right needle in front of the first stitch, then knit the first stitch

Braided Basketweave Stitch

Number of stitches needed for symmetry: multiple of 4 + 1 selvedge stitch at each end. This pattern consists of a minimum of 10 stitches.

Row 1 (right side of work): 1 selvedge stitch, k2, *knit 4 right cross stitches (2 and 2: sl 2 on a cable needle behind work, k2 from left needle, then k2 from cable needle)*; repeat from * to *; end with k2, 1 selvedge stitch.

Row 2 and all even numbered rows: all purl.

Row 3: 1 selvedge stitch, *knit 4 left cross stitches (2 and 2: sl 2 on a cable needle in front of work, k2 from left needle, then k2 from cable needle)*; repeat from * to *; end with 1 selvedge stitch.

Keep repeating these 4 rows.

☐ knit stitch on right side or purl stitch on wrong side

⟩✕⟨ 4 left cross stitches: sl 2 on a cable needle in front of work, k2 from left needle, then k2 from cable needle

⟩✕⟨ 4 right cross stitches: sl 2 on a cable needle behind work, k2 from left needle, then k2 from cable needle

sl: slip stitch from one needle to another without knitting it

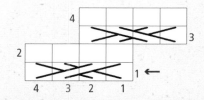

Cable Ribbing (4)

The directions for this pattern consist of 10 stitches on a background of purled stockinette stitch.

Note: uses 2 cable needles.

Rows 1 (right side of work), 5, 7, and 11: *k2, p2*; repeat from * to * 2 times, k2.

Row 2 and all even numbered rows: knit the stitches as they appear (i.e., knit a knit, purl a purl).

Row 3: 6 left cross stitches (k2, p2, k2: sl 2 on a cable needle in front of work, sl 2 on a second cable needle behind work, k2 from left needle, p2 from second cable needle, then k2 from first cable needle), p2, k2.

Row 9: k2, p2, 6 left cross stitches (k2, p2, k2).

Keep repeating these 12 rows.

Crossed Ribbing k2/p2

Number of stitches needed for joining: multiple of 12 + 1 selvedge stitch at each end.

Note: uses 2 cable needles.

Row 1 (right side of work), 5, 7, and 11: 1 selvedge stitch, *p1, °k2, p2°; repeat from ° to ° 2 times, k2, p1*; repeat from * to *; end with 1 selvedge stitch.

Row 2 and all even numbered rows: knit each stitch as it appears in previous row (i.e., knit a knit stitch, purl a purl stitch).

Row 3: 1 selvedge stitch, *p1, 6 right cross stitches (k2, p2, k2: sl 4 on a cable needle behind work, k2 from left needle, sl the fourth and third stitches on the cable needle back to the left needle, purl them while passing them behind the 2 stitches on the cable needle, then k2 from cable needle), p2, k2, p1*; repeat from * to *; end with 1 selvedge stitch.

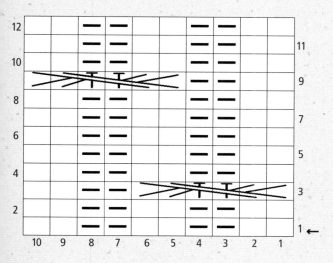

knit stitch on right side or purl stitch on wrong side
— purl stitch on right side or knit stitch on wrong side
6 left cross stitches: sl 2 on a cable needle in front of work, sl 2 on a second cable needle behind work, k2 from left needle, p2 from second cable needle, then k2 from first cable needle
sl: slip stitch from one needle to another without knitting it

Row 9: 1 selvedge stitch, *p1, k2, p2, 6 left cross stitches (k2, p2, k2: sl 2 on a cable needle in front of work, sl 2 on a second cable needle behind work, k2 from left needle, p2 from second cable needle, then k2 from first cable needle), p1*; repeat from * to *; end with 1 selvedge stitch.

Keep repeating these 12 rows.

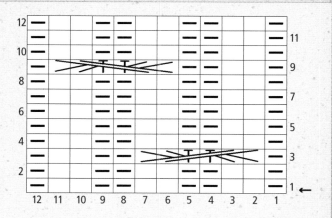

knit stitch on right side or purl stitch on wrong side
— purl stitch on right side or knit stitch on wrong side
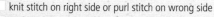 6 left cross stitches: sl 2 on a cable needle in front of work, sl 2 on a second cable needle behind work, k2 from left needle, p2 from second cable needle, then k2 from first cable needle

6 right cross stitches: sl 4 on a cable needle behind work, k2 from left needle, sl the fourth and third stitches on the cable needle back to the left needle, purl them while passing them behind the 2 stitches on the cable needle, then k2 from cable needle
sl: slip stitch from one needle to another without knitting it

Crossed Ribbing (1)

Number of stitches needed for joining: multiple of 8 + 2 + 1 selvedge stitch at each end.

Rows 1 (right side of work), 3, 5, 9, 11, and 13: 1 selvedge stitch, *k2, p2*; repeat from * to *; end with k2, 1 selvedge stitch.

Row 2 and all even numbered rows: knit each stitch as it appears in previous row (i.e., knit a knit stitch, purl a purl stitch).

Row 7: 1 selvedge stitch, *6 right cross stitches (k2, p2, k2: sl 4 on a cable needle behind work, k2 from left needle, sl the fourth and third stitches on the cable needle back to the left needle, purl them while passing them behind the 2 stitches on the cable needle, then k2 from cable needle), p2*; repeat from * to *; end with k2, 1 selvedge stitch.

Row 15: 1 selvedge stitch, k2, *p2, 6 right cross stitches (k2, p2, k2)*; repeat from * to *; end with 1 selvedge stitch.

Keep repeating these 16 rows.

☐ knit stitch on right side or purl stitch on wrong side
— purl stitch on right side or knit stitch on wrong side
⨝ 6 right cross stitches: sl 4 on a cable needle behind work, k2 from left needle, sl the fourth and third stitches on the cable needle back to the left needle, purl them while passing them behind the 2 stitches on the cable needle, then k2 from cable needle
sl: slip stitch from one needle to another without knitting it

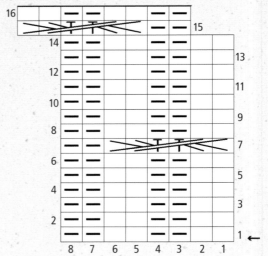

Hearts

The directions for this pattern consist of 13 stitches on a background of purled stockinette stitch.

Row 1 (right side of work): p3, 3 right cross stitches (p1, k2: sl 1 on a cable needle behind work, k2 from left needle, then p1 from cable needle), k1, 3 left cross stitches (k2, p1: sl 2 on a cable needle in front of work, p1 from left needle, then k2 from cable needle), p3.

Row 2: k3, p3, k1, p3, k3.

Row 3: p2, knit 3 right cross stitches (1 and 2: sl 1 on a cable needle behind work, k2 from left needle, then k1 from cable needle), p1, k1, p1, knit 3 left cross stitches (2 and 1: sl 2 on a cable needle in front of work, k1 from left needle, then k2 from cable needle), p2.

Row 4: k2, p2, *k1, p1*; repeat from * to * 2 times, k1, p2, k2.

Row 5: p1, 3 right cross stitches (p1, k2), *k1, p1*; repeat from * to * 2 times, k1, 3 left cross stitches (k2, p1), p1.

Row 6: k1, p3, *k1, p1*; repeat from * to * 2 times, k1, p3, k1.

Row 7: knit 3 right cross stitches (1 and 2), *p1, k1*; repeat from * to * 3 times, p1, knit 3 left cross stitches (2 and 1).

Row 8: p2, *k1, p1*; repeat from * to * 4 times, k1, p2.

Row 9: 3 left cross stitches (k2, p1), *p1, k1*; repeat from * to * 3 times, p1, 3 right cross stitches (p1, k2).

Row 10: k1, p3, *k1, p1*; repeat from * to * 2 times, k1, p3, k1.

Row 11: k1, 3 left cross stitches (k2, p1), k5, 3 right cross stitches (p1, k2), k1.

Row 12: k2, p4, k1, p4, k2.

Keep repeating these 12 rows.

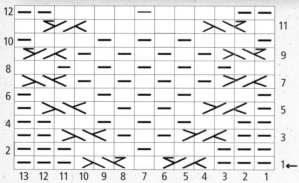

☐ knit stitch on right side or purl stitch on wrong side

– purl stitch on right side or knit stitch on wrong side

⟩⟨ 3 left cross stitches: sl 2 on a cable needle in front of work, p1 from left needle, then k2 from cable needle

⟩⟨ 3 right cross stitches: sl 1 on a cable needle behind work, k2 from left needle, then p1 from cable needle

⟩⟨ 3 left cross stitches: sl 2 on a cable needle in front of work, k1 from left needle, then k2 from cable needle

⟩⟨ 3 right cross stitches: sl 1 on a cable needle behind work, k2 from left needle, then k1 from cable needle

sl: slip stitch from one needle to another without knitting it

Cable Stitches

Cut Cables

The directions for this pattern consist of 12 stitches on a background of purled stockinette stitch.

Row 1 (right side of work): p3, knit 3 right cross stitches (1 and 2: sl 1 on a cable needle behind work, k2 from left needle, then k1 from cable needle), knit 3 left cross stitches (2 and 1: sl 2 on a cable needle in front of work, k1 from left needle, then k2 from cable needle), p3.

Row 2 and all even numbered rows: knit each stitch as it appears in previous row (i.e., knit a knit stitch, purl a purl stitch).

Row 3: p2, knit 3 right cross stitches (1 and 2), k2, knit 3 left cross stitches (2 and 1), p2.

Row 5: p1, 3 right cross stitches (p1, k2: sl 1 on a cable needle behind work, k2 from left needle, then p1 from cable needle), k4, 3 left cross stitches (k2, p1: sl 2 on a cable needle in front of work, p1 from left needle, then k2 from cable needle), p1.

Row 7: 3 right cross stitches (p1, k2), p1, knit 4 right cross stitches (2 and 2: sl 2 on a cable needle behind work, k2 from left needle, then k2 from cable needle), p1, 3 left cross stitches (k2, p1).

Keep repeating these 8 rows.

Rings

The directions for this pattern consist of 8 stitches on a background of purled stockinette stitch.

Rows 1 (right side of work), 5, and 7: k2, p4, k2.

Row 2 and all even numbered rows: knit each stitch as it appears in previous row (i.e., knit a knit stitch, purl a purl stitch).

Row 3: knit 4 left cross stitches (2 and 2: sl 2 on a cable needle in front of work, k2 from left needle, then k2 from cable needle), knit 4 right cross stitches (2 and 2: sl 2 on a cable needle behind work, k2 from left needle, then k2 from cable needle).

Keep repeating these 8 rows.

☐ knit stitch on right side or purl stitch on wrong side
− purl stitch on right side or knit stitch on wrong side
⟩⟨ 4 left cross stitches: sl 2 on a cable needle in front of work, k2 from left needle, then k2 from cable needle
⟩⟨ 4 right cross stitches: sl 2 on a cable needle behind work, k2 from left needle, then k2 from cable needle
sl: slip stitch from one needle to another without knitting it

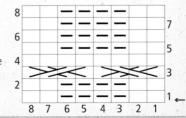

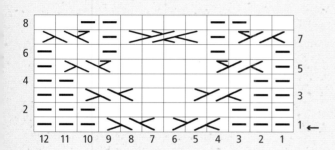

knit stitch on right side or purl stitch on wrong side

− purl stitch on right side or knit stitch on wrong side

⟩⟨ 3 left cross stitches: sl 2 on a cable needle in front of work, p1 from left needle, then k2 from cable needle

⟩⟨ 3 right cross stitches: sl 1 on a cable needle behind work, k2 from left needle, then p1 from cable needle

⟩⟨ 3 left cross stitches: sl 2 on a cable needle in front of work, k1 from left needle, then k2 from cable needle

⟩⟨ 3 right cross stitches: sl 1 on a cable needle behind work, k2 from left needle, then k1 from cable needle

⟩⟨ 4 right cross stitches: sl 2 on a cable needle behind work, k2 from left needle, then k2 from cable needle

sl: slip stitch from one needle to another without knitting it

Braid

The directions for this pattern consist of 16 stitches on a background of knit stockinette stitch.

Rows 1 (right side of work) and 5: p2, k12, p2.
Row 2 and all even numbered rows: k2, p12, k2.
Row 3: p2, knit 6 left cross stitches (3 and 3: sl 3 on a cable needle in front of work, k3 from left needle, then k3 from cable needle), knit 6 left cross stitches (3 and 3), p2.
Row 7: p2, k3, knit 6 right cross stitches (3 and 3: sl 3 on a cable needle behind work, k3 from left needle, then k3 from cable needle), k3, p2.
Keep repeating these 8 rows.

☐ knit stitch on right side or purl stitch on wrong side

⊟ purl stitch on right side or knit stitch on wrong side

⟩⟩⟨ 6 left cross stitches: sl 3 on a cable needle in front of work, k3 from left needle, then k3 from cable needle

⟩⟩⟨ 6 right cross stitches: sl 3 on a cable needle behind work, k3 from left needle, then k3 from cable needle

sl: slip stitch from one needle to another without knitting it

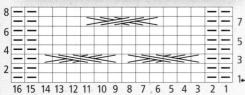

Double Moss Stitch "V"

The directions for this pattern consist of 17 stitches on a background of purled stockinette stitch.

Row 1 (right side of work): k2, p4, k2, p1, k2, p4, k2.

Row 2: k6, p2, k1, p2, k6.

Row 3: p6, 5 right cross stitches (k2, p1, k2: sl 3 on a cable needle behind work, k2 from left needle, sl the third stitch back to the left needle, knit it while passing it behind the 2 stitches on the cable needle, then k2 from cable needle), p6.

Rows 4, 6, 8, 10, 12, 14, and 16: knit each stitch as it appears in previous row (i.e., knit a knit stitch, purl a purl stitch).

Row 5: p5, 3 right cross stitches (p1, k2: sl 1 on a cable needle behind work, k2 from left needle, then p1 from cable needle), k1, 3 left cross stitches (k2, p1: sl 2 on a cable needle in front of work, p1 from left needle, then k2 from cable needle), p5.

Row 7: p4, 3 right cross stitches (p1, k2), k1, p1, k1, 3 left cross stitches (k2, p1), p4.

Row 9: p3, 3 right cross stitches (p1, k2), *k1, p1*; repeat from * to * 2 times, k1, 3 left cross stitches (k2, p1), p3.

Row 11: p2, 3 right cross stitches (p1, k2), *k1, p1*; repeat from * to * 3 times, k1, 3 left cross stitches (k2, p1), p2.

Row 13: p1, 3 right cross stitches (p1, k2), *k1, p1*; repeat from * to * 4 times, k1, 3 left cross stitches (k2, p1), p1.

Row 15: 3 right cross stitches (p1, k2), *k1, p1*; repeat from * to * 5 times, k1, 3 left cross stitches (k2, p1).

Keep repeating these 16 rows.

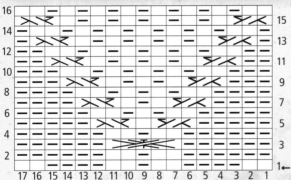

□ knit stitch on right side or purl stitch on wrong side

− purl stitch on right side or knit stitch on wrong side

⟩⟨ 3 left cross stitches: sl 2 on a cable needle in front of work, p1 from left needle, then k2 from cable needle

⟩⟨ 3 right cross stitches: sl 1 on a cable needle behind work, k2 from left needle, then p1 from cable needle

⟩⟨ 5 right cross stitches: sl 3 on a cable needle behind work, k2 from left needle, sl the third stitch back to the left needle, knit it while passing it behind the 2 stitches on the cable needle, then k2 from cable needle

sl: slip stitch from one needle to another without knitting it

Lozenges in Relief

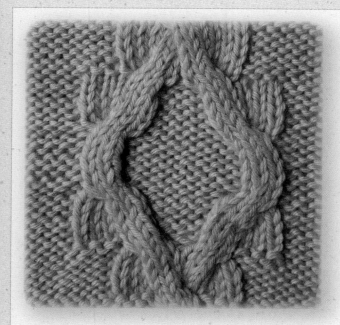

The directions for this pattern consist of 18 stitches on a background of purled stockinette stitch.

Row 1 (right side of work): p6, k6, p6.

Row 2 and all even numbered rows: knit each stitch as it appears in previous row (i.e., knit a knit stitch, purl a purl stitch).

Row 3: p3, k3, knit 6 left cross stitches (3 and 3: sl 3 on a cable needle in front of work, k3 from left needle, then k3 from cable needle), k3, p3.

Rows 5, 7, 11, 13, 17, 19, 23, 25, 29, 31, and 35: knit each stitch as it appears in previous row (i.e., knit a knit stitch, purl a purl stitch).

Row 9: k3, 6 right cross stitches (p3, k3: sl 3 on a cable needle behind work, k3 from left needle, then p3 from cable needle), 6 left cross stitches (k3, p3: sl 3 on a cable needle in front of work, p3 from left needle, then k3 from cable needle), k3.

Row 15: 6 right cross stitches (p3, k3), p6, 6 left cross stitches (k3, p3).

Row 21: knit 6 left cross stitches (3 and 3), p6, knit 6 right cross stitches (3 and 3: sl 3 on a cable needle behind work, k3 from left needle, then k3 from cable needle).

Row 27: p3, knit 6 left cross stitches (3 and 3), knit 6 right cross stitches (3 and 3), p3.

Row 33: p6, knit 6 left cross stitches (3 and 3), p6.

Keep repeating these 36 rows.

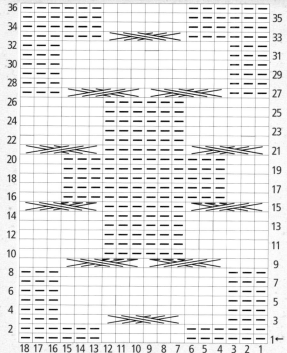

☐ knit stitch on right side or purl stitch on wrong side

⊟ purl stitch on right side or knit stitch on wrong side

⟩⟩⟩⟩⟨ 6 left cross stitches: sl 3 on a cable needle in front of work, k3 from left needle, then k3 from cable needle

⟩⟩⟩⟩⟨ 6 right cross stitches: sl 3 on a cable needle behind work, k3 from left needle, then k3 from cable needle

⟩⟩⟩⟩⟨ 6 left cross stitches: sl 3 on a cable needle in front of work, p3 from left needle, then k3 from cable needle

⟩⟩⟩⟩⟨ 6 right cross stitches: sl 3 on a cable needle behind work, k3 from left needle, then p3 from cable needle

sl: slip stitch from one needle to another without knitting it

Half-Hearts

The directions for this pattern consist of 24 stitches on a background of purled stockinette stitch.

Row 1 (right side of work): k2, p4, 4 left cross stitches (k2, p2: sl 2 on a cable needle in front of work, p2 from left needle, then k2 from cable needle), p1, knit 2 right cross stitches (knit the second stitch on the left needle first, passing the right needle in front of the first stitch, then knit the first stitch), p1, 4 right cross stitches (p2, k2: sl 2 on a cable needle behind work, k2 from left needle, then p2 from cable needle), p4, k2.

Row 2 and all even numbered rows: knit each stitch as it appears in previous row (i.e., knit a knit stitch, purl a purl stitch).

Row 3: 4 left cross stitches (k2, p2), p4, 4 left cross stitches (k2, p2), 4 right cross stitches (p2, k2), p4, 4 right cross stitches (p2, k2).

Row 5: p2, knit 4 left cross stitches (2 and 2: sl 2 on a cable needle in front of work, k2 from left needle, then k2 from cable needle), p4, 2 left cross stitches (k1, p1: purl the second stitch on the left needle first, passing the right needle behind the first stitch, then knit the first stitch), 2 right cross stitches (p1, k1: knit the second stitch on the left needle first, passing the right needle in front of the first stitch, then purl the first stitch), p4, knit 4 right cross stitches (2 and 2: sl 2 on a cable needle behind work, k2 from left needle, then k2 from cable needle), p2.

Row 7: 4 right cross stitches (p2, k2), 4 left cross stitches (k2, p2), p3, knit 2 right cross stitches, p3, 4 right cross stitches (p2, k2), 4 left cross stitches (k2, p2).

Keep repeating these 8 rows.

☐ knit stitch on right side or purl stitch on wrong side

⊟ purl stitch on right side or knit stitch on wrong side

╳ 2 right cross stitches: knit the second stitch on the left needle first, passing the right needle in front of the first stitch, then knit the first stitch

╲ 2 left cross stitches: purl the second stitch on the left needle first, passing the right needle behind the first stitch, then knit the first stitch

╳ 2 right cross stitches: knit the second stitch on the left needle first, passing the right needle in front of the first stitch, then purl the first stitch

▷◁ 4 left cross stitches: sl 2 on a cable needle in front of work, k2 from left needle, then k2 from cable needle

▷◁ 4 right cross stitches: sl 2 on a cable needle behind work, k2 from left needle, then k2 from cable needle

▷◁ 4 left cross stitches: sl 2 on a cable needle in front of work, p2 from left needle, then k2 from cable needle

▷◁ 4 right cross stitches: sl 2 on a cable needle behind work, k2 from left needle, then p2 from cable needle

sl: slip stitch from one needle to another without knitting it

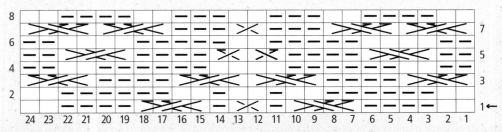

Fancy "V"

☐ knit stitch on right side or purl stitch on wrong side

⊟ purl stitch on right side or knit stitch on wrong side

⤛⤜ 5 right cross stitches: sl 2 on a cable needle behind work, k3 from left needle, p1 and k1 from cable needle

⤛⤜ 5 right cross stitches: sl 2 on a cable needle behind work, k3 from left needle, then p2 from cable needle

⤛⤜ 3 left cross stitches: sl 1 on a cable needle in front of work, p2 from left needle, then k1 from cable needle

sl: slip stitch from one needle to another without knitting it

Number of stitches needed for joining: multiple of 22 + 1 + 1 selvedge stitch at each end.

Row 1 (right side of work): 1 selvedge stitch, *k1, p1, k3, p7, k3, p7*; repeat from * to *; end with k1, 1 selvedge stitch.

Rows 2, 4, 6, 8, and 10: knit each stitch as it appears in previous row (i.e., knit a knit stitch, purl a purl stitch).

Row 3: 1 selvedge stitch, *5 right cross stitches (p2, k3: sl 2 on a cable needle behind work, k3 from left needle, then p2 from cable needle), p5, 5 right cross stitches (p1, k1, k3: sl 2 on a cable needle behind work, k3 from left needle, p1 and k1 from cable needle), p7*; repeat from * to *; end with k1, 1 selvedge stitch.

Row 5: 1 selvedge stitch, *p8, 5 right cross stitches (p2, k3), p1, 3 left cross stitches (k1, p2: sl 1 on a cable needle in front of work, p2 from left needle, then k1 from cable needle), p5*; repeat from * to *; end with p1, 1 selvedge stitch.

Row 7: 1 selvedge stitch, *p6, 5 right cross stitches (p2, k3), p5, 3 left cross stitches (k1, p2), p3*; repeat from * to *; end with p1, 1 selvedge stitch.

Row 9: 1 selvedge stitch, *p4, 5 right cross stitches (p2, k3), p9, 3 left cross stitches (k1, p2), p1*; repeat from * to *; end with p1, 1 selvedge stitch.

Row 11: 1 selvedge stitch, k1, *p1, 5 right cross stitches (p2, k3), p13, 3 left cross stitches (k1, p2)*; repeat from * to *; end with 1 selvedge stitch.

Row 12: 1 selvedge stitch, *p1, k7, p3, k7, p3, k1*; repeat from * to *; end with p1, 1 selvedge stitch.

Keep repeating Rows 3 through 12.

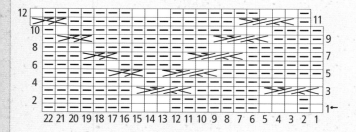

Cable Stitches

"V" Cable

The directions for this pattern consist of 30 stitches on a background of purled stockinette stitch.

Row 1 (right side of work): k9, knit 6 right cross stitches (3 and 3: sl 3 on a cable needle behind work, k3 from left needle, then k3 from cable needle), knit 6 left cross stitches (3 and 3: sl 3 on a cable needle in front of work, k3 from left needle, then k3 from cable needle), k9.

Row 2 and all even numbered rows: knit each stitch as it appears in previous row (i.e., knit a knit stitch, purl a purl stitch).

Row 3: k6, knit 6 right cross stitches (3 and 3), k6, knit 6 left cross stitches (3 and 3), k6.

Row 5: k3, knit 6 right cross stitches (3 and 3), k12, knit 6 left cross stitches (3 and 3), k3.

Row 7: knit 6 right cross stitches (3 and 3), k18, knit 6 left cross stitches (3 and 3).

Keep repeating these 8 rows.

Fancy Cables with Ribbing

The directions for this pattern consist of 22 stitches on a background of knit stockinette stitch.

Rows 1 (right side of work), 3, 5, 7, and 15: p4, k4, p2, k2, p2, k4, p4.

Rows 2, 4, 6, 8, 10, 12, and 16: knit each stitch as it appears in previous row (i.e., knit a knit stitch, purl a purl stitch).

Row 9: p4, knit 4 left cross stitches (2 and 2: sl 2 on a cable needle in front of work, k2 from left needle, then k2 from cable needle), p2, k2, p2, knit 4 right cross stitches (2 and 2: sl 2 on a cable needle behind work, k2 from left needle, then k2 from cable needle), p4.

Row 11: p4, k2, knit 4 left cross stitches (2 and 2), k2, knit 4 right cross stitches (2 and 2), k2, p4.

Row 13: p4, k4, knit 3 left cross stitches (2 and 1: sl 2 on a cable needle in front of work, k1 from left needle, then k2 from cable needle), knit 3 right cross stitches (1 and 2: sl 1 on a cable needle behind work, k2 from left needle, then k1 from cable needle), k4, p4.

Row 14: k4, p4, k2, purl 2 left cross stitches (purl the second stitch on the left needle first, passing the right needle behind the first stitch, then the first stitch), k2, p4, k4.

Keep repeating these 16 rows.

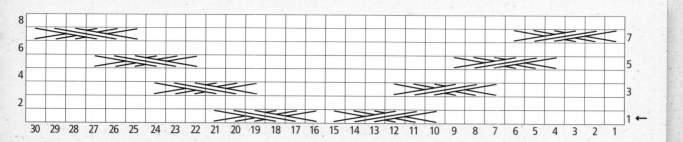

□ knit stitch on right side or purl stitch on wrong side

⊃⋉ 6 left cross stitches: sl 3 on a cable needle in front of work, k3 from left needle, then k3 from cable needle

⊃⋉ 6 right cross stitches: sl 3 on a cable needle behind work, k3 from left needle, then k3 from cable needle

sl: slip stitch from one needle to another without knitting it

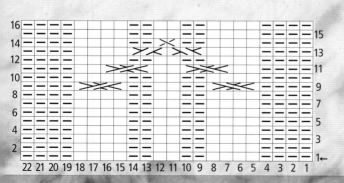

□ knit stitch on right side or purl stitch on wrong side

– purl stitch on right side or knit stitch on wrong side

⋉ 2 left cross stitches: purl the second stitch on the left needle first, passing the right needle behind the first stitch, then the first stitch

⊃⋉ 3 right cross stitches: sl 1 on a cable needle behind work, k2 from left needle, then k1 from cable needle

⋊⋉ 3 left cross stitches: sl 2 on a cable needle in front of work, k1 from left needle, then k2 from cable needle

⊃⋉ 4 right cross stitches: sl 2 on a cable needle behind work, k2 from left needle, then k2 from cable needle

⊃⋉ 4 left cross stitches: sl 2 on a cable needle in front of work, k2 from left needle, then k2 from cable needle

sl: slip stitch from one needle to another without knitting it

Cable Diagonals

The directions for this pattern consist of 16 stitches on a background of purled stockinette stitch.

Row 1 (right side of work): all knit.

Row 2 and all even numbered rows: all purl.

Row 3: knit 4 left cross stitches (2 and 2: sl 2 on a cable needle in front of work, k2 from left needle, then k2 from cable needle), k12.

Row 5: k2, knit 4 left cross stitches (2 and 2), k10.

Row 7: k4, knit 4 left cross stitches (2 and 2), k8.

Row 9: k6, knit 4 left cross stitches (2 and 2), k6.

Row 11: k8, knit 4 left cross stitches (2 and 2), k4.

Row 13: k10, knit 4 left cross stitches (2 and 2), k2.

Row 15: k12, knit 4 right cross stitches (2 and 2: sl 2 on a cable needle behind work, k2 from left needle, then k2 from cable needle).

Row 17: k10, knit 4 right cross stitches (2 and 2), k2.

Row 19: k8, knit 4 right cross stitches (2 and 2), k4.

Row 21: k6, knit 4 right cross stitches (2 and 2), k6.

Row 23: k4, knit 4 right cross stitches (2 and 2), k8.

Row 25: k2, knit 4 right cross stitches (2 and 2), k10.

Row 27: knit 4 right cross stitches (2 and 2), k12.

Keep repeating Rows 3 through 28.

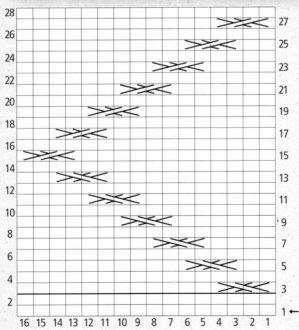

☐ knit stitch on right side or purl stitch on wrong side

⧓ 4 left cross stitches: sl 2 on a cable needle in front of work, k2 from left needle, then k2 from cable needle

⧓ 4 right cross stitches: sl 2 on a cable needle behind work, k2 from left needle, then k2 from cable needle

sl: slip stitch from one needle to another without knitting it

Plait

The directions for this pattern consist of 16 stitches on a background of purled stockinette stitch.

Row 1 (right side of work): k4, knit 4 right cross stitches (2 and 2: sl 2 on a cable needle behind work, k2 from left needle, then k2 from cable needle), knit 4 left cross stitches (2 and 2: sl 2 on a cable needle in front of work, k2 from left needle, then k2 from cable needle), k4.

Row 2 and all even numbered rows: knit each stitch as it appears in previous row (i.e., knit a knit stitch, purl a purl stitch).

Row 3: k2, knit 4 right cross stitches (2 and 2), k4, knit 4 left cross stitches (2 and 2), k2.

Row 5: knit 4 right cross stitches (2 and 2), k8, knit 4 left cross stitches (2 and 2).

Keep repeating these 6 rows.

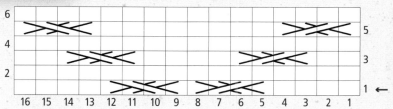

☐ knit stitch on right side or purl stitch on wrong side

✂ 4 left cross stitches: sl 2 on a cable needle in front of work, k2 from left needle, then k2 from cable needle

✂ 4 right cross stitches: sl 2 on a cable needle behind work, k2 from left needle, then k2 from cable needle

sl: slip stitch from one needle to another without knitting it

Fancy Lozenges

□ knit stitch on right side or purl stitch on wrong side

− purl stitch on right side or knit stitch on wrong side

⟩⟨ 3 left cross stitches: sl 2 on a cable needle in front of work, p1 from left needle, then k2 from cable needle

⟩⟨ 3 right cross stitches: sl 1 on a cable needle behind work, k2 from left needle, then p1 from cable needle

⟩⟨ 4 right cross stitches: sl 2 on a cable needle behind work, k2 from left needle, then k2 from cable needle

sl: slip stitch from one needle to another without knitting it

Number of stitches needed for symmetry and joining: multiple of 12 + 1 selvedge stitch at each end.

Row 1 (right side of work): 1 selvedge stitch, *p4, k4, p4*; repeat from * to *; end with 1 selvedge stitch.

Row 2 and all even numbered rows: knit each stitch as it appears in previous row (i.e., knit a knit stitch, purl a purl stitch).

Row 3: 1 selvedge stitch, *p4, knit 4 right cross stitches (2 and 2: sl 2 on a cable needle behind work, k2 from left needle, then k2 from cable needle), p4*; repeat from * to *; end with 1 selvedge stitch.

Row 5: 1 selvedge stitch, *p3, 3 right cross stitches (p1, k2: sl 1 on a cable needle behind work, k2 from left needle, then p1 from cable needle), 3 left cross stitches (k2, p1: sl 2 on a cable needle in front of work, p1 from left needle, then k2 from cable needle), p3*; repeat from * to *; end with 1 selvedge stitch.

Row 7: 1 selvedge stitch, *p2, 3 right cross stitches (p1, k2), p2, 3 left cross stitches (k2, p1), p2*; repeat from * to *; end with 1 selvedge stitch.

Row 9: 1 selvedge stitch, *p1, 3 right cross stitches (p1, k2), p4, 3 left cross stitches (k2, p1), p1*; repeat from * to *; end with 1 selvedge stitch.

Row 11: 1 selvedge stitch, *3 right cross stitches (p1, k2), p6, 3 left cross stitches (k2, p1)*; repeat from * to *; end with 1 selvedge stitch.

Row 13: 1 selvedge stitch, k2, *p8, knit 4 right cross stitches (2 and 2)*; repeat from * to *; end with p8, k2, 1 selvedge stitch.

Row 15: 1 selvedge stitch, k2, *p8, k4*; repeat from * to *; end with p8, k2, 1 selvedge stitch.

Row 17: 1 selvedge stitch, k2, *p8, knit 4 right cross stitches (2 and 2)*; repeat from * to *; end with p8, k2, 1 selvedge stitch.

Row 19: 1 selvedge stitch, *3 left cross stitches (k2, p1), p6, 3 right cross stitches (p1, k2)*; repeat from * to *; end with 1 selvedge stitch.

Row 21: 1 selvedge stitch, *p1, 3 left cross stitches (k2, p1), p4, 3 right cross stitches (p1, k2), p1*; repeat from * to *; end with 1 selvedge stitch.

Row 23: 1 selvedge stitch, *p2, 3 left cross stitches (k2, p1), p2, 3 right cross stitches (p1, k2), p2*; repeat from * to *; end with 1 selvedge stitch.

Row 25: 1 selvedge stitch, *p3, 3 left cross stitches (k2, p1), 3 right cross stitches (p1, k2), p3*; repeat from * to *; end with 1 selvedge stitch.

Row 27: 1 selvedge stitch, *p4, knit 4 right cross stitches (2 and 2), p4*; repeat from * to *; end with 1 selvedge stitch.

Keep repeating these 28 rows.

Cable Lozenges (3)

The directions for this pattern consist of 16 stitches on a background of purled stockinette stitch.

Rows 1 (right side of work) and 5: p2, knit 4 left cross stitches (2 and 2: sl 2 on a cable needle in front of work, k2 from left needle, then k2 from cable needle), p4, knit 4 left cross stitches (2 and 2), p2.

Row 2 and all even numbered rows: knit each stitch as it appears in previous row (i.e., knit a knit stitch, purl a purl stitch).

Row 3: p2, k4, p4, k4, p2.

Row 7: *4 right cross stitches (p2, k2: sl 2 on a cable needle behind work, k2 from left needle, then p2 from cable needle), 4 left cross stitches (k2, p2: sl 2 on a cable needle in front of work, p2 from left needle, then k2 from cable needle)*; repeat from * to * 2 times.

Rows 9, 13, 17, and 21: k2, p4, knit 4 left cross stitches (2 and 2), p4, k2.

Rows 11, 15, and 19: k2, p4, k4, p4, k2.

Row 23: *4 left cross stitches (k2, p2), 4 right cross stitches (p2, k2)*; repeat from * to * 2 times.

Keep repeating these 24 rows.

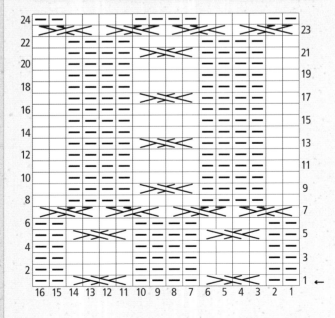

☐ knit stitch on right side or purl stitch on wrong side

— purl stitch on right side or knit stitch on wrong side

⧓ 4 left cross stitches: sl 2 on a cable needle in front of work, k2 from left needle, then k2 from cable needle

⧓ 4 left cross stitches: sl 2 on a cable needle in front of work, p2 from left needle, then k2 from cable needle

⧓ 4 right cross stitches: sl 2 on a cable needle behind work, k2 from left needle, then p2 from cable needle

sl: slip stitch from one needle to another without knitting it

Interlaced Ropes

Number of stitches needed for symmetry: multiple of 16 + 4 + 1 selvedge stitch at each end.

Row 1 (right side of work): 1 selvedge stitch, *knit 4 right cross stitches (2 and 2: sl 2 on a cable needle behind work, k2 from left needle, then k2 from cable needle), p4, knit 4 right cross stitches (2 and 2), p4*; repeat from * to *; end with 4 knit right cross stitches (2 and 2), 1 selvedge stitch.

Row 2 and all even numbered rows: knit each stitch as it appears in previous row (i.e., knit a knit stitch, purl a purl stitch).

Row 3: 1 selvedge stitch, k2, *4 left cross stitches (k2, p2: sl 2 on a cable needle in front of work, p2 from left needle, then k2 from cable needle), 4 right cross stitches (p2, k2: sl 2 on a cable needle behind work, k2 from left needle, then p2 from cable needle), 4 left cross stitches (k2, p2), 4 right cross stitches (p2, k2)*; repeat from * to *; end with k2, 1 selvedge stitch.

Row 5: 1 selvedge stitch, k2, *p2, knit 4 left cross stitches (2 and 2: sl 2 on a cable needle in front of work, k2 from left needle, then k2 from cable needle), p4, knit 4 left cross stitches (2 and 2), p2*; repeat from * to *; end with k2, 1 selvedge stitch.

Row 7: 1 selvedge stitch, k2, *4 right cross stitches (p2, k2), 4 left cross stitches (k2, p2), 4 right cross stitches (p2, k2), 4 left cross stitches (k2, p2)*; repeat from * to *; end with k2, 1 selvedge stitch.

Row 9: 1 selvedge stitch, *knit 4 right cross stitches (2 and 2), p4, knit 4 right cross stitches (2 and 2), p4*; repeat from * to *; end with knit 4 right cross stitches (2 and 2), 1 selvedge stitch.

Row 11: 1 selvedge stitch, *k4, p2, 4 right cross stitches (p2, k2), 4 left cross stitches (k2 and p2), p2*; repeat from * to *; end with k4, 1 selvedge stitch.

Row 13: 1 selvedge stitch, *knit 4 right cross stitches (2 and 2), p2, k2, p4, k2, p2*; repeat from * to *; end with knit 4 right cross stitches (2 and 2), 1 selvedge stitch.

Row 15: 1 selvedge stitch, *k4, p2, 4 left cross stitches (k2, p2), 4 right cross stitches (p2, k2), p2*; repeat from * to *; end with k4, 1 selvedge stitch.

Keep repeating these 16 rows.

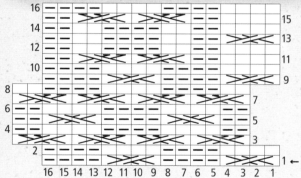

☐ knit stitch on right side or purl stitch on wrong side

– purl stitch on right side or knit stitch on wrong side

4 left cross stitches: sl 2 on a cable needle in front of work, k2 from left needle, then k2 from cable needle

4 right cross stitches: sl 2 on a cable needle behind work, k2 from left needle, then p2 from cable needle

4 left cross stitches: sl 2 on a cable needle in front of work, p2 from left needle, then k2 from cable needle

4 right cross stitches: sl 2 on a cable needle behind work, k2 from left needle, then k2 from cable needle

sl: slip stitch from one needle to another without knitting it

Cables and Ropes

Number of stitches needed for symmetry and joining: multiple of 12 + 6 + 1 selvedge stitch at each end.

Row 1 (right side of work): 1 selvedge stitch, p2, k2, *3 left cross stitches (k2, p1: sl 2 on a cable needle in front of work, p1 from left needle, then k2 from cable needle), p1, knit 2 right cross stitches (knit the second stitch on the left needle first, passing the right needle in front of the first stitch, then the first stitch), p1, 3 right cross stitches (p1, k2: sl 1 on a cable needle behind work, k2 from left needle, then p1 from cable needle), k2*; repeat from * to *; end with p2, 1 selvedge stitch.

Rows 2, 4, 6, 8, 9, 10, 12, 14, 16, 20, 22, 23, 24, 26, and 28: knit each stitch as it appears in previous row (i.e., knit a knit stitch, purl a purl stitch).

Row 3: 1 selvedge stitch, p2, knit 2 right cross stitches, *p1, 3 left cross stitches (k2, p1), k2, 3 right cross stitches (p1, k2), p1, knit 2 right cross stitches*; repeat from * to *; end with p2, 1 selvedge stitch.

Row 5: 1 selvedge stitch, p2, k2, *p2, knit 4 right cross stitches (2 and 2: sl 2 on a cable needle behind work, k2 from left needle, then k2 from cable needle), k2, p2, k2*; repeat from * to *; end with p2, 1 selvedge stitch.

Row 7: 1 selvedge stitch, p2, knit 2 right cross stitches, *p2, k2, knit 4 left cross stitches (2 and 2: sl 2 on a cable needle in front of work, k2 from left needle, then k2 from cable needle), p2, knit 2 right cross stitches*; repeat from * to *; end with p2, 1 selvedge stitch.

Row 11: 1 selvedge stitch, p2, knit 2 right cross stitches, *p2, knit 4 right cross stitches (2 and 2), k2, p2, knit 2 right cross stitches*; repeat from * to *; end with p2, 1 selvedge stitch.

Row 13: 1 selvedge stitch, p2, k2, *p2, k2, knit 4 left cross stitches (2 and 2), p2, k2*; repeat from * to *; end with p2, 1 selvedge stitch.

Row 15: 1 selvedge stitch, p2, knit 2 right cross stitches, *p1, 3 right cross stitches (p1, k2), k2, 3 left cross stitches (k2, p1), p1, knit 2 right cross stitches*; repeat from * to *; end with p2, 1 selvedge stitch.

Row 17: 1 selvedge stitch, p2, k2, *3 right cross stitches (p1, k2), p1, knit 2 right cross stitches, p1, 3 left cross stitches (k2, p1), k2*; repeat from * to *; end with p2, 1 selvedge stitch.

Row 18: 1 selvedge stitch, p6, *k2, p2, k2, p6*; repeat from * to *; end with 1 selvedge stitch.

Row 19: 1 selvedge stitch, *knit 4 right cross stitches (2 and 2), k2, p2, k2, p2*; repeat from * to *; end with knit 4 right cross stitches (2 and 2), k2, 1 selvedge stitch.

Row 21: 1 selvedge stitch, *k2, knit 4 left cross stitches (2 and 2), p2, knit 2 right cross stitches, p2*; repeat from * to *; end with k2, knit 4 left cross stitches (2 and 2), 1 selvedge stitch.

Row 25: 1 selvedge stitch, *knit 4 right cross stitches (2 and 2), k2, p2, knit 2 right cross stitches, p2*; repeat from * to *; end with knit 4 right cross stitches (2 and 2), k2, 1 selvedge stitch.

Row 27: 1 selvedge stitch, *k2, knit 4 left cross stitches (2 and 2), p2, k2, p2*; repeat from * to *; end with k2, knit 4 left cross stitches (2 and 2), 1 selvedge stitch.

Keep repeating these 28 rows.

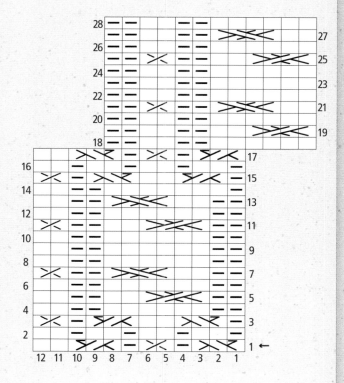

☐ knit stitch on right side or purl stitch on wrong side

− purl stitch on right side or knit stitch on wrong side

✕ 2 right cross stitches: knit the second stitch on the left needle first, passing the right needle in front of the first stitch, then the first stitch

⟩✕ 3 left cross stitches: sl 2 on a cable needle in front of work, p1 from left needle, then k2 from cable needle

⟩✕ 3 right cross stitches: sl 1 on a cable needle behind work, k2 from left needle, then p1 from cable needle),

⟩✕ 4 left cross stitches: 2 and 2: sl 2 on a cable needle in front of work, k2 from left needle, then k2 from cable needle

⟩✕ 4 right cross stitches: sl 2 on a cable needle behind work, k2 from left needle, then k2 from cable needle

sl: slip stitch from one needle to another without knitting it

Half-Lozenges and Ribbing

The directions for this pattern consist of 12 stitches on a background of purled stockinette stitch.

Row 1 (right side of work): 4 left cross stitches (k2, p1, k1: sl 2 on a cable needle in front of work, p1 and k1 from left needle, then k2 from cable needle), *p1, k1*; repeat from * to * 4 times.

Rows 2, 4, 16, 18, and 20: knit each stitch as it appears in previous row (i.e., knit a knit stitch, purl a purl stitch).

Row 3: 2 right cross stitches (p1, k1: knit the second stitch on the left needle first, passing the right needle in front of the first stitch, then purl the first stitch), 4 left cross stitches (k2, p1, k1), *p1, k1*; repeat from * to * 3 times.

Row 5: 2 left cross stitches (k1, p1: purl the second stitch on the left needle first, passing the right needle behind the first stitch, then knit the first stitch), 2 right cross stitches (p1, k1), 4 left cross stitches (k2, p1, k1), *p1, k1*; repeat from * to * 2 times.

Row 6: *p1, k1*; repeat from * to * 2 times, p3, k2, purl 2 left cross stitches (purl the second stitch on the left needle first, passing the right needle behind the first stitch, then the first stitch), k1.

Row 7: 2 right cross stitches (p1, k1), 2 left cross stitches (k1, p1), 2 right cross stitches (p1, k1), 4 left cross stitches (k2, p1, k1), p1, k1.

Row 8: p1, k1, p3, k2, purl 2 left cross stitches (purl the second stitch on the left needle first, passing the right needle behind the first stitch, then the first stitch), k2, p1.

Row 9: *2 left cross stitches (k1, p1), 2 right cross stitches (p1, k1)*; repeat from * to * 2 times, 4 left cross stitches (k2, p1, k1).

Row 10: p3, k2, purl 2 left cross stitches, k2, purl 2 left cross stitches, k1.

Row 11: *2 right cross stitches (p1, k1), 2 left cross stitches (k1, p1)*; repeat from * to * 2 times, 4 right cross stitches (p1, k1, k2: sl 2 on a cable needle behind work, k2 from left needle, p1 and k1 from cable needle).

Row 12: p1, k1, p3, k2, purl 2 right cross stitches, k2, p1.
Row 13: 2 left cross stitches (k1, p1), 2 right cross stitches (p1, k1), 2 left cross stitches (k1, p1), 4 right cross stitches (p1, k1, k2), p1, k1.
Row 14: *p1, k1*; repeat from * to * 2 times, p3, k2, purl 2 left cross stitches, k1.
Row 15: 2 right cross stitches (p1, k1), 2 left cross stitches (k1, p1), 4 right cross stitches (p1, k1, k2), *p1, k1*; repeat from * to * 2 times.
Row 17: 2 left cross stitches (k1, p1), 4 right cross stitches (p1, k1, k2), *p1, k1*; repeat from * to * 3 times.
Row 19: 4 right cross stitches (p1, k1, k2), *p1, k1*; repeat from * to * 4 times.
Keep repeating these 20 rows.

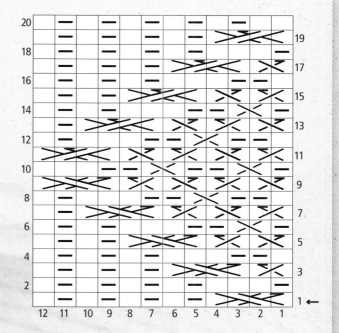

knit stitch on right side or purl stitch on wrong side
− purl stitch on right side or knit stitch on wrong side
2 left cross stitches: purl the second stitch on the left needle first, passing the right needle behind the first stitch, then knit the first stitch
2 right cross stitches: knit the second stitch on the left needle first, passing the right needle in front of the first stitch, then purl the first stitch
2 left cross stitches: knit the second stitch on the left needle first, passing the right needle behind the first stitch, then knit the first stitch
2 right cross stitches: knit the second stitch on the left needle first, passing the right needle in front of the first stitch, then knit the first stitch
4 left cross stitches: sl 2 on a cable needle in front of work, p1 and k1 from left needle, then k2 from cable needle
4 right cross stitches: sl 2 on a cable needle behind work, k2 from left needle, p1 and k1 from cable needle
sl: slip stitch from one needle to another without knitting it

Cable Stitches

Cables and Garter Stripes

Number of stitches needed for symmetry: multiple of 15 + 6 + 1 selvedge stitch at each end.

Rows 1 (right side of work), 3, and 7: 1 selvedge stitch, *p1, k4, p1, k9*; repeat from * to *; end with p1, k4, p1, 1 selvedge stitch.

Rows 2 and 8: knit each stitch as it appears in previous row (i.e., knit a knit stitch, purl a purl stitch).

Rows 4 and 6: 1 selvedge stitch, k1, p4, k1, *k10, p4, k1*; repeat from * to *; end with 1 selvedge stitch.

Row 5: 1 selvedge stitch, *p1, knit 4 left cross stitches (2 and 2: sl 2 on a cable needle in front of work, k2 from left needle, then k2 from cable needle), p1, k9*; repeat from * to *; end with p1, knit 4 left cross stitches (2 and 2), p1, 1 selvedge stitch.

Keep repeating these 8 rows.

Garter Stripes and Twists

Number of stitches needed for symmetry: multiple of 18 + 8 + 1 selvedge stitch at each end.

Rows 1 (right side of work), 3, 5, 7, 11, 13, 15, 17, 19, 21, 23, 27, 29, and 31: all knit.

Rows 2, 4, 12, 14, 16, 18, 20, 28, 30, and 32: all purl.

Rows 6, 8, and 10: 1 selvedge stitch, k1, p6, k1, *k11, p6, k1*; repeat from * to *; end with 1 selvedge stitch.

Row 9: 1 selvedge stitch, *k1, knit 6 left cross stitches (3 and 3: sl 3 on a cable needle in front of work, k3 from left needle, then k3 from cable needle), k11*; repeat from * to *; end with k1, knit 6 left cross stitches (3 and 3), k1, 1 selvedge stitch.

Rows 22, 24, and 26: 1 selvedge stitch, k8, *k2, p6, k10*; repeat from * to *; end with 1 selvedge stitch.

Row 25: 1 selvedge stitch, *k10, knit 6 left cross stitches (3 and 3), k2*; repeat from * to *; end with k8, 1 selvedge stitch.

Keep repeating these 32 rows.

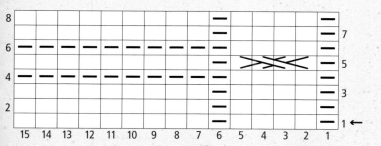

knit stitch on right side or purl stitch on wrong side
− purl stitch on right side or knit stitch on wrong side
4 left cross stitches: sl 2 on a cable needle in front of work, k2
from left needle, then k2 from cable needle
sl: slip stitch from one needle to another without knitting it

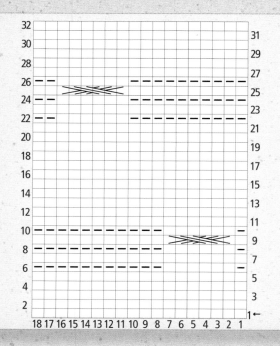

knit stitch on right side or purl stitch on wrong side
− purl stitch on right side or knit stitch on wrong side
6 left cross stitches: sl 3 on a cable needle in front of
work, k3 from left needle, then k3 from cable needle
sl: slip stitch from one needle to another without knitting it

Cable Stitches

Staggered Ribbed Cables

Number of stitches needed for symmetry: multiple of 10 + 6 + 1 selvedge stitch at each end.

Row 1 (right side of work): 1 selvedge stitch, *p1, k4, p2, k2, p1*; repeat from * to *; end with p1, k4, p1, 1 selvedge stitch.

Row 2 and all even numbered rows: knit each stitch as it appears in previous row (i.e., knit a knit stitch, purl a purl stitch).

Rows 3, 7, 11, and 15: knit each stitch as it appears in previous row (i.e., knit a knit stitch, purl a purl stitch).

Row 5: 1 selvedge stitch, *p1, knit 4 right cross stitches (2 and 2: sl 2 on a cable needle behind work, k2 from left needle, then k2 from cable needle), p2, k2, p1*; repeat from * to *; end with p1, knit 4 right cross stitches (2 and 2), p1, 1 selvedge stitch.

Row 9: 1 selvedge stitch, *p2, k2, p2, k4*; repeat from * to *; end with p2, k2, p2, 1 selvedge stitch.

Row 13: 1 selvedge stitch, *p2, k2, p2, knit 4 right cross stitches (2 and 2)*; repeat from * to *; end with p2, k2, p2, 1 selvedge stitch.

Keep repeating Rows 1 through 16.

Granite Stitch Ribbing

Number of stitches needed for symmetry: multiple of 3 + 1 + 1 selvedge stitch at each end.

Row 1 (right side of work): 1 selvedge stitch, *p1, k1, p1*; repeat from * to *; end with p1, 1 selvedge stitch.

Rows 2 and 4: knit each stitch as it appears in previous row (i.e., knit a knit stitch, purl a purl stitch).

Row 3: 1 selvedge stitch, *p1, knit 2 right cross stitches (knit the second stitch on the left needle first, passing the right needle in front of the first stitch, then knit the first stitch)*; repeat from * to *; end with p1, 1 selvedge stitch.

Keep repeating these 4 rows.

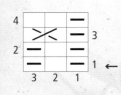

knit stitch on right side or purl stitch on wrong side

− purl stitch on right side or knit stitch on wrong side

✕ 2 right cross stitches: knit the second stitch on the left needle first, passing the right needle in front of the first stitch, then knit the first stitch

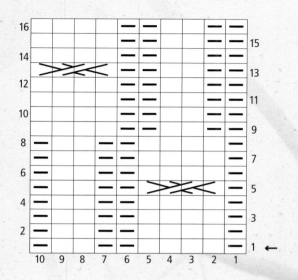

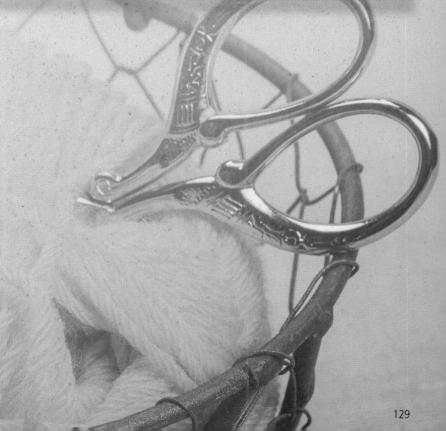

☐ knit stitch on right side or purl stitch on wrong side

– purl stitch on right side or knit stitch on wrong side

⊃⊂ 4 right cross stitches: sl 2 on a cable needle behind work, k2 from left needle, then k2 from cable needle

sl: slip stitch from one needle to another without knitting it

Cable Stitches

Large Cable with k2/p2 Ribbing

The directions for this pattern consist of 16 stitches on a background of purled stockinette stitch.

Rows 1 (right side of work), 5, 7, 9, 11, 13, 17, 19, 21, and 23: *k1, p2, k1*; repeat from * to *4 times.

Row 2 and all even numbered rows: knit each stitch as it appears in previous row (i.e., knit a knit stitch, purl a purl stitch).

Row 3: 8 right cross stitches (sl 4 on a cable needle behind work, work the next 4 stitches as they appear: k1, p2, k1, then the 4 stitches on the cable needle: k1, p2, k1), 8 left cross stitches (sl 4 on a cable needle in front of work, work the next 4 stitches as they appear: k1, p2, k1, then the 4 stitches on the cable needle: k1, p2, k1).

Row 15: 8 left cross stitches (sl 4 on a cable needle in front of work, work the next 4 stitches as they appear: k1, p2, k1, then the 4 stitches on the cable needle: k1, p2, k1), 8 right cross stitches (sl 4 on a cable needle behind work, work the next 4 stitches as they appear: k1, p2, k1, then the 4 stitches on the cable needle: k1, p2, k1).

Keep repeating these 24 rows.

Medallions in Relief

Number of stitches needed for symmetry and joining: multiple of 7 + 1 selvedge stitch at each end.

Row 1 (right side of work): 1 selvedge stitch, *k1, p5, k1*; repeat from * to *; end with 1 selvedge stitch.

Row 2 and all even numbered rows: knit each stitch as it appears in previous row (i.e., knit a knit stitch, purl a purl stitch).

Row 3: 1 selvedge stitch, *knit 2 left cross stitches (knit the second stitch on the left needle first, passing the right needle behind the first stitch, then knit the first stitch), p3, knit 2 right cross stitches (knit the second stitch on the left needle first, passing the right needle in front of the first stitch, then knit the first stitch)*; repeat from * to *; end with 1 selvedge stitch.

Row 5: 1 selvedge stitch, *k1, knit 2 left cross stitches, p1, knit 2 right cross stitches, k1*; repeat from * to *; end with 1 selvedge stitch.

Row 7: knit each stitch as it appears in previous row (i.e., knit a knit stitch, purl a purl stitch).

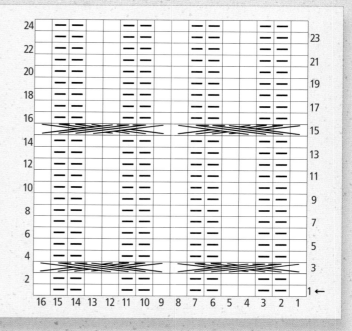

knit stitch on right side or purl stitch on wrong side

− purl stitch on right side or knit stitch on wrong side

8 left cross stitches: sl 4 on a cable needle in front of work, work the next 4 stitches as they appear: k1, p2, k1, then the 4 stitches on the cable needle: k1, p2, k1

8 right cross stitches: sl 4 on a cable needle behind work, work the next 4 stitches as they appear: k1, p2, k1, then the 4 stitches on the cable needle: k1, p2, k1

sl: slip stitch from one needle to another without knitting it

Row 9: 1 selvedge stitch, *k1, 2 right cross stitches (p1, k1: knit the second stitch on the left needle first, passing the right needle in front of the first stitch, then purl the first stitch), p1, 2 left cross stitches (k1, p1: purl the second stitch on the left needle first, passing the right needle behind the first stitch, then knit the first stitch), k1*; repeat from * to *; end with 1 selvedge stitch.

Row 11: 1 selvedge stitch, *2 right cross stitches (p1, k1), p3, 2 left cross stitches (k1, p1)*; repeat from * to *; end with 1 selvedge stitch.

Keep repeating Rows 1 through 12.

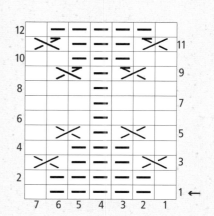

knit stitch on right side or purl stitch on wrong side

− purl stitch on right side or knit stitch on wrong side

2 left cross stitches: knit the second stitch on the left needle first, passing the right needle behind the first stitch, then knit the first stitch

2 right cross stitches: knit the second stitch on the left needle first, passing the right needle in front of the first stitch, then knit the first stitch

2 left cross stitches: purl the second stitch on the left needle first, passing the right needle behind the first stitch, then knit the first stitch

2 right cross stitches: knit the second stitch on the left needle first, passing the right needle in front of the first stitch, then purl the first stitch

Cable Stitches

Fancy Cables with k2/p2 Ribbing

The directions for this pattern consist of 16 stitches on a background of purled stockinette stitch.

Rows 1 (right side of work), 3, 5, and 9: *k1, p2, k1*; repeat from * to * 4 times.

Row 2 and all even numbered rows: p1, *k2, p2*; repeat from * to * 3 times, k2, p1.

Row 7: knit 8 right cross stitches (4 and 4: sl 4 on a cable needle behind work, k4 from left needle, then k4 from cable needle), knit 8 left cross stitches (4 and 4: sl 4 on a cable needle in front of work, k4 from left needle, then k4 from cable needle).

Keep repeating these 10 rows.

Lattices

Number of stitches needed for symmetry and joining: multiple of 6 + 1 selvedge stitch at each end.

Rows 1 (right side of work) and 3: 1 selvedge stitch, *p2, k2, p2*; repeat from * to *; end with 1 selvedge stitch.

Row 2 and all even numbered rows: knit each stitch as it appears in previous row (i.e., knit a knit stitch, purl a purl stitch).

Row 5: 1 selvedge stitch, *3 right cross stitches (p2, k1: sl 2 on a cable needle behind work, k1 from left needle, then p2 from cable needle), 3 left cross stitches (k1, p2: sl 1 on a cable needle in front of work, p2 from left needle, then k1 from cable needle)*; repeat from * to *; end with 1 selvedge stitch.

Rows 7 and 9: 1 selvedge stitch, *k1, p4, k1*; repeat from * to *; end with 1 selvedge stitch.

Row 11: 1 selvedge stitch, *3 left cross stitches (k1, p2), 3 right cross stitches (p2, k1)*; repeat from * to *; end with 1 selvedge stitch.

Keep repeating these 12 rows.

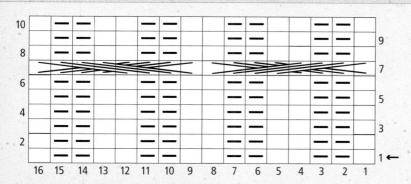

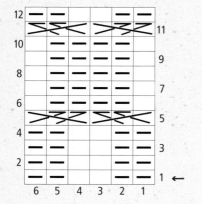

knit stitch on right side or purl stitch on wrong side

− purl stitch on right side or knit stitch on wrong side

8 left cross stitches: sl 4 on a cable needle in front of work, k4 from left needle, then k4 from cable needle

8 right cross stitches: sl 4 on a cable needle behind work, k4 from left needle, then k4 from cable needle

sl: slip stitch from one needle to another without knitting it

knit stitch on right side or purl stitch on wrong side

− purl stitch on right side or knit stitch on wrong side

3 left cross stitches: sl 1 on a cable needle in front of work, p2 from left needle, then k1 from cable needle

3 right cross stitches: sl 2 on a cable needle behind work, k1 from left needle, then p2 from cable needle

sl: slip stitch from one needle to another without knitting it

Cable Stitches

Crossed Ribbing (2)

Number of stitches needed for symmetry and joining: multiple of 4 + 1 selvedge stitch at each end.

Rows 1 (right side of work), 3, and 5: 1 selvedge stitch, *k1, p2, k1*; repeat from * to *; end with 1 selvedge stitch.

Row 2 and all even numbered rows: knit each stitch as it appears in previous row (i.e., knit a knit stitch, purl a purl stitch).

Row 7: 1 selvedge stitch, *2 left cross stitches (k1, p1: purl the second stitch on the left needle first, passing the right needle behind the first stitch, then knit the first stitch), 2 right cross stitches (p1, k1: knit the second stitch on the left needle first, passing the right needle in front of the first stitch, then purl the first stitch)*; repeat from * to *; end with 1 selvedge stitch.

Row 9: knit each stitch as it appears in previous row (i.e., knit a knit stitch, purl a purl stitch).

Row 11: 1 selvedge stitch, *2 right cross stitches (p1, k1), 2 left cross stitches (k1, p1)*; repeat from * to *; end with 1 selvedge stitch.

Keep repeating Rows 1 through 12.

☐ knit stitch on right side or purl stitch on wrong side

– purl stitch on right side or knit stitch on wrong side

⨯ 2 left cross stitches: purl the second stitch on the left needle first, passing the right needle behind the first stitch, then knit the first stitch

⨯ 2 right cross stitches: knit the second stitch on the left needle first, passing the right needle in front of the first stitch, then purl the first stitch

Braid of Diagonals

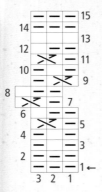

☐ knit stitch on right side or purl stitch on wrong side

– purl stitch on right side or knit stitch on wrong side

⨯ 2 left cross stitches: purl the second stitch on the left needle first, passing the right needle behind the first stitch, then knit the first stitch

The directions for this pattern consist of 15 rows, on a background of knit stockinette stitch.

Number of stitches needed for joining: multiple of 3 + 1 selvedge stitch at each end.

Rows 1 (right side of work) and 15: all purl.

Rows 2, 13, and 14: all knit.

Row 3: 1 selvedge stitch, *p1, k1, p1*; repeat from * to *; end with 1 selvedge stitch.

Rows 4, 6, 8, 10, and 12: knit each stitch as it appears in previous row (i.e., knit a knit stitch, purl a purl stitch).

Rows 5 and 11: 1 selvedge stitch, *p1, 2 left cross stitches (k1, p1: purl the second stitch on the left needle first, passing the right needle behind the first stitch, then knit the first stitch)*; repeat from * to *; end with 1 selvedge stitch.

Row 7: Note: for the first 2 crossed stitches, cross the selvedge stitch with the next stitch; for the last 2 crossed stitches, cross the stitch that precedes the selvedge stitch with the selvedge stitch: 2 left cross stitches (k1, p1), *p1, 2 left cross stitches (k1, p1)*; repeat from * to *; end with p1, 2 left cross stitches (k1, p1).

Row 9: 1 selvedge stitch, *2 left cross stitches (k1, p1), p1*; repeat from * to *; end with 1 selvedge stitch.

Wishbones

Number of stitches needed for symmetry and joining: multiple of 8 + 1 selvedge stitch at each end.

Rows 1 (right side of work), 3, and 5: 1 selvedge stitch, *k1, p6, k1*; repeat from * to *; end with 1 selvedge stitch.

Row 2 and all even numbered rows: knit each stitch as it appears in previous row (i.e., knit a knit stitch, purl a purl stitch).

Row 7: 1 selvedge stitch, *2 left cross stitches (k1, p1: purl the second stitch on the left needle first, passing the right needle behind the first stitch, then knit the first stitch), p4, 2 right cross stitches (p1, k1: knit the second stitch on the left needle first, passing the right needle in front of the first stitch, then purl the first stitch)*; repeat from * to *; end with 1 selvedge stitch.

Row 9: 1 selvedge stitch, *p1, 2 left cross stitches (k1, p1), p2, 2 right cross stitches (p1, k1), p1*; repeat from * to *; end with 1 selvedge stitch.

Row 11: 1 selvedge stitch, *p2, 2 left cross stitches (k1, p1), 2 right cross stitches (p1, k1), p2*; repeat from * to *; end with 1 selvedge stitch.

Rows 13 and 15: 1 selvedge stitch, *p3, k2, p3*; repeat from * to *; end with 1 selvedge stitch.

Keep repeating Rows 1 through 16.

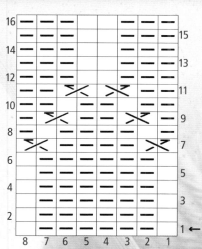

☐ knit stitch on right side or purl stitch on wrong side

– purl stitch on right side or knit stitch on wrong side

⟩⟨ 2 left cross stitches: purl the second stitch on the left needle first, passing the right needle behind the first stitch, then knit the first stitch

⟨⟩ 2 right cross stitches: knit the second stitch on the left needle first, passing the right needle in front of the first stitch, then purl the first stitch

Palmettos

Number of stitches needed for symmetry: multiple of 12 + 1 selvedge stitch at each end.

Row 1 (right side of work): all knit.

Row 2: 1 selvedge stitch, *k5, p2, k5*; repeat from * to *; end with 1 selvedge stitch.

Row 3: 1 selvedge stitch, *p4, knit 2 right cross stitches (knit the second stitch on the left needle first, passing the right needle in front of the first stitch, then knit the first stitch), knit 2 left cross stitches (knit the second stitch on the left needle first, passing the right needle behind the first stitch, then knit the first stitch), p4*; repeat from * to *; end with 1 selvedge stitch.

Row 4: 1 selvedge stitch, *k4, p4, k4*; repeat from * to *; end with 1 selvedge stitch.

Row 5: 1 selvedge stitch, *p3, 2 right cross stitches (p1, k1: knit the second stitch on the left needle first, passing the right needle in front of the first stitch, then purl the first stitch), k2, 2 left cross stitches (k1, p1: purl the second stitch on the left needle first, passing the right needle behind the first stitch, then knit the first stitch), p3*; repeat from * to *; end with 1 selvedge stitch.

Row 6: 1 selvedge stitch, *k3, p1, k1, p2, k1, p1, k3*; repeat from * to *; end with 1 selvedge stitch.

Row 7: 1 selvedge stitch, *p2, 2 right cross stitches (p1, k1), p1, k2, p1, 2 left cross stitches (k1, p1), p2*; repeat from * to *; end with 1 selvedge stitch.

Row 8: 1 selvedge stitch, *k1, 2 left cross stitches (k1, p1), k2, p2, k2, 2 right cross stitches (p1, k1), k1*; repeat from * to *; end with 1 selvedge stitch.

Keep repeating Rows 3 through 8.

☐ knit stitch on right side or purl stitch on wrong side

− purl stitch on right side or knit stitch on wrong side

⟩⟨ 2 left cross stitches: knit the second stitch on the left needle first, passing the right needle behind the first stitch, then knit the first stitch

⟩⟨ 2 right cross stitches: knit the second stitch on the left needle first, passing the right needle in front of the first stitch, then knit the first stitch

⟩⟨ 2 left cross stitches: purl the second stitch on the left needle first, passing the right needle behind the first stitch, then knit the first stitch

⟩⟨ 2 right cross stitches: knit the second stitch on the left needle first, passing the right needle in front of the first stitch, then purl the first stitch

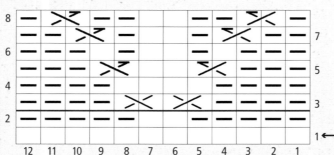

Zigzags and Bobbles

The directions for this pattern consist of 6 stitches on a background of purled stockinette stitch.

Row 1 (right side of work): p1, 1 bobble (inc 3 in 1 st [k1, p1, k1], turn work: p3, turn work: k3, turn work: p3, turn work: sl 1 on right needle, k2tog, psso), p1, 3 right cross stitches (p1, k2: sl 1 on a cable needle behind work, k2 from left needle, then p1 from cable needle).

Row 2 and all even numbered rows: knit each stitch as it appears in previous row (i.e., knit a knit stitch, purl a purl stitch).

Row 3: p2, 3 right cross stitches (p1, k2), p1.

Row 5: p1, 3 right cross stitches (p1, k2), p2.

Row 7: 3 right cross stitches (p1, k2), p3.

Row 9: 3 left cross stitches (k2, p1: sl 2 on a cable needle in front of work, p1 from left needle, then k2 from cable needle), p1, 1 bobble, p1.

Row 11: p1, 3 left cross stitches (k2, p1), p2.

Row 13: p2, 3 left cross stitches (k2, p1), p1.

Row 15: p3, 3 left cross stitches (k2, p1).

Keep repeating these 16 rows.

☐ knit stitch on right side or purl stitch on wrong side

– purl stitch on right side or knit stitch on wrong side

● bobble: inc 3 in 1 st (k1, p1, k1), turn work: p3, turn work: k3, turn work: p3, turn work: sl 1 on right needle, k2tog, psso

⨞ 3 left cross stitches: sl 2 on a cable needle in front of work, p1 from left needle, then k2 from cable needle

⨞ 3 right cross stitches: sl 1 on a cable needle behind work, k2 from left needle, then p1 from cable needle

inc 3 in 1 st (k1, p1, k1): make 3 stitches in 1 stitch, alternating knit, purl

sl: slip stitch from one needle to another without knitting it

k2tog: knit 2 together

psso: pass slipped stitch over stitches/yarn overs and off the needle

Lozenges and Ropes

Number of stitches needed for symmetry: multiple of 15 + 4 + 1 selvedge stitch at each end.

Note: Uses 2 cable needles.

Row 1 (right side of work): 1 selvedge stitch, *p1, knit 2 left cross stitches (knit the second stitch on the left needle first, passing the right needle behind the first stitch, then knit the first stitch), p1, k1, p1, knit 3 left cross stitches (2 and 1: sl 2 on a cable needle in front of work, k1 from left needle, then k2 from cable needle), p1, knit 3 right cross stitches (1 and 2: sl 1 on a cable needle behind work, k2 from left needle, then k1 from cable needle), p1, k1*; repeat from * to *; end with p1, knit 2 left cross stitches, p1, 1 selvedge stitch.

Rows 2, 4, 6, 12, and 14: knit each stitch as it appears in previous row (i.e., knit a knit stitch, purl a purl stitch).

Row 3: 1 selvedge stitch, *p1, knit 2 left cross stitches, p2, k1, p1, 5 left cross stitches (k2, p1, k2: sl 2 on a cable needle in front of work, sl 1 on a second cable needle behind work, k2 from left needle, p1 from second cable needle, then k2 from first cable needle), p1, k1, p1*; repeat from * to *; end with p1, knit 2 left cross stitches, p1, 1 selvedge stitch.

Row 5: 1 selvedge stitch, *p1, knit 2 left cross stitches, p1, k1, p1, 3 right cross stitches (p1, k2: sl 1 on a cable needle behind work, k2 from left needle, then p1 from cable needle), p1, 3 left cross stitches (k2, p1: sl 2 on a cable needle in front of work, p1 from left needle, then k2 from cable needle), p1, k1*; repeat from * to *; end with p1, knit 2 left cross stitches, p1, 1 selvedge stitch.

Row 7: 1 selvedge stitch, *p1, knit 2 left cross stitches, p2, 3 right cross stitches (p1, k2), p1, inc 3 in 1 st (k1, p1, k1), p1, 3 left cross stitches (k2, p1), p1*; repeat from * to *; end with p1, knit 2 left cross stitches, p1, 1 selvedge stitch.

Row 8: 1 selvedge stitch, k1, p2, k1, *k1, p2, k2, p3, k2, p2, k2, p2, k1*; repeat from * to *; end with 1 selvedge stitch.

Row 9: 1 selvedge stitch, *p1, knit 2 left cross stitches, p1, 3 right cross stitches (p1, k2), p2, k3, p2, 3 left cross stitches (k2, p1)*; repeat from * to *; end with p1, knit 2 left cross stitches, p1, 1 selvedge stitch.

　knit stitch on right side or purl stitch on wrong side

− purl stitch on right side or knit stitch on wrong side

⯗ inc 3 in 1 st (k1, p1, k1): make 3 stitches in 1 stitch, alternating knit, purl

III k3 on right side or p3 on wrong side

⋏ k3tog: knit 3 together on right side (or purl on wrong side)

⤬ 2 left cross stitches: knit the second stitch on the left needle first, passing the right needle behind the first stitch, then knit the first stitch

⤫ 3 left cross stitches: sl 2 on a cable needle in front of work, k1 from left needle, then k2 from cable needle

⤬ 3 right cross stitches: sl 1 on a cable needle behind work, k2 from left needle, then k1 from cable needle

⤫ 3 left cross stitches: sl 2 on a cable needle in front of work, p1 from left needle, then k2 from cable needle

⤬ 3 right cross stitches: sl 1 on a cable needle behind work, k2 from left needle, then p1 from cable needle

⤫ 5 left cross stitches: sl 2 on a cable needle in front of work, sl 1 on a second cable needle behind work, k2 from left needle, p1 from second cable needle, then k2 from first cable needle

sl: slip stitch from one needle to another without knitting it

p3tog: purl 3 together

Row 10: 1 selvedge stitch, k1, p2, k1, *p2, k3, p3tog, k3, p2, k1, p2, k1*; repeat from * to *; end with 1 selvedge stitch.

Row 11: 1 selvedge stitch, *p1, knit 2 left cross stitches, p1, knit 3 left cross stitches (2 and 1), p5, knit 3 right cross stitches (1 and 2)*; repeat from * to *; end with p1, knit 2 left cross stitches, p1, 1 selvedge stitch.

Row 13: 1 selvedge stitch, *p1, knit 2 left cross stitches, p2, knit 3 left cross stitches (2 and 1), p3, knit 3 right cross stitches (1 and 2), p1*; repeat from * to *; end with p1, knit 2 left cross stitches, p1, 1 selvedge stitch.

Keep repeating these 14 rows.

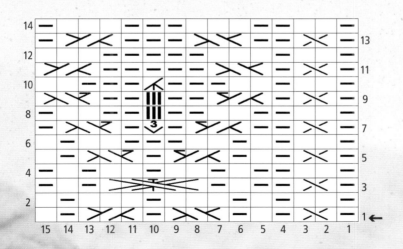

Lozenges and Bobbles

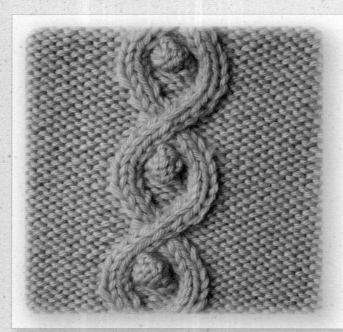

The directions for this pattern consist of 9 stitches on a background of purled stockinette stitch.

Row 1 (right side of work): p1, 3 right cross stitches (p1, k2: sl 1 on a cable needle behind work, k2 from left needle, then p1 from cable needle), p1, 3 left cross stitches (k2, p1: sl 2 on a cable needle in front of work, p1 from left needle, then k2 from cable needle), p1.

Row 2 and all even numbered rows: knit each stitch as it appears in previous row (i.e., knit a knit stitch, purl a purl stitch).

Row 3: 3 right cross stitches (p1, k2), p3, 3 left cross stitches (k2, p1).

Row 5: k2, p2, 1 bobble (inc 4 in 1 st [k1, p1, k1, p1], turn work: p4, turn work: k4, turn work: p4, turn work: sl 1 on right needle, k3tog, psso), p2, k2.

Row 7: 3 left cross stitches (k2, p1), p3, 3 right cross stitches (p1, k2).

Row 9: p1, 3 left cross stitches (k2, p1), p1, 3 right cross stitches (p1, k2), p1.

Rice Stitch Diamonds and Bobbles

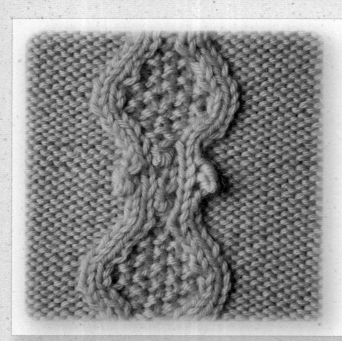

The directions for this pattern consist of 11 stitches on a background of purled stockinette stitch.

Rows 1 (right side of work) and 5: p3, k2, 1 bobble (inc 3 in 1 st [k1, p1, k1], turn work: p3, turn work: sl 1 on right needle, k2tog, psso), k2, p3.

Rows 2, 4, 6, and 20: knit each stitch as it appears in previous row (i.e., knit a knit stitch, purl a purl stitch).

Row 3: p3, 1 bobble, k3, 1 bobble, p3.

Row 7: p2, 3 right cross stitches (p1, k2: sl 1 on a cable needle behind work, k2 from left needle, then p1 from cable needle), p1, 3 left cross stitches (k2, p1: sl 2 on a cable needle in front of work, p1 from left needle, then k2 from cable needle), p2.

Rows 8 and 18: k2, p2, k1, p1, k1, p2, k2.

Row 9: p1, 3 right cross stitches (p1, k2), k1, p1, k1, 3 left cross stitches (k2, p1), p1.

Rows 10 and 16: k1, p3, k1, p1, k1, p3, k1.

Row 11: 3 right cross stitches (p1, k2), *p1, k1*; repeat from * to * 2 times, p1, 3 left cross stitches (k2, p1).

Row 11: p2, 5 right cross stitches (k2, p1, k2: sl 3 on a cable needle behind work, k2 from left needle, slip the third stitch on the cable needle back to the left needle, knit it while passing it behind the 2 stitches on the cable needle, then k2 from cable needle), p2.
Keep repeating these 12 rows.

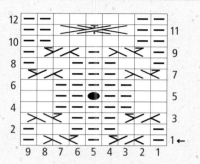

knit stitch on right side or purl stitch on wrong side
− purl stitch on right side or knit stitch on wrong side
● bobble: inc 4 in 1 st (k1, p1, k1, p1), turn work: p4, turn work: k4, turn work: p4, turn work: sl 1 on right needle, k3tog, psso
3 left cross stitches: sl 2 on a cable needle in front of work, p1 from left needle, then k2 from cable needle
3 right cross stitches: sl 1 on a cable needle behind work, k2 from left needle, then p1 from cable needle

5 right cross stitches: sl 3 on a cable needle behind work, k2 from left needle, slip the third stitch on the cable needle back to the left needle, knit it while passing it behind the 2 stitches on the cable needle, then k2 from cable needle
sl: slip stitch from one needle to another without knitting it
k3tog: knit 3 together
psso: pass slipped stitch over stitches/yarn overs and off the needle

Rows 12 and 14: p2, *k1, p1*; repeat from * to * 3 times, k1, p2.
Row 13: k3, *p1, k1*; repeat from * to * 2 times, p1, k3.
Row 15: 3 left cross stitches (k2, p1), *p1, k1*; repeat from * to * 2 times, p1, 3 right cross stitches (p1, k2).
Row 17: p1, 3 left cross stitches (k2, p1), k1, p1, k1, 3 right cross stitches (p1, k2), p1.
Row 19: p2, 3 left cross stitches (k2, p1), p1, 3 right cross stitches (p1, k2), p2.
Keep repeating these 20 rows.

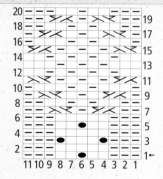

knit stitch on right side or purl stitch on wrong side
− purl stitch on right side or knit stitch on wrong side
● bobble: inc 3 in 1 st (k1, p1, k1), turn work: p3, turn work: k3, turn work: p3, turn work: sl 1 on right needle, k2tog, psso
3 left cross stitches: sl 2 on a cable needle in front of work, p1 from left needle, then k2 from cable needle

3 right cross stitches: sl 1 stitch on a cable needle behind work, k2 from left needle, then p1 from cable needle
inc 3 in 1 st (k1, p1, k1): make 3 stitches in 1 stitch, alternating knit, purl
sl: slip stitch from one needle to another without knitting it
k2tog: knit 2 together
psso: pass slipped stitch over stitches/yarn overs and off the needle

Cherries

The directions for this pattern consist of 11 stitches on a background of purled stockinette stitch.

Twisted stitches created by knitting/purling through the back of the loop, or k tbl/p tbl: For a knit stitch, insert the right needle into the back of the loop (behind the work) instead of the front, and knit as usual; for a purl stitch, insert the right needle into the back of the loop, slide it in front of the left needle, and purl as usual. This creates a twisted stitch.

Row 1 (right side of work): all purl.

Row 2: all knit.

Row 3: p5, 1 bobble (inc 5 in 1 st [k1, p1, k1, p1, k1], turn work: p5, turn work: k5, turn work: p5, turn work: k5tog), p5.

Rows 4 and 6: k5, p1 tbl, k5.

Row 5: p2, 1 bobble, p2, k1 tbl, p2, 1 bobble, p2.

Row 7: 1 bobble, p4, k1 tbl, p4, 1 bobble.

Row 8: p1 tbl, k2, *p1 tbl, k1*; repeat from * to * 3 times, k1, p1 tbl.

Row 9: 2 left cross stitches (k1, p1: purl the second stitch on the left needle first, passing the right needle behind the first stitch, then knit the first stitch), p1, 2 left cross stitches (k1, p1), k1 tbl, 2 right cross stitches (p1, k1: knit the second stitch on the left needle first, passing the right needle in front of the first stitch, then purl the first stitch), p1, 2 right cross stitches (p1, k1).

Row 10: k1, 2 right cross stitches (p1, k1), k1, p3 tbl, k1, 2 left cross stitches (k1, p1), k1.

Row 11: p2, 2 left cross stitches (k1, p1), m1, sl 1 kwise, k2tog, psso, m1, 2 right cross stitches (p1, k1), p2.

Row 12: k3, 2 right cross stitches (p1, k1), p1 tbl, 2 left cross stitches (k1, p1), k3.

Row 13: p4, m1, sl 1 kwise, k2tog, psso, m1, p4.

Row 14: k5, p1 tbl, k5.

Row 15: all purl.

Row 16: all knit.

Keep repeating these 16 rows.

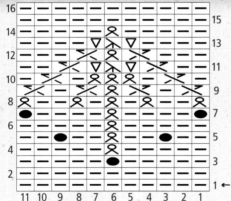

☐ knit stitch on right side or purl stitch on wrong side

– purl stitch on right side or knit stitch on wrong side

● bobble: inc 5 in 1 st (k1, p1, k1, p1, k1), turn work: p5, turn work: k5, turn work: p5, turn work, k5tog

꒑ k tbl: knit through the back of the loop on right side, creating a twisted stitch, or purl through the back of the loop on wrong side

▽ m1: using the left needle, pick up the strand between 2 stitches from back to front and knit normally to increase 1

⅄ sl 1 kwise, k2tog, psso: slip 1 stitch knitwise, knit the next 2 stitches together, pass the slipped stitch over the stitch obtained and off the needle

⤫ 2 left cross stitches: purl the second stitch on the left needle first, passing the right needle behind the first stitch, then knit the first stitch

⤬ 2 right cross stitches: knit the second stitch on the left needle first, passing the right needle in front of the first stitch, then purl the first stitch

inc 5 in 1 st (k1, p1, k1, p1, k1): make 5 stitches in 1 stitch, alternating knit, purl

k5tog: knit 5 together

Twists

TWISTED INWARD (LEFT CABLE)

The directions for this pattern consist of 9 stitches on a background of purled stockinette stitch.

Rows 1 (right side of work) and 5: k9.

Row 2 and all even numbered rows: knit each stitch as it appears in previous row (i.e., knit a knit stitch, purl a purl stitch).

Row 3: knit 4 left cross stitches (1 and 3: sl 1 on a cable needle in front of work, k3 from left needle, then k1 from cable needle), k1, knit 4 right cross stitches (3 and 1: sl 3 on a cable needle behind work, k1 from left needle, then k3 from cable needle).

Keep repeating these 6 rows.

TWISTED OUTWARD (RIGHT CABLE)

The directions for this pattern consist of 9 stitches on a background of purled stockinette stitch.

Rows 1 (right side of work) and 5: k9.

Row 2 and all even numbered rows: knit each stitch as it appears in previous row (i.e., knit a knit stitch, purl a purl stitch).

Row 3: knit 4 right cross stitches (3 and 1: sl 3 on a cable needle behind work, k1 from left needle, then k3 from cable needle), k1, knit 4 left cross stitches (1 and 3: sl 1 on a cable needle in front of work, k3 from left needle, then k1 from cable needle).

Keep repeating these 6 rows.

TWISTED INWARD

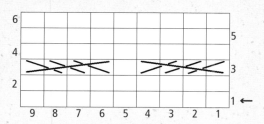

TWISTED OUTWARD

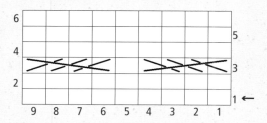

☐ knit stitch on right side or purl stitch on wrong side

✕ 4 right cross stitches: sl 3 on a cable needle behind work, k1 from left needle, then k3 from cable needle

✕ 4 left cross stitches: sl 1 on a cable needle in front of work, k3 from left needle, then k1 from cable needle

sl: slip stitch from one needle to another without knitting it

Cable Stitches

Little Zigzags

Number of stitches needed for joining: multiple of 6 + 1 selvedge stitch at each end.

Row 1 (right side of work): 1 selvedge stitch, *knit 3 left cross stitches (2 and 1: sl 2 on a cable needle in front of work, k1 from left needle, then k2 from cable needle), k3*; repeat from * to *; end with 1 selvedge stitch.

Row 2 and all even numbered rows: all purl.

Row 3: 1 selvedge stitch, *k1, knit 3 left cross stitches (2 and 1), k2*; repeat from * to *; end with 1 selvedge stitch.

Row 5: 1 selvedge stitch, *k2, knit 3 left cross stitches (2 and 1), k1*; repeat from * to *; end with 1 selvedge stitch.

Row 7: 1 selvedge stitch, *k3, knit 3 left cross stitches (2 and 1)*; repeat from * to *; end with 1 selvedge stitch.

Row 9: 1 selvedge stitch, *k3, knit 3 right cross stitches (1 and 2: sl 1 on a cable needle in front of work, k2 from left needle, then k1 from cable needle)*; repeat from * to *; end with 1 selvedge stitch.

Zigzags

Number of stitches needed for joining: multiple of 6 + 1 selvedge stitch at each end.

Row 1 (right side of work): 1 selvedge stitch, *p3, 3 right cross stitches (p1, k2: sl 1 on a cable needle behind work, k2 from left needle, then p1 from cable needle)*; repeat from * to *; end with 1 selvedge stitch.

Row 2 and all even numbered rows: knit each stitch as it appears in previous row (i.e., knit a knit stitch, purl a purl stitch).

Row 3: 1 selvedge stitch, *p2, 3 right cross stitches (p1, k2), p1*; repeat from * to *; end with 1 selvedge stitch.

Row 5: 1 selvedge stitch, *p1, 3 right cross stitches (p1, k2), p2*; repeat from * to *; end with 1 selvedge stitch.

Row 7: 1 selvedge stitch, *3 right cross stitches (p1, k2), p3*; repeat from * to *; end with 1 selvedge stitch.

Row 9: 1 selvedge stitch, *3 left cross stitches (k2, p1: sl 2 on a cable needle in front of work, p1 from left needle, then k2 from cable needle), p3*; repeat from * to *; end with 1 selvedge stitch.

Row 11: 1 selvedge stitch, *k2, knit 3 right cross stitches (1 and 2), k1*; repeat from * to *; end with 1 selvedge stitch.
Row 13: 1 selvedge stitch, *k1, knit 3 right cross stitches (1 and 2), k2*; repeat from * to *; end with 1 selvedge stitch.
Row 15: 1 selvedge stitch, *knit 3 right cross stitches (1 and 2), k3*; repeat from * to *; end with 1 selvedge stitch.
Keep repeating these 16 rows.

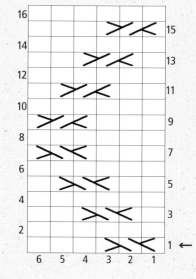

⟩⟨ 3 left cross stitches: sl 2 on a cable needle in front of work, k1 from left needle, then k2 from cable needle

⟩⟨ 3 right cross stitches: sl 1 on a cable needle in front of work, k2 from left needle, then k1 from cable needle

sl: slip stitch from one needle to another without knitting it

---

Row 11: 1 selvedge stitch, *p1, 3 left cross stitches (k2, p1), p2*; repeat from * to *; end with 1 selvedge stitch.
Row 13: 1 selvedge stitch, *p2, 3 left cross stitches (k2, p1), p1*; repeat from * to *; end with 1 selvedge stitch.
Row 15: 1 selvedge stitch, *p3, 3 left cross stitches (k2, p1)*; repeat from * to *; end with 1 selvedge stitch.
Keep repeating these 16 rows.

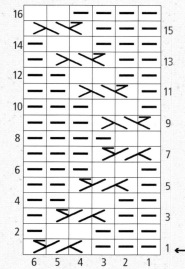

☐ knit stitch on right side or purl stitch on wrong side

− purl stitch on right side or knit stitch on wrong side

⟩⟨ 3 left cross stitches: sl 2 on a cable needle in front of work, p1 from left needle, then k2 from cable needle

⟩⟨ 3 right cross stitches: sl 1 on a cable needle behind work, k2 from left needle, then p1 from cable needle

sl: slip stitch from one needle to another without knitting it

Lozenges and Cables

Number of stitches needed for symmetry and joining: multiple of 8 + 1 selvedge stitch at each end.

Rows 1 (right side of work) and 5: 1 selvedge stitch, *p2, k4, p2*; repeat from * to *; end with 1 selvedge stitch.

Row 2 and all even numbered rows: knit each stitch as it appears in previous row (i.e., knit a knit stitch, purl a purl stitch).

Rows 3 and 7: 1 selvedge stitch, *p2, knit 4 right cross stitches (2 and 2: sl 2 on a cable needle behind work, k2 from left needle, then k2 from cable needle), p2*; repeat from * to *; end with 1 selvedge stitch.

Row 9: 1 selvedge stitch, *4 right cross stitches (p2, k2: sl 2 on a cable needle behind work, k2 from left needle, then p2 from cable needle), 4 left cross stitches (k2, p2: sl 2 on a cable needle in front of work, p2 from left needle, then k2 from cable needle)*; repeat from * to *; end with 1 selvedge stitch.

Row 11: 1 selvedge stitch, k2, *p4, knit 4 left cross stitches (2 and 2: sl 2 on a cable needle in front of work, k2 from left needle, then k2 from cable needle)*; repeat from * to *; end with p4, k2, 1 selvedge stitch.

Row 13: 1 selvedge stitch, *4 left cross stitches (k2, p2), 4 right cross stitches (p2, k2)*; repeat from * to *; end with 1 selvedge stitch.

Row 15: 1 selvedge stitch, *p2, knit 4 right cross stitches (2 and 2), p2*; repeat from * to *; end with 1 selvedge stitch.

Keep repeating these 16 rows.

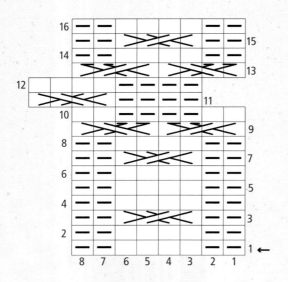

☐ knit stitch on right side or purl stitch on wrong side

− purl stitch on right side or knit stitch on wrong side

⟩⟨ 4 left cross stitches: sl 2 on a cable needle in front of work, k2 from left needle, then k2 from cable needle

⟩⟨ 4 right cross stitches: sl 2 on a cable needle behind work, k2 from left needle, then k2 from cable needle

⟩⟨ 4 left cross stitches: sl 2 on a cable needle in front of work, p2 from left needle, then k2 from cable needle

⟩⟨ 4 right cross stitches: sl 2 on a cable needle behind work, k2 from left needle, then p2 from cable needle

sl: slip stitch from one needle to another without knitting it

Lozenges

The directions for this pattern consist of 16 stitches on a background of purled stockinette stitch.

Row 1 (right side of work): k2, p3, 3 right cross stitches (p1, k2: sl 1 on a cable needle behind work, k2 from left needle, then p1 from cable needle), 3 left cross stitches (k2, p1: sl 2 on a cable needle in front of work, p1 from left needle, then k2 from cable needle), p3, k2.

Row 2 and all even numbered rows: knit each stitch as it appears in previous row (i.e., knit a knit stitch, purl a purl stitch).

Row 3: k2, p2, 3 right cross stitches (p1, k2), p2, 3 left cross stitches (k2, p1), p2, k2.

Row 5: k2, p1, 3 right cross stitches (p1, k2), p4, 3 left cross stitches (k2, p1), p1, k2.

Row 7: k2, 3 right cross stitches (p1, k2), p6, 3 left cross stitches (k2, p1), k2.

Row 9: knit 4 left cross stitches (2 and 2: sl 2 on a cable needle in front of work, k2 from left needle, then k2 from cable needle), p8, knit 4 right cross stitches (2 and 2: sl 2 on a cable needle behind work, k2 from left needle, then k2 from cable needle).

Row 11: k2, 3 left cross stitches (k2, p1), p6, 3 right cross stitches (p1, k2), k2.

Row 13: k2, p1, 3 left cross stitches (k2, p1), p4, 3 right cross stitches (p1, k2), p1, k2.

Row 15: k2, p2, 3 left cross stitches (k2, p1), p2, 3 right cross stitches (p1, k2), p2, k2.

Row 17: k2, p3, 3 left cross stitches (k2, p1), 3 right cross stitches (p1, k2), p3, k2.

Row 19: k2, p4, knit 4 right cross stitches (2 and 2), p4, k2.

Keep repeating these 20 rows.

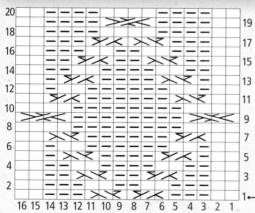

☐ knit stitch on right side or purl stitch on wrong side

− purl stitch on right side or knit stitch on wrong side

⟩⟨ 3 left cross stitches: sl 2 on a cable needle in front of work, p1 from left needle, then k2 from cable needle

⟩⟨ 3 right cross stitches: sl 1 on a cable needle behind work, k2 from left needle, then p1 from cable needle

⟩⟨ 4 left cross stitches: sl 2 on a cable needle in front of work, k2 from left needle, then k2 from cable needle

⟩⟨ 4 right cross stitches: sl 2 on a cable needle behind work, k2 from left needle, then k2 from cable needle

sl: slip stitch from one needle to another without knitting it

Moss Stitch Diamonds

knit stitch on right side or purl stitch on wrong side

− purl stitch on right side or knit stitch on wrong side

3 left cross stitches: sl 2 on a cable needle in front of work, p1 from left needle, then k2 from cable needle

3 right cross stitches: sl 1 on a cable needle behind work, k2 from left needle, then p1 from cable needle

3 left cross stitches: sl 2 on a cable needle in front of work, k1 from left needle, then k2 from cable needle

3 right cross stitches: sl 1 on a cable needle behind work, k2 from left needle, then k1 from cable needle

5 right cross stitches: sl 3 on a cable needle behind work, k2 from left needle, sl the third stitch back to the left needle, knit it while passing it behind the 2 stitches on the cable needle, then k2 from cable needle

sl: slip stitch from one needle to another without knitting it

The directions for this pattern consist of 13 stitches on a background of purled stockinette stitch.

Row 1 (right side of work): 3 left cross stitches (k2, p1: sl 2 on a cable needle in front of work, p1 from left needle, then k2 from cable needle), *p1, k1*; repeat from * to * 3 times, p1, 3 right cross stitches (p1, k2: sl 1 on a cable needle behind work, k2 from left needle, then p1 from cable needle).

Row 2 and all even numbered rows: knit each stitch as it appears in previous row (i.e., knit a knit stitch, purl a purl stitch).

Row 3: p1, 3 left cross stitches (k2, p1), *p1, k1*; repeat from * to * 2 times, p1, 3 right cross stitches (p1, k2), p1.

Row 5: p2, 3 left cross stitches (k2, p1), p1, k1, p1, 3 right cross stitches (p1, k2), p2.

Row 7: p3, 3 left cross stitches (k2, p1), p1, 3 right cross stitches (p1, k2), p3.

Row 9: p4, knit 5 right cross stitches (2, 1, and 2: sl 3 on a cable needle behind work, k2 from left needle, sl the third stitch back to the left needle, knit it while passing it behind the 2 stitches on the cable needle, then k2 from cable needle), p4.

Row 11: p3, knit 3 right cross stitches (1 and 2: sl 1 on a cable needle behind work, k2 from left needle, then k1 from cable needle), p1, knit 3 left cross stitches (2 and 1: sl 2 on a cable needle in front of work, k1 from left needle, then k2 from cable needle), p3.

Row 13: p2, knit 3 right cross stitches (1 and 2), p1, k1, p1, knit 3 left cross stitches (2 and 1), p2.

Row 15: p1, knit 3 right cross stitches (1 and 2), *p1, k1*; repeat from * to * 2 times, p1, knit 3 left cross stitches (2 and 1), p1.

Row 17: knit 3 right cross stitches (1 and 2), *p1, k1*; repeat from * to * 3 times, p1, knit 3 left cross stitches (2 and 1).

Row 19: k2, *p1, k1*; repeat from * to * 4 times, p1, k2.

Keep repeating these 20 rows.

Slip Stitches

Slip stitches allow
a broad variety of textures
and motifs.

Slip Stitches

Double Stockinette

Number of stitches: multiple of 2.

Row 1: *k1, sl 1 pwise wyif*; repeat from * to *.

Keep repeating this row. You therefore knit the stitch that was slipped in the previous row, and slip the stitch that was knitted.
The wrong and right sides of the work look similar.

☐ knit stitch on right side or purl stitch on wrong side

– purl stitch on right side or knit stitch on wrong side

⊻ sl 1 pwise wyib: stitch slipped purlwise on right side with yarn in back or purlwise on wrong side with yarn in front

⊻ sl 1 pwise wyif: stitch slipped purlwise on right side with yarn in front or purlwise on wrong side with yarn in back

Half Linen Stitch

Number of stitches needed for symmetry: multiple of 2 + 1 + 1 selvedge stitch at each end.

Row 1 (right side of work): 1 selvedge stitch, *k1, sl 1 pwise wyif*; repeat from * to *; end with k1, 1 selvedge stitch.

Rows 2 and 4: all purl.

Row 3: 1 selvedge stitch, *sl 1 pwise wyif, k1*; repeat from * to *; end with sl 1 pwise wyif, 1 selvedge stitch.

Keep repeating these 4 rows.

☐ knit stitch on right side or purl stitch on wrong side

⊻ sl 1 pwise wyif: stitch slipped purlwise on right side with yarn in front or purlwise on wrong side with yarn in back

Linen Stitch

Number of stitches needed for symmetry: multiple of 2 + 1 + 1 selvedge stitch at each end.

Row 1 (right side of work): 1 selvedge stitch, *k1, sl 1 pwise wyif*; repeat from * to *; end with k1, 1 selvedge stitch.

Row 2: 1 selvedge stitch, sl 1 pwise wyib, *p1, sl 1 pwise wyib*; repeat from * to *; end with 1 selvedge stitch.

Keep repeating these 2 rows.

☐ knit stitch on right side or purl stitch on wrong side

⊻ sl 1 pwise wyif: stitch slipped purlwise on right side with yarn in front or purlwise on wrong side with yarn in back

sl 1 pwise wyib: slip 1 purlwise with yarn in back

Suiting Stitch

Number of stitches needed for symmetry: multiple of 2 + 1 + 1 selvedge stitch at each end.

Row 1 (right side of work): 1 selvedge stitch, *p1, sl 1 pwise wyib*; repeat from * to *; end with p1, 1 selvedge stitch.

Row 2 and all even numbered rows: all purl.

Row 3: 1 selvedge stitch, *sl 1 pwise wyib, p1*; repeat from * to *; end with sl 1 pwise wyib, 1 selvedge stitch.

Keep repeating these 4 rows.

☐ knit stitch on right side or purl stitch on wrong side

– purl stitch on right side or knit stitch on wrong side

⊻ sl 1 pwise wyib: stitch slipped purlwise on right side with yarn in back or purlwise on wrong side with yarn in front

Eye of Partridge Stitch

Number of stitches needed for symmetry: multiple of 2 + 1 + 1 selvedge stitch at each end.

Row 1 (right side of work): 1 selvedge stitch, *k1, sl 1 pwise wyib*; repeat from * to *; end with k1, 1 selvedge stitch.

Row 2 and all even numbered rows: all purl.

Row 3: 1 selvedge stitch, *sl 1 pwise wyib, k1*; repeat from * to *; end with sl 1 pwise wyib, 1 selvedge stitch.

Keep repeating these 4 rows.

☐ knit stitch on right side or purl stitch on wrong side

⊻ sl 1 pwise wyib: stitch slipped purlwise on right side with yarn in back or purlwise on wrong side with yarn in front

Stamen Stitch

Number of stitches needed for symmetry: multiple of 2 + 1 + 1 selvedge stitch at each end.

Rows 1 (right side of work) and 3: all knit.

Row 2: 1 selvedge stitch, k1, *sl 1 pwise wyib, k1*; repeat from * to *; end with 1 selvedge stitch.

Row 4: 1 selvedge stitch, sl 1 pwise wyib, *k1, sl 1 pwise wyib*; repeat from * to *; end with 1 selvedge stitch.

Keep repeating these 4 rows.

LOOSE-KNIT STAMEN STITCH: knit according for the instructions for Stamen Stitch above, but using large needles and a fine yarn.

☐ knit stitch on right side or purl stitch on wrong side

– purl stitch on right side or knit stitch on wrong side

⊼ sl 1 pwise wyif: stitch slipped purlwise on right side with yarn in front or purlwise on wrong side with yarn in back

sl 1 pwise wyib: slip 1 purlwise with yarn in back

Wisteria Stitch

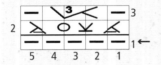

Photo: wrong side of work

Number of stitches needed for symmetry: multiple of 5 + 1 selvedge stitch at each end.

Row 1 (right side of work): all purl.

Row 2: 1 selvedge stitch, *skp, yo1 bringing yarn to front (wrong side), sl 1 pwise, bring yarn to back, k2tog*; repeat from * to *; end with 1 selvedge stitch.

Row 3: 1 selvedge stitch, *p1, knit slipped stitch and yarn over together k1, p1, k1 to obtain 3 stitches, p1*; repeat from * to *; end with 1 selvedge stitch.

Keep repeating Rows 2 and 3.

− purl stitch on right side or knit stitch on wrong side

⅄ ○ ⅃ ⅂ on wrong side of work: skp, yo1 bringing yarn to front (wrong side of work), sl 1 pwise, bring yarn to back, k2tog

⅂< on right side of work: knit slipped stitch and yarn over together k1, p1, k1 to obtain 3 stitches

skp: slip 1 stitch knitwise, knit the next stitch, then pass the slipped stitch over the knit stitch and off the needle

sl 1 pwise: slip 1 purlwise

k2tog: knit 2 together

Grass Stitch

Number of stitches needed for symmetry and joining: multiple of 4 + 1 selvedge stitch at each end.

Row 1 (right side of work): 1 selvedge stitch, *k1, sl 1 pwise wyib, k1, yo1, psso, k1*; repeat from * to *; end with 1 selvedge stitch.

Row 2: all purl.

Keep repeating these 2 rows.

☐ knit stitch on right side or purl stitch on wrong side

○⅂ on right side of work: sl 1 pwise wyib, k1, yo1, psso

sl 1 pwise wyib: slip 1 purlwise with yarn in back

psso: pass slipped stitch over stitches/yarn overs and off the needle

Slip Stitch Honeycomb

Number of stitches needed for symmetry: multiple of 2 + 1 selvedge stitch at each end.

Row 1 (right side of work): 1 selvedge stitch, *sl 1 pwise wyif, yo1, p1*; repeat from * to *; end with 1 selvedge stitch.

Row 2: 1 selvedge stitch, *k1, yo1, sl 2 pwise wyib*; repeat from * to *; end with 1 selvedge stitch.

Row 3: 1 selvedge stitch, *sl 3 pwise wyif, p1*; repeat from * to *; end with 1 selvedge stitch.

Row 4: 1 selvedge stitch, *k1, knit the 3 slipped stitches together*; repeat from * to *; end with 1 selvedge stitch.

Row 5: 1 selvedge stitch, *p1, sl 1 pwise wyif, yo1*; repeat from * to *; end with 1 selvedge stitch.

Row 6: 1 selvedge stitch, *yo1, sl 2 pwise wyib, k1*; repeat from * to *; end with 1 selvedge stitch.

Row 7: 1 selvedge stitch, *p1, sl 3 pwise wyif*; repeat from * to *; end with 1 selvedge stitch.

Row 8: 1 selvedge stitch, *knit the 3 slipped stitches together, k1*; repeat from * to *; end with 1 selvedge stitch.

Keep repeating these 8 rows.

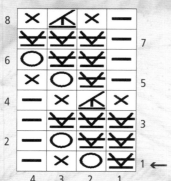

− purl stitch on right side or knit stitch on wrong side

× stitch that does not exist

O yo: yarn over

⤛ sl 1 pwise wyif: stitch slipped purlwise on right side with yarn in front or purlwise on wrong side with yarn in back

⟁ 3 knitwise slipped stitches knit together on wrong side of work

sl 1 pwise wyib: slip 1 purlwise with yarn in back

Slip Stitches

Cross Stitch

Number of stitches needed for the connection: multiple of 2 + 1 selvedge stitch at each end.

Row 1 (right side of work): 1 selvedge stitch, *sl 1 pwise wyib, k1, yo1, psso*; repeat from * to *; end with 1 selvedge stitch.

Row 2: all purl.

Keep repeating these two rows.

☐ knit stitch on right side or purl stitch on wrong side

⟆⟈ on the right side of the work: sl 1 pwise wyib, k1, yo1, psso

sl 1 pwise wyib: slip 1 purlwise with yarn in back

psso: pass slipped stitch over stitches/yarn overs and off the needle

Wild Oats

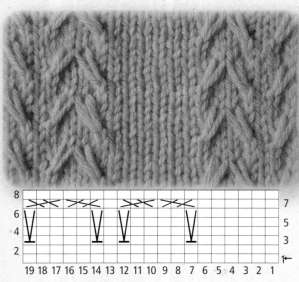

Number of stitches needed for symmetry: multiple of 19 + 6 + 1 selvedge stitch at each end.

Row 1 (right side of work): all knit.

Row 2: all purl.

Row 3: 1 selvedge stitch, *k6, sl 1 pwise wyib, k4, sl 1 pwise wyib, k1, sl 1 pwise wyib, k4, sl 1 pwise wyib*; repeat from * to *; end with k6, 1 selvedge stitch.

Rows 4 and 6: all purl, slipping the slipped stitches (yarn in front) of the preceding row.

Row 5: all knit, slipping the slipped stitches (yarn behind) of the preceding row.

Row 7: 1 selvedge stitch, *k6, 3 left cross stitches (1 and 2: sl 1 on a cable needle in front of work, k2 from left needle, then k1 from cable needle), 3 right cross stitches (2 and 1: sl 2 on a cable needle behind work, k1 from left needle, then k2 from cable needle), k1, 3 left cross stitches (1 and 2), 3 right cross stitches (2 and 1)*; repeat from * to *; end with k6, 1 selvedge stitch.

Row 8: all purl.

Keep repeating Rows 3 through 8.

☐ knit stitch on right side or purl stitch on wrong side

⋁ sl 1 pwise wyib: stitch slipped purlwise on right side with yarn in back or purlwise on wrong side with yarn in front

⤫ 3 left cross stitches: sl 1 on a cable needle in front of work, k2 from left needle, then k1 from cable needle

⤬ 3 right cross stitches: sl 2 on a cable needle behind work, k1 from left needle, then k2 from cable needle

sl: slip stitch from one needle to another without knitting it

"X" Stitch

Number of stitches needed for symmetry: multiple of 8 + 2 + 1 selvedge stitch at each end.

Row 1 (right side of work): all knit.

Row 2: 1 selvedge stitch, k2, *6 long purl stitches (insert right needle into stitch as if to purl, yo2 on right needle to make 1 purl stitch), k2*; repeat from * to *; end with 1 selvedge stitch.

Row 3: 1 selvedge stitch, *k2, knit 6 long right cross stitches (sl 6 on right needle letting yarn overs slide off, slip stitches back to left needle, move the last 3 over the first 3 while leaving them on the left needle, knit these 6 stitches)*; repeat from * to *; end with k2, 1 selvedge stitch.

Row 4: 1 selvedge stitch, p4, k2, *6 long purl stitches, k2*; repeat from * to *; end with p4, 1 selvedge stitch.

Row 5: 1 selvedge stitch, k4, *k2, 6 long left cross stitches (sl 6 on right needle letting yarn overs slide off, move the first 3 over the last 3 while leaving them on the right needle, replace stitches in this position on left needle, knit these 6 stitches)*; repeat from * to *; end with k6, 1 selvedge stitch.

Keep repeating Rows 2 through 5.

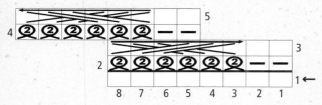

☐ knit stitch on right side or purl stitch on wrong side

– purl stitch on right side or knit stitch on wrong side

☒ long knit stitch on right side or purl stitch on wrong side: insert right needle into stitch as if to purl, yo2 on right needle, knit or purl as usual

⟩⟩⟩⟨ 6 long left cross stitches: sl 6 on right needle letting yarn overs slide off, move the first 3 over the last 3 while leaving them on the right needle, replace stitches in this position on left needle, knit these 6 stitches

⟩⟩⟩⟨ 6 long right cross stitches: sl 6 on right needle letting yarn overs slide off, slip stitches back to left needle, move the last 3 over the first 3 while leaving them on the left needle, knit these 6 stitches

sl: slip stitch from one needle to another without knitting it

Seedlings

Number of stitches needed for symmetry: multiple of 4 + 1 + 1 selvedge stitch at each end.

Row 1 (right side of work): 1 selvedge stitch, *k2, sl 1 pwise wyib, k1*; repeat from * to *; end with k1, 1 selvedge stitch.

Row 2: 1 selvedge stitch, p1, *p1, sl 1 pwise wyif, p2*; repeat from * to *; end with 1 selvedge stitch.

Row 3: 1 selvedge stitch, *knit 3 right cross stitches (2 and 1: sl 2 on a cable needle behind work, k1 from left needle, then k2 from cable needle), k1*; repeat from * to *; end with k1, 1 selvedge stitch.

Rows 4 and 8: all purl.

Row 5: 1 selvedge stitch, k1, *k1, sl 1 pwise wyib, k2*; repeat from * to *; end with 1 selvedge stitch.

Row 6: 1 selvedge stitch, *p2, sl 1 pwise wyif, p1*; repeat from * to *; end with p1, 1 selvedge stitch.

Row 7: 1 selvedge stitch, k1, *k1, knit 3 left cross stitches (1 and 2: sl 1 on a cable needle in front of work, k2 from left needle, then k1 from cable needle)*; repeat from * to *; end with 1 selvedge stitch.

Keep repeating these 8 rows.

Wings

Number of stitches needed for symmetry: multiple of 4 + 1 + 1 selvedge stitch at each end.

Row 1 (right side of work): 1 selvedge stitch, k1, *k1, sl 1 pwise wyib, k2*; repeat from * to *; end with 1 selvedge stitch.

Row 2: 1 selvedge stitch, *p2, sl 1 pwise wyif, p1*; repeat from * to *; end with p1, 1 selvedge stitch.

Row 3: 1 selvedge stitch, k1, *k1, 3 left cross stitches (sl 1 pwise, k2: sl 1 on a cable needle in front of work, k2 from left needle, then sl the stitch on the cable needle pwise wyib*; repeat from * to *; end with 1 selvedge stitch.

Rows 4, 6, 10, and 12: all purl.

Rows 5 and 11: all knit.

Row 7: 1 selvedge stitch, *k2, sl 1 pwise wyib, k1*; repeat from * to *; end with k1, 1 selvedge stitch.

Row 8: 1 selvedge stitch, p1, *p1, sl 1 pwise wyif, p2*; repeat from * to *; end with 1 selvedge stitch.

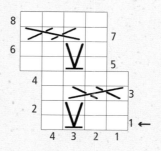

knit stitch on right side or purl stitch on wrong side

$\underline{V}$ sl 1 pwise wyib: stitch slipped purlwise on right side with yarn in back or purlwise on wrong side with yarn in front for 2 rows

3 left cross stitches: sl 1 on a cable needle in front of work, k2 from left needle, then k1 from cable needle

3 right cross stitches: sl 2 on a cable needle behind work, k1 from left needle, then k2 from cable needle

sl 1 pwise wyif: slip 1 purlwise with yarn in front

sl: slip stitch from one needle to another without knitting it

Row 9: 1 selvedge stitch, *3 right cross stitches (k2, sl 1 pwise: sl 2 on a cable needle behind work, sl 1 pwise wyib from left needle, then k2 from cable needle), k1*; repeat from * to *; end with k1, 1 selvedge stitch.

Keep repeating these 12 rows.

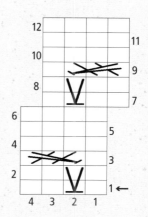

knit stitch on right side or purl stitch on wrong side

$\underline{V}$ sl 1 pwise wyib: stitch slipped purlwise on right side with yarn in back or purlwise on wrong side with yarn in front for 2 rows

3 left cross stitches: sl 1 on a cable needle in front of work, k2 from left needle, then sl the stitch on the cable needle pwise wyib

3 right cross stitches: sl 2 on a cable needle behind work, sl 1 pwise wyib from left needle, then k2 from cable needle

sl 1 pwise wyif: slip 1 purlwise with yarn in front

sl: slip stitch from one needle to another without knitting it

Giant Honeycomb Stitch

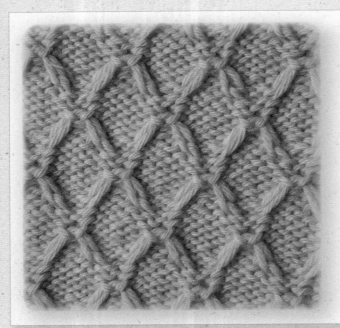

Number of stitches needed for symmetry: multiple of 6 + 3 + 1 selvedge stitch at each end.

Rows 1 (right side of work), 7, and 15: all purl.

Row 2 and all even numbered rows: all knit.

Rows 3 and 5: 1 selvedge stitch, *p3, sl 3 pwise wyif*; repeat from * to *; end with p3, 1 selvedge stitch.

Row 9: 1 selvedge stitch, *p4, p1 while lifting strands from slipped stitches (insert right needle into front of next stitch and the 2 strands in front of slipped stitches below at the same time, and purl all together), p1*; repeat from * to *; end with p3, 1 selvedge stitch.

Rows 11 and 13: 1 selvedge stitch, *sl 3 pwise wyif, p3*; repeat from * to *; end with sl 3 pwise wyif, 1 selvedge stitch.

Row 17: 1 selvedge stitch, *p1, p1 while lifting strands from slipped stitches, p4*; repeat from * to *; end with p1, p1 while lifting strands from slipped stitches, p1, 1 selvedge stitch.

Keep repeating Rows 3 through 18.

Slip Stitch Diamonds

Number of stitches needed for symmetry and joining: multiple of 6 + 1 selvedge stitch at each end.

Rows 1 (wrong side of work) and 7: all purl.

Rows 2 and 4: 1 selvedge stitch, *sl 1 pwise wyib, k4, sl 1 pwise wyib*; repeat from * to *; end with 1 selvedge stitch.

Rows 3 and 5: 1 selvedge stitch, *sl 1 pwise wyif, p4, sl 1 pwise wyif*; repeat from * to *; end with 1 selvedge stitch.

Row 6: 1 selvedge stitch, *3 left cross stitches (sl 1 pwise, k2: sl 1 on a cable needle in front of work, k2 from left needle, then sl 1 pwise wyib from cable needle), 3 right cross stitches (k2, sl 1 pwise: sl 2 on a cable needle behind work, sl 1 pwise wyib, then k2 from cable needle)*; repeat from * to *; end with 1 selvedge stitch.

Rows 8 and 10: 1 selvedge stitch, *k2, sl 2 pwise wyib, k2*; repeat from * to *; end with 1 selvedge stitch.

Rows 9 and 11: 1 selvedge stitch, *p2, sl 2 pwise wyif, p2*; repeat from * to *; end with 1 selvedge stitch.

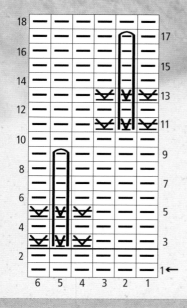

- purl stitch on right side or knit stitch on wrong side

⊻ sl 1 pwise wyif: stitch slipped purlwise on right side with yarn in front or purlwise on wrong side with yarn in back

⋒ purl stitch lifting strands from slipped stitches (yarn in front of stitches): insert right needle into next stitch and the 2 strands in front of slipped stitches below at the same time, and purl all together

Row 12: 1 selvedge stitch, *3 right cross stitches (k2, sl 1 pwise), 3 left cross stitches (sl 1 pwise, k2)*; repeat from * to *; end with 1 selvedge stitch.

Keep repeating these 12 rows.

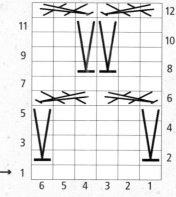

□ knit stitch on right side or purl stitch on wrong side

V sl 1 pwise wyib: stitch slipped purlwise on right side with yarn in back or purlwise on wrong side with yarn in front for 4 rows

⤫ 3 left cross stitches: sl 1 on a cable needle in front of work, k2 from left needle, then sl 1 pwise wyib from cable needle

⤫ 3 right cross stitches: sl 2 on a cable needle behind work, sl 1 pwise wyib, then k2 from cable needle

sl 1 pwise wyif: slip 1 purlwise with yarn in front

sl: slip stitch from one needle to another without knitting it

Slip Stitches

Broderie Anglaise

Number of stitches needed for symmetry: multiple of 8 + 4 + 1 selvedge stitch at each end.

Note: The number of stitches will not be the same as the number at the beginning except in rows 5 and 9.

Rows 1 (wrong side of work), 3, 5, 7, and 9: all purl.

Row 2: 1 selvedge stitch, *k4, k2tog, skp*; repeat from * to *; end with k4, 1 selvedge stitch.

Row 4: 1 selvedge stitch, *k4, 1 long knit stitch (insert the right needle into the space 2 rows below between the k2tog and the skp, and k1, creating a loop), k2, 1 long knit stitch*; repeat from * to *; end with k4, 1 selvedge stitch.

Row 6: 1 selvedge stitch, *k2tog, skp, k4*; repeat from * to *; end with k2tog, skp, 1 selvedge stitch.

Row 8: 1 selvedge stitch, *1 long knit stitch as in row 4, k2, 1 long knit stitch as in row 4, k4*; repeat from * to *; end with 1 long knit stitch as in row 4, k2, 1 long stitch as in row 4, 1 selvedge stitch.

Keep repeating Rows 2 through 9.

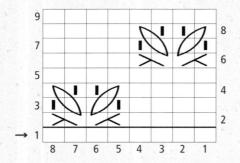

☐ knit stitch on right side or purl stitch on wrong side

on right side of work: 1 long knit stitch (insert the right needle into the space 2 rows below between the k2tog and the skp, and k1, creating a loop), k2, 1 long knit stitch

k2tog: knit 2 together

skp: slip 1 stitch knitwise, knit the next stitch, then pass the slipped stitch over the knit stitch and off the needle

Rows of Petals

Number of stitches needed for symmetry: multiple of 4 + 1 + 1 selvedge stitch at each end.

Note: During the 8 rows that comprise the repeat, the number of stitches differs from row to row. For each group of 4 stitches in Row 1, you will have 6 stitches in Row 8.

Rows 1 (right side of work), 3, and 5: all purl.

Rows 2, 4, and 6: all knit.

Row 7: 1 selvedge stitch, *p2, 1 long knit stitch (insert the right needle not into the next stitch on the left needle, but into the stitch 3 rows below it, and k1, creating a loop), k1, 1 long knit stitch into the same stitch below as the previous long stitch, p1*; repeat from * to *; end with p1, 1 selvedge stitch.

Row 8: 1 selvedge stitch, k1, *k1, p3, k2*; repeat from * to *; end with 1 selvedge stitch.

Row 9: 1 selvedge stitch, *p1, p2tog, p1, sl 2 kwise, return slipped stitches to left needle, p2tog tbl*; repeat from * to *; end with p1, 1 selvedge stitch.

Keep repeating Rows 2 through 9.

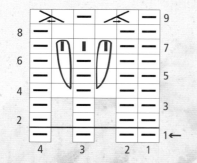

☐   knit stitch on right side or purl stitch on wrong side

−   purl stitch on right side or knit stitch on wrong side

on right side of work: 1 long knit stitch (insert the right needle not into the next stitch on the left needle, but into the stitch 3 rows below it, and k1, creating a loop), k1, 1 long knit stitch into the same stitch below as the previous long stitch

⤰ sl 2 kwise, return slipped stitches to left needle, p2tog tbl: slip 2 stitches knitwise onto the right needle, slip them back to the left needle, and purl them together through the back loops

⤲ p2tog: purl 2 together on right side or knit 2 together on wrong side

Butterfly Stitch

Number of stitches needed for symmetry: multiple of 10 + 5 + 1 selvedge stitch at each end.

Rows 1 (right side of work), 3, 5, 9, and 11: all knit.

Rows 2, 4, and 6: 1 selvedge stitch, p5, *sl 5 pwise wyib, p5*; repeat from * to *; end with 1 selvedge stitch.

Row 7: 1 selvedge stitch, *k7, k1 while lifting strands from slipped stitches (insert right needle under 3 strands in front of slipped stitches below, then into next stitch, and knit them together), k2*; repeat from * to *; end with k5, 1 selvedge stitch.

Rows 8, 10, and 12: 1 selvedge stitch, sl 5 pwise wyib, *p5, sl 5 pwise wyib*; repeat from * to *; end with 1 selvedge stitch.

Row 13: 1 selvedge stitch, *k2, k1 while lifting the strands from the slipped stitches, k7*; repeat from * to *; end with k2, k1 while lifting the strands from the slipped stitches, k2, 1 selvedge stitch.

Keep repeating Rows 2 through 13.

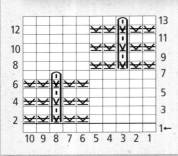

☐ knit stitch on right side or purl stitch on wrong side

⊻ sl 1 pwise wyif: stitch slipped purlwise on right side with yarn in front or purlwise on wrong side with yarn in back

⊻ knit stitch lifting strands from slipped stitches (yarn in front of stitches): insert right needle under 3 strands in front of slipped stitches below, then into next stitch, and knit them together

sl 1 pwise wyib: slip 1 purlwise with yarn in back

Butterfly Stitch Ribbing

Number of stitches needed for symmetry: multiple of 10 + 5 + 1 selvedge stitch at each end.

Rows 1 (right side of work), 3, 5, 7, and 9: all knit.

Rows 2 and 12: 1 selvedge stitch, k5, *p5, k5*; repeat from * to *; end with 1 selvedge stitch.

Rows 4, 6, 8, and 10: 1 selvedge stitch, k5, *sl 5 pwise wyib, k5*; repeat from * to *; end with 1 selvedge stitch.

Row 11: 1 selvedge stitch, *k7, k1 while lifting the strands from the slipped stitches (insert the right needle under the 4 strands in front of the slipped stitches below, then into the next stitch, and knit them together), k2*; repeat from * to *; end with k5, 1 selvedge stitch.

Keep repeating these 12 rows.

☐ knit stitch on right side or purl stitch on wrong side

⊻ sl 1 pwise wyif: stitch slipped purlwise on right side with yarn in front or purlwise on wrong side with yarn in back

⊻ knit stitch lifting strands from slipped stitches (yarn in front of stitches): insert the right needle under the 4 strands in front of the slipped stitches below, then into the next stitch, and knit them together

sl 1 pwise wyib: slip 1 purlwise with yarn in back

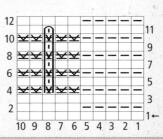

Twig Stitch

Number of stitches needed for symmetry: multiple of 13 + 1 selvedge stitch at each end.

Row 1 (right side of work): 1 selvedge stitch, *k1, 2 right cross stitches (k1, sl 1 pwise: sl 1 on a cable needle behind work, sl 1 pwise wyib from left needle, then k1 from cable needle), k2, 2 right cross stitches (k1, sl 1 pwise), k1, 2 left cross stitches (sl 1 pwise, k1: sl 1 on a cable needle in front of work, k1 from left needle, then sl 1 pwise wyib), k3*; repeat from * to *; end with 1 selvedge stitch.

Row 2 and all even numbered rows: all purl.

Row 3: 1 selvedge stitch, *k4, 2 right cross stitches (k1, sl 1 pwise), k3, 2 left cross stitches (sl 1 pwise, k1), k2*; repeat from * to *; end with 1 selvedge stitch.

Row 5: 1 selvedge stitch, *k3, 2 right cross stitches (k1, sl 1 pwise), k1, 2 left cross stitches (sl 1 pwise, k1), k2, 2 left cross stitches (sl 1 pwise, k1), k1*; repeat from * to *; end with 1 selvedge stitch.

Row 7: 1 selvedge stitch, *k2, 2 right cross stitches (k1, sl 1 pwise), k3, 2 left cross stitches (sl 1 pwise, k1), k4*; repeat from * to *; end with 1 selvedge stitch.

Keep repeating these 8 rows.

knit stitch on right side or purl stitch on wrong side

⤲ 2 left cross stitches: sl 1 on a cable needle in front of work, k1 from left needle, then sl 1 pwise wyib

⤲ 2 right cross stitches: sl 1 on a cable needle behind work, sl 1 pwise wyib from left needle, then k1 from cable needle

sl 1 pwise wyib: slip 1 purlwise with yarn in back

sl: slip stitch from one needle to another without knitting it

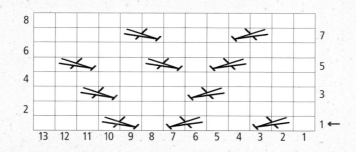

Vice-Versa

Number of stitches needed for symmetry: multiple of 28 + 1 selvedge stitch at each end.

Row 1 (right side of work): 1 selvedge stitch, *k6, 2 right cross stitches (k1, sl 1 pwise: sl 1 on a cable needle behind work, sl 1 pwise wyib from left needle, then k1 from cable needle), 2 left cross stitches (sl 1 pwise, k1: sl 1 on a cable needle in front of work, k1 from left needle, then sl 1 pwise wyib from cable needle), k6, 2 left cross stitches (sl 1 pwise, k1), k8, 2 right cross stitches (k1, sl 1 pwise)*; repeat from * to *; end with 1 selvedge stitch.

Row 2 and all even numbered rows: all purl.

Row 3: 1 selvedge stitch, *k5, 2 right cross stitches (k1, sl 1 pwise), k2, 2 left cross stitches (sl 1 pwise, k1), k6, 2 left cross stitches (sl 1 pwise, k1), k6, 2 right cross stitches (k1, sl 1 pwise), k1*; repeat from * to *; end with 1 selvedge stitch.

Row 5: 1 selvedge stitch, *k4, 2 right cross stitches (k1, sl 1 pwise), k4, 2 left cross stitches (sl 1 pwise, k1), k6, 2 left cross stitches (sl 1 pwise, k1), k4, 2 right cross stitches (k1, sl 1 pwise), k2*; repeat from * to *; end with 1 selvedge stitch.

Row 7: 1 selvedge stitch, *k3, 2 right cross stitches (k1, sl 1 pwise), k6, 2 left cross stitches (sl 1 pwise, k1), k6, 2 left cross stitches (sl 1 pwise, k1), k2, 2 right cross stitches (k1, sl 1 pwise), k3*; repeat from * to *; end with 1 selvedge stitch.

Row 9: 1 selvedge stitch, *k2, 2 right cross stitches (k1, sl 1 pwise), k8, 2 left cross stitches (sl 1 pwise, k1), k6, 2 left cross stitches (sl 1 pwise, k1), 2 right cross stitches (k1, sl 1 pwise), k4*; repeat from * to *; end with 1 selvedge stitch.

Keep repeating these 10 rows.

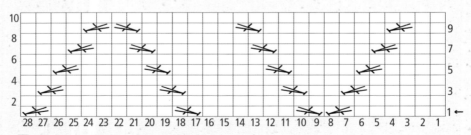

knit stitch on right side or purl stitch on wrong side

2 left cross stitches: sl 1 on a cable needle in front of work, k1 from left needle, then sl 1 pwise wyib from cable needle

2 right cross stitches: sl 1 on a cable needle behind work, sl 1 pwise wyib from left needle, then k1 from cable needle

sl 1 pwise wyib: slip 1 purlwise with yarn in back

sl: slip stitch from one needle to another without knitting it

Garter Stitch Triangles

Number of stitches needed for joining: multiple of 8 + 1 selvedge stitch at each end.

Row 1 (right side of work): 1 selvedge stitch, *k2, 2 right cross stitches (k1, sl 1 pwise: sl 1 on a cable needle behind work, sl 1 pwise wyib from left needle, then k1 from cable needle), k4*; repeat from * to *; end with 1 selvedge stitch.

Row 2: 1 selvedge stitch, *p4, k1, p3*; repeat from * to *; end with 1 selvedge stitch.

Row 3: 1 selvedge stitch, *k1, 2 right cross stitches (k1, sl 1 pwise), k5*; repeat from * to *; end with 1 selvedge stitch.

Row 4: 1 selvedge stitch, *p4, k2, p2*; repeat from * to *; end with 1 selvedge stitch.

Row 5: 1 selvedge stitch, *2 right cross stitches (k1, sl 1 pwise), k6*; repeat from * to *; end with 1 selvedge stitch.

Row 6: 1 selvedge stitch, *p4, k3, p1*; repeat from * to *; end with 1 selvedge stitch.

Rows 7 and 15: all knit.

Rows 8 and 16: all purl.

Row 9: 1 selvedge stitch, *k4, 2 left cross stitches (sl 1 pwise, k1: sl 1 on a cable needle in front of work, k1 from left needle, then sl 1 pwise wyib from cable needle), k2*; repeat from * to *; end with 1 selvedge stitch.

Row 10: 1 selvedge stitch, *p3, k1, p4*; repeat from * to *; end with 1 selvedge stitch.

Row 11: 1 selvedge stitch, *k5, 2 left cross stitches (sl 1 pwise, k1), k1*; repeat from * to *; end with 1 selvedge stitch.

Row 12: 1 selvedge stitch, *p2, k2, p4*; repeat from * to *; end with 1 selvedge stitch.

Row 13: 1 selvedge stitch, *k6, 2 left cross stitches (sl 1 pwise, k1)*; repeat from * to *; end with 1 selvedge stitch.

Row 14: 1 selvedge stitch, *p1, k3, p4*; repeat from * to *; end with 1 selvedge stitch.

Keep repeating these 16 rows.

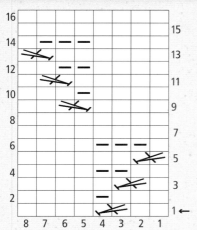

☐ knit stitch on right side or purl stitch on wrong side

– purl stitch on right side or knit stitch on wrong side

✕ 2 left cross stitches: sl 1 on a cable needle in front of work, k1 from left needle, then sl 1 pwise wyib from cable needle

✕ 2 right cross stitches: sl 1 on a cable needle behind work, sl 1 pwise wyib from left needle, then k1 from cable needle

sl 1 pwise wyib: slip 1 purlwise with yarn in back

sl: slip stitch from one needle to another without knitting it

Diamonds (with slipped stitches)

Number of stitches needed for symmetry: multiple of 16 + 1 selvedge stitch at each end.

Row 1 (right side of work): 2 right cross stitches (k1, sl 1 pwise: sl 1 on a cable needle behind work, sl 1 pwise wyib from left needle, then k1 from cable needle), *k14, 2 right cross stitches (k1, sl 1 pwise)*; repeat from * to *.

Row 2 and all even numbered rows: all purl.

Row 3: 1 selvedge stitch, *2 left cross stitches (sl 1 pwise, k1: sl 1 on a cable needle in front of work, k1 from left needle, then sl 1 pwise wyib from cable needle), k12, 2 right cross stitches (k1, sl 1 pwise)*; repeat from * to *; end with 1 selvedge stitch.

Row 5: 1 selvedge stitch, *k1, 2 left cross stitches (sl 1 pwise, k1), k10, 2 right cross stitches (k1, sl 1 pwise), k1*; repeat from * to *; end with 1 selvedge stitch.

Row 7: 1 selvedge stitch, *k2, 2 left cross stitches (sl 1 pwise, k1), k8, 2 right cross stitches (k1, sl 1 pwise), k2*; repeat from * to *; end with 1 selvedge stitch.

Row 9: 1 selvedge stitch, *k3, 2 left cross stitches (sl 1 pwise, k1), k6, 2 right cross stitches (k1, sl 1 pwise), k3*; repeat from * to *; end with 1 selvedge stitch.

Row 11: 1 selvedge stitch, *k4, 2 left cross stitches (sl 1 pwise, k1), k4, 2 right cross stitches (k1, sl 1 pwise), k4*; repeat from * to *; end with 1 selvedge stitch.

Row 13: 1 selvedge stitch, *k5, 2 left cross stitches (sl 1 pwise, k1), k2, 2 right cross stitches (k1, sl 1 pwise), k5*; repeat from * to *; end with 1 selvedge stitch.

Row 15: 1 selvedge stitch, *k6, 2 left cross stitches (sl 1 pwise, k1), 2 right cross stitches (k1, sl 1 pwise), k6*; repeat from * to *; end with 1 selvedge stitch.

Row 17: 1 selvedge stitch, *k7, 2 right cross stitches (k1, sl 1 pwise), k7*; repeat from * to *; end with 1 selvedge stitch.

Row 19: 1 selvedge stitch, *k6, 2 right cross stitches (k1, sl 1 pwise), 2 left cross stitches (sl 1 pwise, k1), k6*; repeat from * to *; end with 1 selvedge stitch.

Row 21: 1 selvedge stitch, *k5, 2 right cross stitches (k1, sl 1 pwise), k2, 2 left cross stitches (sl 1 pwise, k1), k5*; repeat from * to *; end with 1 selvedge stitch.

Row 23: 1 selvedge stitch, *k4, 2 right cross stitches (k1, sl 1 pwise), k4, 2 left cross stitches (sl 1 pwise, k1), k4*; repeat from * to *; end with 1 selvedge stitch.

Row 25: 1 selvedge stitch, *k3, 2 right cross stitches (k1, sl 1 pwise), k6, 2 left cross stitches (sl 1 pwise, k1), k3*; repeat from * to *; end with 1 selvedge stitch.

Row 27: 1 selvedge stitch, *k2, 2 right cross stitches (k1, sl 1 pwise), k8, 2 left cross stitches (sl 1 pwise, k1), k2*; repeat from * to *; end with 1 selvedge stitch.

Row 29: 1 selvedge stitch, *k1, 2 right cross stitches (k1, sl 1 pwise), k10, 2 left cross stitches (sl 1 pwise, k1), k1*; repeat from * to *; end with 1 selvedge stitch.

Row 31: 1 selvedge stitch, *2 right cross stitches (k1, sl 1 pwise), k12, 2 left cross stitches (sl 1 pwise, k1)*; repeat from * to *; end with 1 selvedge stitch.

Keep repeating these 32 rows.

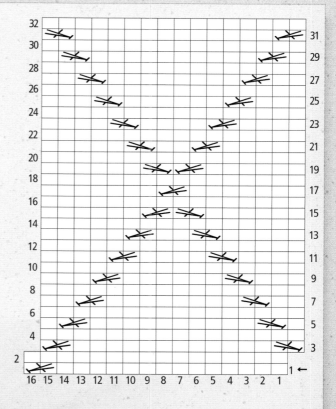

☐ knit stitch on right side or purl stitch on wrong side

⤸ 2 left cross stitches: sl 1 on a cable needle in front of work, k1 from left needle, then sl 1 pwise wyib from cable needle

⤲ 2 right cross stitches: sl 1 on a cable needle behind work, sl 1 pwise wyib from left needle, then k1 from cable needle

sl 1 pwise wyib: slip 1 purlwise with yarn in back

sl: slip stitch from one needle to another without knitting it

Woven Chevrons

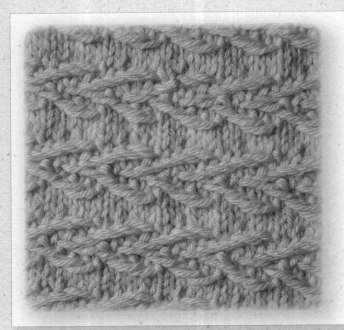

Number of stitches needed for symmetry: multiple of 5 + 1 selvedge stitch at each end.

Rows 1 (right side of work) and 11: 1 selvedge stitch, *k1, sl 3 pwise wyif, k1*; repeat from * to *; end with 1 selvedge stitch.

Rows 2 and 10: 1 selvedge stitch, *sl 3 pwise wyib, p2*; repeat from * to *; end with 1 selvedge stitch.

Rows 3 and 9: 1 selvedge stitch, *sl 1 pwise wyif, k2, sl 2 pwise wyif*; repeat from * to *; end with 1 selvedge stitch.

Rows 4 and 8: 1 selvedge stitch, *sl 1 pwise wyib, p2, sl 2 pwise wyib*; repeat from * to *; end with 1 selvedge stitch.

Rows 5 and 7: 1 selvedge stitch, *sl 3 pwise wyif, k2*; repeat from * to *; end with 1 selvedge stitch.

Row 6: 1 selvedge stitch, *p1, sl 3 pwise wyib, p1*; repeat from * to *; end with 1 selvedge stitch.

Rows 12 and 14: all purl.

Row 13: all knit.

Keep repeating these 14 rows.

Twists

Number of stitches needed for symmetry: multiple of 10 + 3 + 1 selvedge stitch at each end.

Row 1 (right side of work): 1 selvedge stitch, *p3, sl 1 pwise wyib, k2, p1, k2, sl 1 pwise wyib*; repeat from * to *; end with p3, 1 selvedge stitch.

Row 2: 1 selvedge stitch, k3, *sl 1 pwise wyif, p2, k1, p2, sl 1 pwise wyif, k3*; repeat from * to *; end with 1 selvedge stitch.

Row 3: 1 selvedge stitch, *p3, knit 3 left cross stitches (1 and 2: sl 1 on a cable needle in front of work, k2 from left needle, then k1 from cable needle), p1, knit 3 right cross stitches (2 and 1: sl 2 on a cable needle behind work, k1 from left needle, then k2 from cable needle)*; repeat from * to *; end with p3, 1 selvedge stitch.

Row 4: 1 selvedge stitch, k3, *p3, k1, p3, k3*; repeat from * to *; end with 1 selvedge stitch.

Keep repeating these 4 rows.

Cobblestone Stitch in Relief

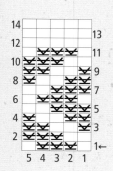

Number of stitches needed for symmetry and joining: multiple of 8 + 1 selvedge stitch at each end.

Rows 1 (right side of work), 3, 11, and 13: all purl.

Rows 2 and 12: all knit.

Rows 4, 6, 8, and 10: 1 selvedge stitch, *p3, sl 2 pwise wyif, p3*; repeat from * to *; end with 1 selvedge stitch.

Rows 5, 7, and 9: 1 selvedge stitch, *k3, sl 2 pwise wyib, k3*; repeat from * to *; end with 1 selvedge stitch.

Rows 14, 16, 18, and 20: 1 selvedge stitch, *sl 1 pwise wyif, p6, sl 1 pwise wyif*; repeat from * to *; end with 1 selvedge stitch.

Rows 15, 17, and 19: 1 selvedge stitch, *sl 1 pwise wyib, k6, sl 1 pwise wyib*; repeat from * to *; end with 1 selvedge stitch.

Keep repeating these 20 rows.

☐ knit stitch on right side or purl stitch on wrong side

⅄ sl 1 pwise wyif: stitch slipped purlwise on right side with yarn in front or purlwise on wrong side with yarn in back

sl 1 pwise wyib: slip 1 purlwise with yarn in back

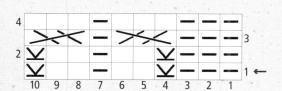

☐ knit stitch on right side or purl stitch on wrong side

– purl stitch on right side or knit stitch on wrong side

⅄ sl 1 pwise wyib: stitch slipped purlwise on right side with yarn in back or purlwise on wrong side with yarn in front

⤢ 3 left cross stitches: sl 1 on a cable needle in front of work, k2 from left needle, then k1 from cable needle

⤡ 3 right cross stitches: sl 2 on a cable needle behind work, k1 from left needle, then k2 from cable needle

sl 1 pwise wyif: slip 1 purlwise with yarn in front

sl: slip stitch from one needle to another without knitting it

---

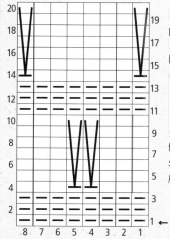

☐ knit stitch on right side or purl stitch on wrong side

– purl stitch on right side or knit stitch on wrong side

V sl 1 pwise wyib: stitch slipped purlwise on right side with yarn in back or purlwise on wrong side with yarn in front for 7 rows

sl 1 pwise wyif: slip 1 purlwise with yarn in front

Fancy Slip Stitch Cables

Number of stitches needed for symmetry: multiple of 10 + 5 + 1 selvedge stitch at each end.

Rows 1 (right side of work) and 7: 1 selvedge stitch, *p5, k5*; repeat from * to *; end with p5, 1 selvedge stitch.

Rows 2 and 6: knit each stitch as it appears in previous row (i.e., knit a knit stitch, purl a purl stitch).

Row 3: 1 selvedge stitch, *p5, sl 1 pwise wyib, k4*; repeat from * to *; end with p5, 1 selvedge stitch.

Row 4: 1 selvedge stitch, k5, *p4, sl slipped stitch from previous row again pwise wyif, k5*; repeat from * to *; end with 1 selvedge stitch.

Row 5: 1 selvedge stitch, *p5, knit 5 left cross stitches (1 and 4: sl slipped stitch from previous row on a cable needle in front of work, k4 from left needle, then k1 from cable needle)*; repeat from * to *; end with p5, 1 selvedge stitch.

Row 8: 1 selvedge stitch, k5, *sl 1 pwise wyif, p4, k5*; repeat from * to *; end with 1 selvedge stitch.

Row 9: 1 selvedge stitch, *p5, k4, sl slipped stitch from the previous row again pwise wyib*; repeat from * to *; end with p5, 1 selvedge stitch.

Row 10: 1 selvedge stitch, k5, *5 right cross stitches (1 and 4: sl slipped stitch from previous row on a cable needle behind work, p4 from left needle, then k1 from cable needle), k5*; repeat from * to *; end with 1 selvedge stitch.

Keep repeating these 10 rows.

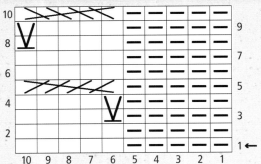

☐ knit stitch on right side or purl stitch on wrong side

– purl stitch on right side or knit stitch on wrong side

V sl 1 pwise wyib: stitch slipped purlwise on right side with yarn in back or purlwise on wrong side with yarn in front for 2 rows

〉〉〉〈 knit 5 left cross stitches: sl slipped stitch from previous row on a cable needle in front of work, k4 from left needle, then k1 from cable needle

〉〉〉〈 purl 5 right cross stitches: sl slipped stitch from previous row on a cable needle behind work, p4 from left needle, then k1 from cable needle

sl 1 pwise wyif: slip 1 purlwise with yarn in front

sl: slip stitch from one needle to another without knitting it

Staggered Fancy Slip Stitch Cables

Number of stitches needed for symmetry: multiple of 18 + 12 + 1 selvedge stitch at each end.

Row 1 (right side of work): 1 selvedge stitch, *p3, k6, p3, k6*; repeat from * to *; end with p3, k6, p3, 1 selvedge stitch.

Rows 2, 4, and 6: 1 selvedge stitch, k3, p6, k3, *p2, sl 2 pwise wyif, p2, k3, p6, k3*; repeat from * to *; end with 1 selvedge stitch.

Rows 3, 5, and 7: 1 selvedge stitch, *p3, k6, p3, knit 3 right cross stitches (2 and 1: sl 2 on a cable needle behind work, k1 from left needle, then k2 from cable needle), knit 3 left cross stitches (1 and 2: sl 1 on a cable needle in front of work, k2 from left needle, then k1 from cable needle)*; repeat from * to *; end with p3, k6, p3, 1 selvedge stitch.

Rows 8, 10, and 12: 1 selvedge stitch, k3, p2, sl 2 pwise wyif, p2, k3, *p6, k3, p2, sl 2 pwise wyif, p2, k3*; repeat from * to *; end with 1 selvedge stitch.

Rows 9, 11, and 13: 1 selvedge stitch, *p3, knit 3 right cross stitches (2 and 1), knit 3 left cross stitches (1 and 2), p3, k6*; repeat from * to *; end with p3, knit 3 right cross stitches (2 and 1), knit 3 left cross stitches (1 and 2), p3, 1 selvedge stitch.

Keep repeating Rows 2 through 13.

knit stitch on right side or purl stitch on wrong side

− purl stitch on right side or knit stitch on wrong side

⟈ sl 1 pwise wyib: stitch slipped purlwise on right side with yarn in back or purlwise on wrong side with yarn in front

✕ 3 left cross stitches: sl 1 on a cable needle in front of work, k2 from left needle, then k1 from cable needle

✕ 3 right cross stitches: sl 2 on a cable needle behind work, k1 from left needle, then k2 from cable needle

sl 1 pwise wyif: slip 1 purlwise with yarn in front

sl: slip stitch from one needle to another without knitting it

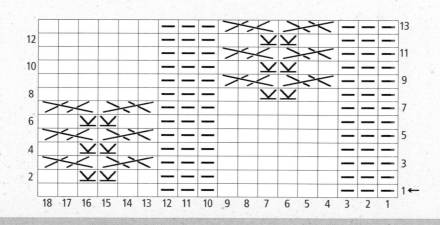

Slip Stitches

Greek Motif

knit stitch on right side or purl stitch on wrong side

⟋ sl 1 pwise wyib: stitch slipped purlwise on right side with yarn in back or purlwise on wrong side with yarn in front

⟋ 2 left cross stitches: knit the second stitch on the left needle first, passing the right needle behind the first stitch, then knit the first stitch

⟋ 2 right cross stitches: knit the second stitch on the left needle first, passing the right needle in front of the first stitch, then knit the first stitch

Number of stitches needed for symmetry and joining: multiple of 4 + 1 selvedge stitch at each end.

Note: To give your work some elasticity, take care not to pull yarn too tightly behind slipped stitches.

Row 1 (right side of work): all knit.

Row 2: all purl.

Row 3: 1 selvedge stitch, *sl 2 pwise wyib, knit 2 left cross stitches (knit the second stitch on the left needle first, passing the right needle behind the first stitch, then knit the first stitch)*; repeat from * to *; end with 1 selvedge stitch.

Row 4: 1 selvedge stitch, *sl 2 pwise wyif, purl 2 right cross stitches (purl the second stitch on the left needle first, passing the right needle in front of the first stitch, then purl the first stitch)*; repeat from * to *; end with 1 selvedge stitch.

Keep repeating these 4 rows.

sl 1 pwise wyif: slip 1 purlwise with yarn in front

Sycamore

Number of stitches needed for symmetry: multiple of 12 + 4 + 1 selvedge stitch at each end.

Knitting/purling through the back of the loop, or k tbl/p tbl: For a knit stitch, insert the right needle into the back of the loop (behind the work) instead of the front, and knit as usual; for a purl stitch, insert the right needle into the back of the loop, slide it in front of the left needle, and purl as usual. This creates a twisted stitch.

Row 1 (right side of work): 1 selvedge stitch, *p4, k2*; repeat from * to *; end with p4, 1 selvedge stitch.

Rows 2, 3, 4, and 5: knit each stitch as it appears in previous row (i.e., knit a knit stitch, purl a purl stitch).

Row 6: 1 selvedge stitch, *sl 2 pwise wyif, k4*; repeat from * to *; end with 1 selvedge stitch.

Row 7: 1 selvedge stitch, *p4, 4 left cross stitches (k2tog, p2 and yo1: sl 2 on a cable needle in front of work, p2 and yo1 from left needle, k2tog tbl from cable needle), 4 right cross stitches (p2, yo1 and k2tog: sl 2 on a cable needle behind work, k2tog and yo1 from left needle, p2 from cable needle)*; repeat from * to *; end with p4, 1 selvedge stitch.

Staggered Grass Stitch

Number of stitches needed for symmetry: multiple of 8 + 6 + 1 selvedge stitch at each end.

Row 1 (right side of work) and 7: all purl.

Rows 2, 4, and 6: 1 selvedge stitch, k6, *p2, k6*; repeat from * to *; end with 1 selvedge stitch.

Rows 3 and 5: 1 selvedge stitch, *p6, sl 1 pwise wyib, k1, yo1, psso*; repeat from * to *; end with p6, 1 selvedge stitch.

Rows 8, 10, and 12: 1 selvedge stitch, k2, p2, k2, *k4, p2, k2*; repeat from * to *; end with 1 selvedge stitch.

Rows 9 and 11: 1 selvedge stitch, *p2, sl 1 pwise wyib, k1, yo1, psso, p4*; repeat from * to *; end with p2, sl 1 pwise wyib, k1, yo1, psso, p2, 1 selvedge stitch.

Keep repeating these 12 rows.

☐ knit stitch on right side or purl stitch on wrong side

– purl stitch on right side or knit stitch on wrong side

� On right side of work: sl 1 pwise wyib, k1, yo1, psso

sl 1 pwise wyib: slip 1 purlwise with yarn in back

psso: pass slipped stitch over stitches/yarn overs and off the needle

---

Row 8: 1 selvedge stitch, k4, *p2, k1 tbl, k2, k1 tbl, p2, k4*; repeat from * to *; end with 1 selvedge stitch.

Keep repeating these 8 rows.

☐ knit stitch on right side or purl stitch on wrong side

– purl stitch on right side or knit stitch on wrong side

⑧ p tbl: purl through the back of the loop on right side, creating a twisted stitch, or knit through the back of the loop on wrong side

⋎ sl 1 pwise wyib: stitch slipped purlwise on right side with yarn in back or purlwise on wrong side with yarn in front

▷▷▷ 4 left cross stitches: sl 2 on a cable needle in front of work, p2 and yo1 from left needle, k2tog tbl from cable needle

▷◁▷ 4 right cross stitches: sl 2 on a cable needle behind work, k2tog and yo1 from left needle, p2 from cable needle

k tbl: knit through the back of the loop, creating a twisted stitch

sl: slip stitch from one needle to another without knitting it

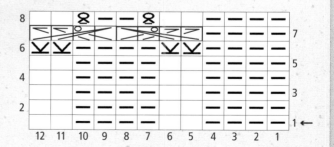

Horizontal Woven Stitch

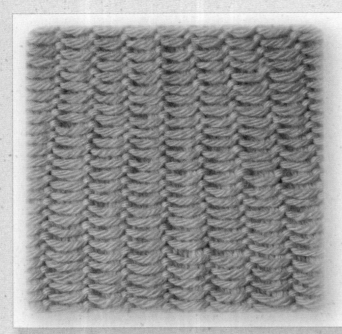

Number of stitches needed for symmetry: multiple of 3 + 1 + 1 selvedge stitch at each end.

Row 1 (right side of work): all knit.

Row 2: 1 selvedge stitch, k1, *sl 2 pwise wyib, k1*; repeat from * to *; end with 1 selvedge stitch.

Keep repeating these 2 rows.

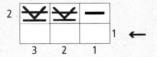

☐ knit stitch on right side or purl stitch on wrong side

– purl stitch on right side or knit stitch on wrong side

⊻ sl 1 pwise wyif: stitch slipped purlwise on right side with yarn in front or purlwise on wrong side with yarn in back

sl 1 pwise wyib: slip 1 purlwise with yarn in back

Diagonal Drapery

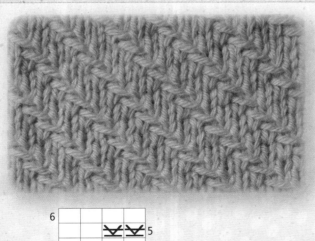

Number of stitches needed for symmetry: multiple of 4 + 2 + 1 selvedge stitch at each end.

Row 1 (right side of work): 1 selvedge stitch, *k2, sl 2 pwise wyif*; repeat from * to *; end with k2, 1 selvedge stitch.

Row 2 and all even numbered rows: all purl.

Row 3: 1 selvedge stitch, *sl 1 pwise wyif, k2, sl 1 pwise wyif*; repeat from * to *; end with sl 1 pwise wyif, k1, 1 selvedge stitch.

Row 5: 1 selvedge stitch, *sl 2 pwise wyif, k2*; repeat from * to *; end with sl 2 pwise wyif, 1 selvedge stitch.

Keep repeating these 6 rows.

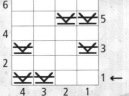

☐ knit stitch on right side or purl stitch on wrong side

⊻ sl 1 pwise wyif: stitch slipped purlwise on right side with yarn in front or purlwise on wrong side with yarn in back

Fancy k3/p3 Ribbing

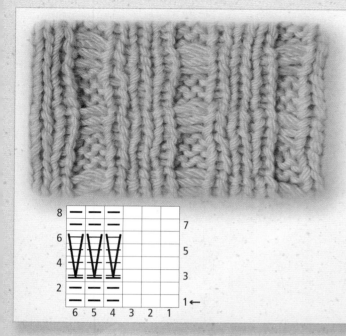

Number of stitches needed for symmetry: multiple of 6 + 3 + 1 selvedge stitch at each end.

Rows 1 (right side of work) and 7: 1 selvedge stitch, *k3, p3*; repeat from * to *; end with k3, 1 selvedge stitch.

Rows 2 and 8: 1 selvedge stitch, p3, *k3, p3*; repeat from * to *; end with 1 selvedge stitch.

Rows 3 and 5: 1 selvedge stitch, *k3, sl 3 pwise wyif*; repeat from * to *; end with k3, 1 selvedge stitch.

Rows 4 and 6: 1 selvedge stitch, p3, *sl 3 pwise wyib, p3*; repeat from * to *; end with 1 selvedge stitch.

Keep repeating these 8 rows.

☐ knit stitch on right side or purl stitch on wrong side

– purl stitch on right side or knit stitch on wrong side

sl 1 pwise wyib: stitch slipped purlwise on right side with yarn in back or purlwise on wrong side with yarn in front for 4 rows

sl 1 pwise wyif: slip 1 purlwise with yarn in front

Mop Ribbing

Number of stitches needed for symmetry: multiple of 4 + 3 + 1 selvedge stitch at each end.

Row 1 (right side of work): 1 selvedge stitch, *p3, k1*; repeat from * to *; end with p3, 1 selvedge stitch.

Row 2 and all even numbered rows: all knit.

Row 3: 1 selvedge stitch, *p3, k1b*; repeat from * to *; end with p3, 1 selvedge stitch.

Row 5: 1 selvedge stitch, *sl 3 pwise wyif, k1b*; repeat from * to *; end with sl 3 pwise wyif, 1 selvedge stitch.

Keep repeating the 4 rows between Row 2 and Row 5.

☐ knit stitch on right side or purl stitch on wrong side

– purl stitch on right side or knit stitch on wrong side

sl 1 pwise wyif: stitch slipped purlwise on right side with yarn in front or purlwise on wrong side with yarn in back

k1b on right side or p1b on wrong side: knit 1 on right side or purl 1 on wrong side by inserting the right needle not into the next stitch on the left needle but into the stitch immediately below it. Let the stitch above slide off the left needle; it will drop down 1 row

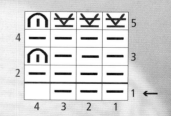

Slip Stitches

Staggered Ladder Stitch

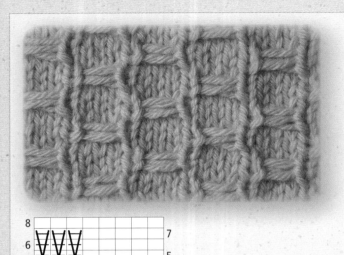

Number of stitches needed for symmetry: multiple of 8 + 5 + 1 selvedge stitch at each end.

Rows 1 (right side of work) and 3: 1 selvedge stitch, *k1, sl 3 pwise wyif, k4*; repeat from * to *; end with k1, sl 3 pwise wyif, k1, 1 selvedge stitch.

Row 2: 1 selvedge stitch, p1, sl 3 pwise wyib, p1, *p4, sl 3 pwise wyib, p1*; repeat from * to *; end with 1 selvedge stitch.

Rows 4 and 8: all purl.

Rows 5 and 7: 1 selvedge stitch, *k5, sl 3 pwise wyif*; repeat from * to *; end with k5, 1 selvedge stitch.

Row 6: 1 selvedge stitch, p5, *sl 3 pwise wyib, p5*; repeat from * to *; end with 1 selvedge stitch.

Keep repeating these 8 rows.

knit stitch on right side or purl stitch on wrong side

sl 1 pwise wyib: stitch slipped purlwise on right side with yarn in back or purlwise on wrong side with yarn in front for 3 rows

sl 1 pwise wyif: slip 1 purlwise with yarn in front

Folds

Number of stitches needed for symmetry: multiple of 2 + 1 + 1 selvedge stitch at each end.

Row 1 (right side of work): 1 selvedge stitch, *k1, p1*; repeat from * to *; end with k1, 1 selvedge stitch.

Row 2: 1 selvedge stitch, p1, *k1, p1*; repeat from * to *; end with 1 selvedge stitch.

Rows 3, 5, 7, and 9: 1 selvedge stitch, *k1, sl 1 pwise wyif*; repeat from * to *; end with k1, 1 selvedge stitch.

Rows 4, 6, 8, and 10: 1 selvedge stitch, p1, *sl 1 pwise wyib, p1*; repeat from * to *; end with 1 selvedge stitch.

Keep repeating these 10 rows.

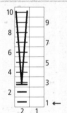

knit stitch on right side or purl stitch on wrong side

— purl stitch on right side or knit stitch on wrong side

sl 1 pwise wyib: stitch slipped purlwise on right side with yarn in back or purlwise on wrong side with yarn in front for 8 rows

sl 1 pwise wyif: slip 1 purlwise with yarn in front

Ribbing with Long Stitches

Number of stitches needed for symmetry: multiple of 8 + 4 + 1 selvedge stitch at each end.

Row 1 (right side of work): 1 selvedge stitch, *p4, knit 4 long stitches (insert right needle into each stitch as if to knit, yo3, knit as usual)*; repeat from * to *; end with p4, 1 selvedge stitch.

Rows 2 and 4: 1 selvedge stitch, k4, *sl 4 pwise wyif, k4*; repeat from * to *; end with 1 selvedge stitch.

Row 3: 1 selvedge stitch, *p4, sl 4 pwise wyib*; repeat from * to *; end with p4, 1 selvedge stitch.

Keep repeating these 4 rows.

− purl stitch on right side or knit stitch on wrong side

③ long knit stitch on right side or purl stitch on wrong side: insert right needle into stitch as if to knit or purl, yo3, knit or purl as usual

⋁ sl 1 pwise wyib: stitch slipped purlwise on right side with yarn in back or purlwise on wrong side with yarn in front for 3 rows

sl 1 pwise wyif: slip 1 purlwise with yarn in front

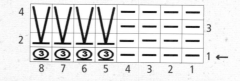

Blister Stitch

Number of stitches needed for symmetry and joining: multiple of 4 + 1 selvedge stitch at each end.

Rows 1 (right side of work) and 9: all purl.

Rows 2 and 10: all knit.

Rows 3, 5, and 7: 1 selvedge stitch, *k1, sl 2 pwise wyib, k1*; repeat from * to *; end with 1 selvedge stitch.

Rows 4, 6, and 8: 1 selvedge stitch, *p1, sl 2 pwise wyif, p1*; repeat from * to *; end with 1 selvedge stitch.

Rows 11, 13, and 15: 1 selvedge stitch, *sl 1 pwise wyib, k2, sl 1 pwise wyib*; repeat from * to *; end with 1 selvedge stitch.

Rows 12, 14, and 16: 1 selvedge stitch, *sl 1 pwise wyif, p2, sl 1 pwise wyif*; repeat from * to *; end with 1 selvedge stitch.

Keep repeating these 16 rows.

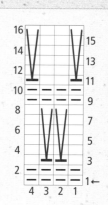

☐ knit stitch on right side or purl stitch on wrong side

− purl stitch on right side or knit stitch on wrong side

⋁ sl 1 pwise wyib: stitch slipped purlwise on right side with yarn in back or purlwise on wrong side with yarn in front for 6 rows

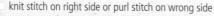

sl 1 pwise wyif: slip 1 purlwise with yarn in front

Lace and Eyelet Stitches

Numerous and varied, lace and eyelet stitches can be knit in almost any yarn.

Lace and Eyelet Stitches

Simple River Pattern

The directions for this pattern consist of any number of stitches.

Rows 1 (right side of work), 3, and 5: all knit.

Rows 2, 4, and 6: all purl.

Row 7: all long knit stitches (insert right needle into each stitch as if to knit, yo3, knit as usual).

Row 8: purl each stitch by inserting right needle into the first loop and letting the 2 others slide off the needle.

Keep repeating these 8 rows.

☐ knit stitch on right side or purl stitch on wrong side

♀ long knit stitch on right side or purl stitch on wrong side: insert right needle into stitch as if to knit or purl, yo3, knit or purl as usual

Bed Jacket

The directions for this pattern consist of any number of stitches.

Row 1 (right side of work): With a right needle of the size recommended for your yarn, all knit.

Row 2: With a right needle at least 2 sizes larger, all purl.

Keep repeating these 2 rows.

Simple River Pattern with Garter Stitch

The directions for this pattern consist of any number of stitches.

Rows 1 (right side of work), 2, 3, and 4: all knit.

Row 5: all long knit stitches (insert right needle into each stitch as if to knit, yo2, knit as usual).

Row 6: knit each stitch by inserting right needle into the first loop and letting the other slide off the needle.

Keep repeating these 6 rows.

− purl stitch on right side or knit stitch on wrong side

♀ long knit stitch on right side or purl stitch on wrong side: insert right needle into stitch as if to knit or purl, yo2, knit or purl as usual

Simple Eyelets

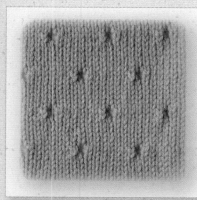

Number of stitches needed for joining: multiple of 8 + 1 selvedge stitch at each end.

Rows 1 (right side of work), 3, 7, 9, 11, and 15: all knit.

Row 2 and all even numbered rows: all purl (stitches and yarn overs).

Row 5: 1 selvedge stitch, *k2, yo1, k2tog, k4*; repeat from * to *; end with 1 selvedge stitch.

Row 13: 1 selvedge stitch, *k6, yo1, k2tog*; repeat from * to *; end with 1 selvedge stitch.

Keep repeating these 16 rows.

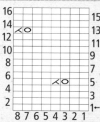

☐ knit stitch on right side or purl stitch on wrong side

⋏ k2tog: knit 2 together on right side or purl 2 together on wrong side

o yo: yarn over

Diamond Eyelets

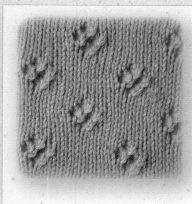

Number of stitches needed for symmetry: multiple of 12 + 7 + 1 selvedge stitch at each end.

Rows 1 (right side of work) and 5: 1 selvedge stitch, *k2, k2tog, yo1, k8*; repeat from * to *; end with k2, k2tog, yo1, k3, 1 selvedge stitch.

Row 2 and all even numbered rows: all purl (stitches and yarn overs).

Row 3: 1 selvedge stitch, *k1, k2tog, yo1, k2tog, yo1, k7*; repeat from * to *; end with k1, k2tog, yo1, k2tog, yo1, k2, 1 selvedge stitch.

Rows 7 and 15: all knit.

Rows 9 and 13: 1 selvedge stitch, *k8, k2tog, yo1, k2*; repeat from * to *; end with k7, 1 selvedge stitch.

Row 11: 1 selvedge stitch, *k7, k2tog, yo1, k2tog, yo1, k1*; repeat from * to *; end with k7, 1 selvedge stitch.

Keep repeating these 16 rows.

☐ knit stitch on right side or purl stitch on wrong side

⋏ k2tog: knit 2 together on right side or purl 2 together on wrong side

o yo: yarn over

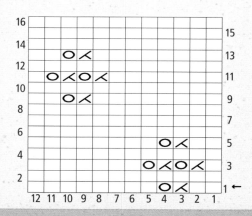

Lace and Eyelet Stitches

Eyelet Squares

Number of stitches needed for symmetry: multiple of 6 + 1 + 1 selvedge stitch at each end.

Rows 1 (right side of work) and 5: 1 selvedge stitch, *k1, k2tog, yo1, k1, yo1, skp*; repeat from * to *; end with k1, 1 selvedge stitch.

Row 2 and all even numbered rows: all purl (stitches and yarn overs).

Rows 3, 7, 9, and 11: all knit.

Keep repeating these 12 rows.

☐ knit stitch on right side or purl stitch on wrong side

o yo: yarn over

⋏ k2tog: knit 2 together on right side or purl 2 together on wrong side

⋋ skp: slip 1 stitch knitwise, knit the next stitch, then pass the slipped stitch over the knit stitch and off the needle

Small Eyelet Stripes

Number of stitches needed for joining: multiple of 2 + 1 selvedge stitch at each end. **Note: Reversible.**

Rows 1 (right side of work), 5, 7, 9, 13, and 15: all knit.

Row 2 and all even numbered rows: all purl (stitches and yarn overs).

Row 3: 1 selvedge stitch, *yo1, skp*; repeat from * to *; end with 1 selvedge stitch.

Row 11: 1 selvedge stitch, *skp, yo1*; repeat from * to *; end with 1 selvedge stitch.

Keep repeating these 16 rows.

☐ knit stitch on right side or purl stitch on wrong side

o yo: yarn over

⋋ skp: slip 1 stitch knitwise, knit the next stitch, then pass the slipped stitch over the knit stitch and off the needle

Eyelet Stripes

Number of stitches needed for symmetry: multiple of 2 + 1 + 1 selvedge stitch at each end.

Rows 1 (right side of work), 3, 5, 7, 8, and 10: all knit.

Rows 2, 4, and 6: all purl.

Row 9: 1 selvedge stitch, *p2tog, yo1*; repeat from * to *; end with p1, 1 selvedge stitch.

Keep repeating these 10 rows.

☐ knit stitch on right side or purl stitch on wrong side

– purl stitch on right side or knit stitch on wrong side

o yo: yarn over

⋌ p2tog: purl 2 together on right side or knit 2 together on wrong side

Vertical Eyelets

Number of stitches needed for symmetry: multiple of 12 + 1 + 1 selvedge stitch at each end.

Row 1 (right side of work): 1 selvedge stitch, *k3, yo1, k2tog, k3, skp, yo1, k2*; repeat from * to *; end with k1, 1 selvedge stitch.

Row 2: all purl.

Keep repeating these 2 rows.

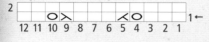

☐ knit stitch on right side or purl stitch on wrong side

⋌ k2tog: knit 2 together on right side or purl 2 together on wrong side

⋋ skp: slip 1 stitch knitwise, knit the next stitch, then pass the slipped stitch over the knit stitch and off the needle

○ yo: yarn over

Eyelet Ribbing

Number of stitches needed for symmetry and joining: multiple of 10 + 1 selvedge stitch at each end.

Row 1 (right side of work): 1 selvedge stitch, *k3, p1, yo1, k2tog, p1, k3*; repeat from * to *; end with 1 selvedge stitch.

Row 2: 1 selvedge stitch, *p3, k1, yo1, p2tog, k1, p3*; repeat from * to *; end with 1 selvedge stitch.

Keep repeating these 2 rows.

☐ knit stitch on right side or purl stitch on wrong side

− purl stitch on right side or knit stitch on wrong side

○ yo: yarn over

⋌ k2tog: knit 2 together on right side or purl 2 together on wrong side

p2tog: purl 2 together

Ladder Eyelets

Number of stitches needed for symmetry: multiple of 6 + 1 + 1 selvedge stitch at each end.

Row 1 (right side of work): 1 selvedge stitch, *k1, skp, yo1, k1, yo1, k2tog*; repeat from * to *; end with k1, 1 selvedge stitch.

Row 2: 1 selvedge stitch, p1, *p2, k1, p3*; repeat from * to *; end with 1 selvedge stitch.

Keep repeating these 2 rows.

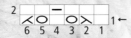

☐ knit stitch on right side or purl stitch on wrong side

− purl stitch on right side or knit stitch on wrong side

○ yo: yarn over

⋌ k2tog: knit 2 together on right side or purl 2 together on wrong side

⋋ skp: slip 1 stitch knitwise, knit the next stitch, then pass the slipped stitch over the knit stitch and off the needle

Lace and Eyelet Stitches

Vertical Eyelet Zigzags

Number of stitches needed for symmetry: multiple of 6 + 4 + 1 selvedge stitch at each end.

Row 1 (right side of work): 1 selvedge stitch, *k4, yo1, skp*, repeat from * to *; end with k4, 1 selvedge stitch.

Rows 2 and 4: all purl.

Row 3: 1 selvedge stitch, *k4, k2tog, yo1*; repeat from * to *; end with k4, 1 selvedge stitch.

Keep repeating these 4 rows.

☐ knit stitch on right side or purl stitch on wrong side

○ yo: yarn over

✗ k2tog: knit 2 together on right side or purl 2 together on wrong side

⋋ skp: slip 1 stitch knitwise, knit the next stitch, then pass the slipped stitch over the knit stitch and off the needle

Eyelet Chevrons (1)

Number of stitches needed for symmetry: multiple of 7 + 8 + 1 selvedge stitch at each end.

Note: Number of stitches varies from one row to another. Every odd row (right side of work) ends with 1 stitch less per group of 7 stitches (because you make 1 yarn over for each double decrease) and every even row (wrong side of work) ends with the number of stitches you started with (because you add back 1 stitch per group of 7 by making 1 yarn over without a corresponding decrease).

Row 1 (right side of work): 1 selvedge stitch, k2tog, k2, *yo1, k2, sl 1 kwise, k2tog, psso, k2*; repeat from * to *; end with yo1, k2, skp, 1 selvedge stitch.

Row 2: 1 selvedge stitch, p4, *yo1, p6*; repeat from * to *; end with yo1, p3, 1 selvedge stitch.

Keep repeating these 2 rows.

☐ knit stitch on right side or purl stitch on wrong side

○ yo: yarn over

⋏ sl 1 kwise, k2tog, psso: slip 1 stitch knitwise, knit the next 2 stitches together, pass the slipped stitch over the stitch obtained and off the needle

× stitch that does not exist

skp: slip 1 stitch knitwise, knit the next stitch, then pass the slipped stitch over the knit stitch and off the needle

Alpine Stitch

Number of stitches needed for symmetry: multiple of 4 + 1 selvedge stitch at each end.
Row 1 (right side of work): 1 selvedge stitch, *yo1, k4*; repeat from * to *; end with 1 selvedge stitch.
Row 2: all purl.
Row 3: 1 selvedge stitch, *yo1, sl 2 on a cable needle behind work, k1 from left needle, then k2tog from cable needle, knit 2 left cross stitches (knit the second stitch on the left needle first, passing the right needle behind the first stitch, then knit the first stitch)*; repeat from * to *; end with 1 selvedge stitch.
Row 4: all purl.
Keep repeating Rows 3 and 4.

☐ knit stitch on right side or purl stitch on wrong side
O yo: yarn over
✕ 2 left cross stitches: knit the second stitch on the left needle first, passing the right needle behind the first stitch, then knit the first stitch
✕O yo1, sl 2 on a cable needle behind work, k1 from left needle, then k2tog from cable needle
sl: slip stitch from one needle to another without knitting it

Wickerwork Stitch

Number of stitches needed for symmetry: multiple of 2 + 1 selvedge stitch at each end.
Row 1 (right side of work): 1 selvedge stitch, *knit the second stitch on the left needle first as a long stitch (insert right needle into stitch as if to knit, yo2, knit as usual), passing the right needle in front of the first stitch, then knit the first stitch normally, and let the 2 stitches slide off the left needle*; repeat from * to *; end with 1 selvedge stitch.
Row 2: 1 selvedge stitch, p1 (to shift), *purl the second stitch on the left needle (the one without the yarn over in previous row) first as a long stitch (insert right needle into stitch as if to knit, yo2, knit as usual), passing the right needle in front of the first stitch, then purl the first stitch normally, and let the 2 stitches and the yarn over slide off the left needle*; repeat from * to *; end with p1, 1 selvedge stitch.
Row 3: 1 selvedge stitch, *knit the second stitch on the left needle (the one without the yarn over in previous row) first as a long stitch (insert right needle into stitch as if to knit, yo2, knit as usual), passing the right needle in front of the first stitch, then knit the first stitch normally, and let the 2 stitches and the yarn over slide off the left needle*; repeat from * to *; end with 1 selvedge stitch.
Keep repeating Rows 2 and 3.

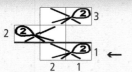

☐ knit stitch on right side or purl stitch on wrong side
o yo: yarn over
✕ on right side of work: knit the second stitch on the left needle first as a long stitch (insert right needle into stitch as if to knit, yo2, knit as usual), passing the right needle in front of the first stitch, then knit the first stitch normally, and let the 2 stitches slide off the left needle
✕ on wrong side of work: purl the second stitch on the left needle first as a long stitch (insert right needle into stitch as if to knit, yo2, knit as usual), passing the right needle in front of the first stitch, then purl the first stitch normally, and let the 2 stitches and the yarn over slide off the left needle

Mock Turkish Stitch

Number of stitches needed for joining: multiple of 2 + 1 selvedge stitch at each end.
Row 1 (right side of work): 1 selvedge stitch, *skp, yo1*; repeat from * to *; end with 1 selvedge stitch.
Row 2: 1 selvedge stitch, *p2tog, yo1*; repeat from * to *; end with 1 selvedge stitch.
Keep repeating these 2 rows.

O yo: yarn over
⟨ k2tog: knit 2 together on right side or purl 2 together on wrong side
⟩ skp: slip 1 stitch knitwise, knit the next stitch, then pass the slipped stitch over the knit stitch and off the needle
p2tog: purl 2 together

Diagonal Eyelets (1)

The directions for this pattern consist of an even number of stitches.
Row 1 (right side of work): 1 selvedge stitch, *yo1, k2tog*; repeat from * to *; end with 1 selvedge stitch.
Rows 2 and 4: all purl.
Row 3: 1 selvedge stitch, k1, *yo1, k2tog*; repeat from * to *; end with k1, 1 selvedge stitch.
Keep repeating these 4 rows.

☐ knit stitch on right side or purl stitch on wrong side
O yo: yarn over
⟨ k2tog: knit 2 together on right side or purl 2 together on wrong side

Purse Stitch

The directions for this pattern consist of an even number of stitches.
Row 1 (right side of work): 1 selvedge stitch, *yo1, p2tog*; repeat from * to *; end with 1 selvedge stitch.
Row 2: As row 1.
Keep repeating these 2 rows.

O yo: yarn over
⟨ k2tog: knit 2 together on right side on right side or purl 2 together on wrong side
⟋ p2tog: purl 2 together on right side or knit 2 together on wrong side

Turkish Stitch

Number of stitches needed for joining: multiple of 2 + 1 selvedge stitch at each end.

Row 1 (right side of work): 1 selvedge stitch, *yo1, skp*; repeat from * to *; end with 1 selvedge stitch.

Row 2: 1 selvedge stitch, *yo1, skp*; repeat from * to *; end with 1 selvedge stitch.

Keep repeating these 2 rows.

○ yo: yarn over

⟂ skp on wrong side: slip 1 stitch knitwise, knit the next stitch, then pass the slipped stitch over the knit stitch and off the needle

⟍ skp: slip 1 stitch knitwise, knit the next stitch, then pass the slipped stitch over the knit stitch and off the needle

Fishnet Stitch (1)

Number of stitches needed for symmetry: multiple of 4 + 5 + 1 selvedge stitch at each end.

Row 1 (right side of work): 1 selvedge stitch, *k1, yo1, sl 1 kwise, k2tog, psso, yo1*; repeat from * to *; end with k1, 1 selvedge stitch.

Rows 2 and 4: all purl (stitches and yarn overs).

Row 3: 1 selvedge stitch, k2tog, yo1, *k1, yo1, sl 1 kwise, k2tog, psso, yo1*; repeat from * to *; end with k1, yo1, skp, 1 selvedge stitch.

Keep repeating these 4 rows.

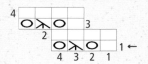

knit stitch on right side or purl stitch on wrong side

○ yo: yarn over

⋋ sl 1 kwise, k2tog, psso: slip 1 stitch knitwise, knit the next 2 stitches together, pass the slipped stitch over the stitch obtained and off the needle

Eyelet Grid

Number of stitches needed for symmetry: multiple of 2 + 1 + 1 selvedge stitch at each end.

Row 1 (right side of work): 1 selvedge stitch, *k2tog, yo1*; repeat from * to *; end with k1, 1 selvedge stitch.

Rows 2 and 4: all purl (stitches and yarn overs).

Row 3: 1 selvedge stitch, k1, *yo1, skp*; repeat from * to *; end with 1 selvedge stitch.

Keep repeating these 4 rows.

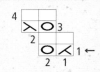

knit stitch on right side or purl stitch on wrong side

○ yo: yarn over

⟋ k2tog: knit 2 together on right side or purl 2 together on wrong side

⟍ skp: slip 1 stitch knitwise, knit the next stitch, then pass the slipped stitch over the knit stitch and off the needle

Perforated Stitch

Number of stitches needed for symmetry: multiple of 3 + 1 + 1 selvedge stitch at each end.

Row 1 (right side of work): 1 selvedge stitch, *k1, yo1, k2tog*; repeat from * to *; end with k1, 1 selvedge stitch.

Row 2: 1 selvedge stitch, p1, *p1, knit the yarn over, p1*; repeat from * to *; end with 1 selvedge stitch.

Row 3: 1 selvedge stitch, *k1, k2tog, yo1*; repeat from * to *; end with k1, 1 selvedge stitch.

Row 4: 1 selvedge stitch, p1, *knit the yarn over, p2*; repeat from * to *; end with 1 selvedge stitch.

Keep repeating these 4 rows.

☐ knit stitch on right side or purl stitch on wrong side

– purl stitch on right side or knit stitch on wrong side

O yo: yarn over

✕ k2tog: knit 2 together on right side or purl 2 together on wrong side

Fishnet Stitch (2)

Number of stitches needed for symmetry: multiple of 3 + 1 + 1 selvedge stitch at each end.

Row 1 (right side of work): 1 selvedge stitch, k1, *yo1, sl 1 kwise wyib, k2, psso*; repeat from * to *; end with 1 selvedge stitch.

Rows 2 and 4: all purl.

Row 3: 1 selvedge stitch, *sl 1 kwise wyib, k2, psso, yo1*; repeat from * to *; end with k1, 1 selvedge stitch.

Keep repeating these 4 rows.

☐ knit stitch on right side or purl stitch on wrong side

⊙ΠΠ▽ sl 1 kwise wyib, k2, psso, yo1: slip 1 stitch knitwise with yarn in back, k2, pass slipped stitch over the knit stitches and off the needle, yo1

ΠΠ▽⊙ yo1, sl 1 kwise wyib, k2, psso: yo1, slip 1 stitch knitwise with yarn in back, k2, pass slipped stitch over the knit stitches and off the needle

Eyelet Wasp's Nest

Number of stitches needed for symmetry and joining: multiple of 4 + 1 selvedge stitch at each end.

Rows 1 (right side of work) and 5: all knit.

Rows 2 and 6: all purl.

Row 3: 1 selvedge stitch, *yo1, skp, k2tog, yo1*; repeat from * to *; end with 1 selvedge stitch.

Rows 4 and 8: all purl. Note: when there are 2 yarn overs in a row, p1 and p1 tbl

Row 7: 1 selvedge stitch, *k2tog, yo2, skp*; repeat from * to *; end with 1 selvedge stitch.

Keep repeating these 8 rows.

☐ knit stitch on right side or purl stitch on wrong side

O yo: yarn over

⟋ k2tog: knit 2 together on right side or purl 2 together on wrong side

⟍ skp: slip 1 stitch knitwise, knit the next stitch, then pass the slipped stitch over the knit stitch and off the needle

Я k tbl: knit through the back of the loop on right side (or purl on wrong side)

Fancy Cables and Eyelets

Number of stitches needed for joining: multiple of 4 + 1 selvedge stitch at each end.

Row 1 (right side of work): all knit.

Row 2: 1 selvedge stitch, *p4, yo1*; repeat from * to *; end with 1 selvedge stitch.

Row 3: 1 selvedge stitch, *yo1, let the yarn over from previous row slide off needle, sl 1 kwise wyib, k3, psso*; repeat from * to *; end with 1 selvedge stitch.

Row 4: all purl.

Keep repeating these 4 rows.

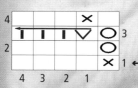

☐ knit stitch on right side or purl stitch on wrong side

O yo: yarn over

✕ stitch that does not exist

↑↑↑▽ sl 1 kwise wyib, k3, psso: slip 1 stitch knitwise with yarn in back, k3, pass slipped stitch over knit stitches and off the needle

Lace and Eyelet Stitches

Tulle Stitch

Number of stitches needed for symmetry: multiple of 2 + 1 + 1 selvedge stitch at each end.

Row 1 (right side of work): 1 selvedge stitch, *k1, yo1, k1*; repeat from * to *; end with k1, 1 selvedge stitch.

Row 2: 1 selvedge stitch, p1, *p3, pass the 1st of the 3 stitches over the following 2 and off the needle*; repeat from * to *; end with 1 selvedge stitch.

Row 3: 1 selvedge stitch, k1, *k1, yo1, k1*; repeat from * to *; end with 1 selvedge stitch.

Row 4: 1 selvedge stitch, *p3, pass the 1st of the 3 stitches over the following 2 and off the needle*; repeat from * to *; end with p1, 1 selvedge stitch.

Keep repeating these 4 rows.

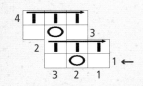

☐ knit stitch on right side or purl stitch on wrong side

O yo: yarn over

⊤⊤⊤ p3, pass the 1st of the 3 stitches over the following 2 and off the needle

Staggered Eyelets

Number of stitches needed for symmetry: multiple of 6 + 5 + 1 selvedge stitch at each end.

Rows 1 (right side of work) and 5: all knit.

Rows 2 and 6: all purl.

Row 3: 1 selvedge stitch, k1, *k3, yo1, sl 1 kwise, k2tog, psso, yo1*; repeat from * to *; end with k4, 1 selvedge stitch.

Row 4: 1 selvedge stitch, p4, *k1, p1, k1, p3*; repeat from * to *; end with p1, 1 selvedge stitch.

Row 7: 1 selvedge stitch, k1, *yo1, sl 1 kwise, k2tog, psso, yo1, k3*; repeat from * to *; end with yo1, sl 1 kwise, k2tog, psso, yo1, k1, 1 selvedge stitch.

Row 8: 1 selvedge stitch, p1, k1, p1, k1, *p3, k1, p1, k1*; repeat from * to *; end with p1, 1 selvedge stitch.

Keep repeating these 8 rows.

☐ knit stitch on right side or purl stitch on wrong side

– purl stitch on right side or knit stitch on wrong side

O yo: yarn over

⋋ sl 1 kwise, k2tog, psso: slip 1 stitch knitwise, knit the next 2 stitches together, pass the slipped stitch over the stitch obtained and off the needle

Reversible Layette Stitch

Number of stitches needed for symmetry: multiple of 4 + 1 + 1 selvedge stitch at each end.

Rows 1 (right side of work) and 3: 1 selvedge stitch, *p1, k3*; repeat from * to *; end with p1, 1 selvedge stitch.

Rows 2 and 6: knit each stitch as it appears in previous row (i.e., knit a knit stitch, purl a purl stitch).

Row 4: 1 selvedge stitch, k1, *yo1, k3tog, yo1, k1*; repeat from * to *; end with 1 selvedge stitch.

Rows 5 and 7: 1 selvedge stitch, k2, *p1, k3*; repeat from * to *; end with p1, k2, 1 selvedge stitch.

Row 8: 1 selvedge stitch, p2tog, yo1, k1, *yo1, k3tog, yo1, k1*; repeat from * to *; end with yo1, p2tog, 1 selvedge stitch.

Keep repeating these 8 rows.

- ☐ knit stitch on right side or purl stitch on wrong side
- − purl stitch on right side or knit stitch on wrong side
- O yo: yarn over
- ⋏ k3tog: knit 3 together on right side or purl 3 together on wrong side

p2tog: purl 2 together

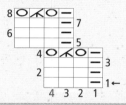

Trellis

- ☐ knit stitch on right side or purl stitch on wrong side
- O yo: yarn over
- ⋏ k2tog: knit 2 together on right side or purl 2 together on wrong side
- ⋌ skp: slip 1 stitch knitwise, knit the next stitch, then pass the slipped stitch over the knit stitch and off the needle (on wrong side, ssp)

Number of stitches needed for symmetry and joining: multiple of 7 + 1 selvedge stitch at each end.

Row 1 (right side of work): 1 selvedge stitch, *k2, k2tog, yo1, k3*; repeat from * to *; end with 1 selvedge stitch.

Row 2: 1 selvedge stitch, *p1, ssp, yo1, p1, yo1, p2tog, p1*; repeat from * to *; end with 1 selvedge stitch.

Row 3: 1 selvedge stitch, *k2tog, yo1, k3, yo1, skp*; repeat from * to *; end with 1 selvedge stitch.

Rows 4 and 8: all purl.

Row 5: 1 selvedge stitch, *yo1, skp, k5*; repeat from * to *; end with 1 selvedge stitch.

Row 6: 1 selvedge stitch, *yo1, p2tog, p2, ssp, yo1, p1*; repeat from * to *; end with 1 selvedge stitch.

Row 7: 1 selvedge stitch, *k2, yo1, skp, k2tog, yo1, k1*; repeat from * to *; end with 1 selvedge stitch.

Keep repeating these 8 rows.

ssp: slip 2 stitches knitwise, place them back on the left needle, and purl them together through the back loops

Embroidery-Style Lozenges

Number of stitches needed for symmetry and joining: multiple of 6 + 7 + 1 selvedge stitch at each end.

Note: The number of stitches will not be the same as the number at the beginning except in rows 10 and 18.

Row 1 (right side of work): all knit.

Row 2 and all even numbered rows: all purl.

Row 3: 1 selvedge stitch, *k3, inc 7 in 1 st (k1, p1, k1, p1, k1, p1, k1), k2*; repeat from * to *; end with k1, 1 selvedge stitch.

Row 5: 1 selvedge stitch, *k2, k2tog, k5, skp, k1*; repeat from * to *; end with k1, 1 selvedge stitch.

Row 7: 1 selvedge stitch, *k1, k2tog, k5, skp*; repeat from * to *; end with k1, 1 selvedge stitch.

Row 9: 1 selvedge stitch, k2tog, *k5, sl 1 kwise, k2tog, psso*; repeat from * to *; end with k5, skp, 1 selvedge stitch.

Row 11: 1 selvedge stitch, inc 4 in 1 st (k1, p1, k1, p1), *k5, inc 7 in 1 st (k1, p1, k1, p1, k1, p1, k1)*; repeat from * to *; end with k5, inc 4 in 1 st (k1, p1, k1, p1), 1 selvedge stitch.

Row 13: 1 selvedge stitch, *k3, skp, k3, k2tog, k2*; repeat from * to *; end with k1, 1 selvedge stitch.

Row 15: 1 selvedge stitch, *k3, skp, k1, k2tog, k2*; repeat from * to *; end with k1, 1 selvedge stitch.

Row 17: 1 selvedge stitch, *k3, sl 1 kwise, k2tog, psso, k2*; repeat from * to *; end with k1, 1 selvedge stitch.

Keep repeating Rows 3 through 18 (16 rows in total).

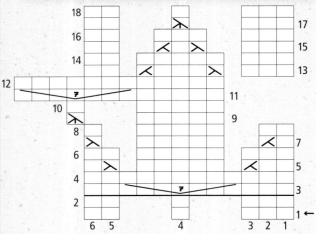

knit stitch on right side or purl stitch on wrong side

⟋ k2tog: knit 2 together on right side or purl 2 together on wrong side

⟍ skp: slip 1 stitch knitwise, knit the next stitch, then pass the slipped stitch over the knit stitch and off the needle

⟰ sl 1 kwise, k2tog, psso: slip 1 stitch knitwise, knit the next 2 stitches together, pass the slipped stitch over the stitch obtained and off the needle

inc 7 in 1 st (k1, p1, k1, p1, k1, p1, k1): make 7 stitches in 1 stitch, alternating knit, purl

inc 4 in 1 st (k1, p1, k1, p1): make 4 stitches in 1 stitch, alternating knit, purl

Tile Stitch

Number of stitches: multiple of 12 + 1 + 1 selvedge stitch at each end.

Row 1 (right side of work): 1 selvedge stitch, k1, *skp, k3, yo1, p2, yo1, k3, k2tog*; repeat from * to *; end with k1, 1 selvedge stitch.

Row 2: 1 selvedge stitch, k1, *p2tog, p2, yo1, k4, yo1, p2, ssp*; repeat from * to *; end with k1, 1 selvedge stitch.

Row 3: 1 selvedge stitch, k1, *skp, k1, yo1, p6, yo1, k1, k2tog*; repeat from * to *; end with k1, 1 selvedge stitch.

Row 4: 1 selvedge stitch, k1, *p2tog, yo1, k8, yo1, ssp*; repeat from * to *; end with k1, 1 selvedge stitch.

Row 5: 1 selvedge stitch, k1, *p1, yo1, k3, k2tog, skp, k3, yo1, p1*; repeat from * to *; end with k1, 1 selvedge stitch.

Row 6: 1 selvedge stitch, k1, *k2, yo1, p2, ssp, p2tog, p2, yo1, k2*; repeat from * to *; end with k1, 1 selvedge stitch.

Row 7: 1 selvedge stitch, k1, *p3, yo1, k1, k2tog, skp, k1, yo1, p3*; repeat from * to *; end with k1, 1 selvedge stitch.

Row 8: 1 selvedge stitch, k1, *k4, yo1, ssp, p2tog, yo1, k4*; repeat from * to *; end with k1, 1 selvedge stitch.

Keep repeating these 8 rows.

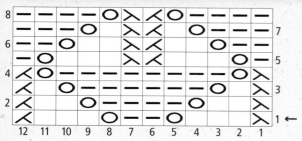

☐ knit stitch on right side or purl stitch on wrong side

– purl stitch on right side or knit stitch on wrong side

O yo: yarn over

╱ k2tog: knit 2 together on right side or purl 2 together on wrong side

╲ skp: slip 1 stitch knitwise, knit the next stitch, then pass the slipped stitch over the knit stitch and off the needle (ssp on wrong side)

p2tog: purl 2 together

ssp: slip 2 stitches knitwise, place them back on the left needle, and purl them together through the back loops

Eyelet Chevrons (2)

Row 13: *skp (at beginning of row, make the skp with selvedge stitch and next stitch), yo1, k5*; repeat from * to *; (skp, yo1, k11, yo1, k2tog – 15 stitches in middle this row); *k5, yo1, k2tog*; repeat from * to * (at end of row knit together selvedge stitch and preceding stitch).
Keep repeating Rows 1 through 14.

Number of stitches needed for symmetry: multiple of 14 + 13 stitches in the middle of the work + 1 selvedge stitch at each end. In each odd row, the work is explained from * to * for the right side up to the middle 13 stitches, then in parentheses ( ) for the middle, and again from * to * for the left side after the 13 middle stitches.

Row 1: 1 selvedge stitch, *k5, skp, yo1*; repeat from * to *; (k6, yo1, k2tog, k5); *yo1, k2tog, k5*; repeat from * to *; end with 1 selvedge stitch.

Row 2 and all even numbered rows: all purl (stitches and yarn overs).

Row 3: 1 selvedge stitch, *k4, skp, yo1, k1*; repeat from * to *; (k4, skp, yo1, k1, yo1, k2tog, k4); *k1, yo1, k2tog, k4*; repeat from * to *; end with 1 selvedge stitch.

Row 5: 1 selvedge stitch, *k3, skp, yo1, k2*; repeat from * to *; (k3, skp, yo1, k3, yo1, k2tog, k3); *k2, yo1, k2tog, k3*; repeat from * to *; end with 1 selvedge stitch.

Row 7: 1 selvedge stitch, *k2, skp, yo1, k3*; repeat from * to *; (k2, skp, yo1, k5, yo1, k2tog, k2); *k3, yo1, k2tog, k2*; repeat from * to *; end with 1 selvedge stitch.

Row 9: 1 selvedge stitch, *k1, skp, yo1, k4*; repeat from * to *; (k1, skp, yo1, k7, yo1, k2tog, k1); *k4, yo1, k2tog, k1*; repeat from * to *; end with 1 selvedge stitch.

Row 11: 1 selvedge stitch, *skp, yo1, k5*; repeat from * to *; (skp, yo1, k9, yo1, k2tog); *k5, yo1, k2tog*; repeat from * to *; end with 1 selvedge stitch.

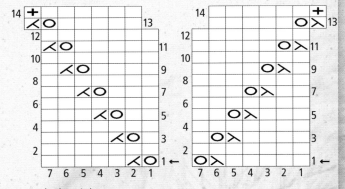

+ selvedge stitch

☐ knit stitch on right side or purl stitch on wrong side

○ yo: yarn over

⋌ k2tog: knit 2 together on right side or purl 2 together on wrong side

⋋ skp: slip 1 stitch knitwise, knit the next stitch, then pass the slipped stitch over the knit stitch and off the needle

Diagonal Eyelets (2)

Number of stitches needed for joining: multiple of 9 + 1 selvedge stitch at each end.

Row 1 (right side of work): 1 selvedge stitch, k4, *m1, k2tog, pass the increase stitch over the stitch obtained, m1, k6*; repeat from * to *; end with m1, k2tog, pass the increase stitch over the stitch obtained, m1, k3, 1 selvedge stitch.

Row 2 and all even numbered rows: all purl.

Row 3: 1 selvedge stitch, k3, *m1, k2tog, pass the increase stitch over the stitch obtained, m1, k6*; repeat from * to *; end with m1, k2tog, pass the increase stitch over the stitch obtained, m1, k4, 1 selvedge stitch.

Continue shifting one stitch to the right.

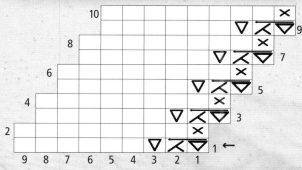

☐ knit stitch on right side or purl stitch on wrong side

▽ m1: using the left needle, pick up the strand between 2 stitches from back to front and knit as usual to increase 1

⃨▽ m1, k2tog, pass the increase stitch over the stitch obtained

✕ stitch that does not exist

k2tog: knit 2 together

Lace and Eyelet Stitches

Small Eyelet Diagonals

Number of stitches needed for joining: multiple of 5 + 1 selvedge stitch at each end.

Note: The directions for this pattern consist of a minimum of 12 stitches.

Row 1 (right side of work): 1 selvedge stitch, *k3, k2tog, yo1*; repeat from * to *; end with 1 selvedge stitch.

Row 2 and all even numbered rows: all purl (stitches and yarn overs).

Row 3: 1 selvedge stitch, k2, k2tog, yo1, *k3, k2tog, yo1*; repeat from * to *; end with k1, 1 selvedge stitch.

Row 5: 1 selvedge stitch, k1, k2tog, yo1, *k3, k2tog, yo1*; repeat from * to *; end with k2, 1 selvedge stitch.

Row 7: 1 selvedge stitch, k2tog, yo1, *k3, k2tog, yo1*; repeat from * to *; end with k3, 1 selvedge stitch.

Row 9: k2tog (at beginning of row, knit together selvedge stitch and next stitch), yo1, *k3, k2tog, yo1*; repeat from * to *; end with k4, 1 selvedge stitch.

Keep repeating these 10 rows.

Diamond Eyelet Stripe

This stripe consists of 16 rows, on a background of knit stockinette stitch.

Number of stitches needed for symmetry and joining: multiple of 9 + 1 selvedge stitch at each end.

Row 1 (right side of work) and 15: all knit.

Row 2 and all even numbered rows: all purl (stitches and yarn overs).

Rows 3 and 13: 1 selvedge stitch, *k3, yo1, sl 1 kwise, k2tog, psso, yo1, k3*; repeat from * to *; end with 1 selvedge stitch.

Row 5: 1 selvedge stitch, *k1, k2tog, yo1, k3, yo1, skp, k1*; repeat from * to *; end with 1 selvedge stitch.

Row 7: 1 selvedge stitch, *k2tog, yo1, k5, yo1, skp*; repeat from * to *; end with 1 selvedge stitch.

Row 9: 1 selvedge stitch, *k1, yo1, skp, k3, k2tog, yo1, k1*; repeat from * to *; end with 1 selvedge stitch.

Row 11: 1 selvedge stitch, *k2, yo1, skp, k1, k2tog, yo1, k2*; repeat from * to *; end with 1 selvedge stitch.

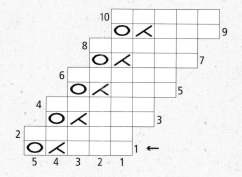

knit stitch on right side or purl stitch on wrong side

O yo: yarn over

⟋ k2tog: knit 2 together on right side or purl 2 together on wrong side

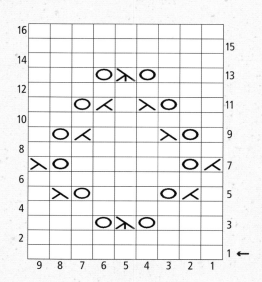

knit stitch on right side or purl stitch on wrong side

O yo: yarn over

⟋ skp: slip 1 stitch knitwise, knit the next stitch, then pass the slipped stitch over the knit stitch and off the needle

⟋ k2tog: knit 2 together on right side or purl 2 together on wrong side

⟋ sl 1 kwise, k2tog, psso: slip 1 stitch knitwise, knit the next 2 stitches together, pass the slipped stitch over the stitch obtained and off the needle

"V" Eyelets

Number of stitches needed for symmetry: multiple of 10 + 1 + 1 selvedge stitch at each end.

Row 1 (right side of work): 1 selvedge stitch, *yo1, skp, k8*; repeat from * to *; end with k1, 1 selvedge stitch.

Row 2 and all even numbered rows: all purl (stitches and yarn overs).

Row 3: 1 selvedge stitch, *k1, yo1, skp, k5, k2tog, yo1*; repeat from * to *; end with k1, 1 selvedge stitch.

Row 5: 1 selvedge stitch, *k2, yo1, skp, k3, k2tog, yo1, k1*; repeat from * to *; end with k1, 1 selvedge stitch.

Row 7: 1 selvedge stitch, *k5, yo1, skp, k3*; repeat from * to *; end with k1, 1 selvedge stitch.

Row 9: 1 selvedge stitch, *k3, k2tog, yo1, k1, yo1, skp, k2*; repeat from * to *; end with k1, 1 selvedge stitch.

Row 11: 1 selvedge stitch, *k2, k2tog, yo1, k3, yo1, skp, k1*; repeat from * to *; end with k1, 1 selvedge stitch.

Keep repeating these 12 rows.

Zigzag Eyelets

Number of stitches needed for joining: multiple of 7 + 1 selvedge stitch at each end.

Row 1 (right side of work): 1 selvedge stitch, *k5, yo1, k2tog*; repeat from * to *; end with 1 selvedge stitch.

Row 2 and all even numbered rows: all purl (stitches and yarn overs).

Rows 3 and 15: 1 selvedge stitch, *k4, yo1, k2tog, k1*; repeat from * to *; end with 1 selvedge stitch.

Rows 5 and 13: 1 selvedge stitch, *k3, yo1, k2tog, k2*; repeat from * to *; end with 1 selvedge stitch.

Rows 7 and 11: 1 selvedge stitch, *k2, yo1, k2tog, k3*; repeat from * to *; end with 1 selvedge stitch.

Row 9: 1 selvedge stitch, *k1, yo1, k2tog, k4*; repeat from * to *; end with 1 selvedge stitch.

Keep repeating these 16 rows.

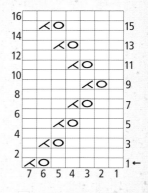

☐ knit stitch on right side or purl stitch on wrong side

O yo: yarn over

⚋ k2tog: knit 2 together on right side or purl 2 together on wrong side

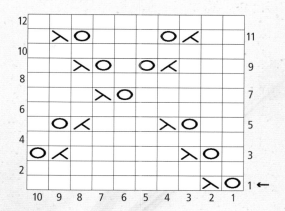

knit stitch on right side or purl stitch on wrong side
O yo: yarn over
k2tog: knit 2 together on right side or purl 2 together on wrong side
skp: slip 1 stitch knitwise, knit the next stitch, then pass the slipped stitch over the knit stitch and off the needle

Falling Leaves

Number of stitches needed for symmetry: multiple of 10 + 11 + 1 selvedge stitch at each end.

Row 1 (right side of work): 1 selvedge stitch, *k1, yo1, k3, sl 1 kwise, k2tog, psso, k3, yo1*; repeat from * to *; end with k1, 1 selvedge stitch.

Row 2 and all even numbered rows: all purl (stitches and yarn overs).

Row 3: 1 selvedge stitch, *k2, yo1, k2, sl 1 kwise, k2tog, psso, k2, yo1, k1*; repeat from * to *; end with k1, 1 selvedge stitch.

Row 5: 1 selvedge stitch, *k3, yo1, k1, sl 1 kwise, k2tog, psso, k1, yo1, k2*; repeat from * to *; end with k1, 1 selvedge stitch.

Row 7: 1 selvedge stitch, *k4, yo1, sl 1 kwise, k2tog, psso, yo1, k3*; repeat from * to *; end with k1, 1 selvedge stitch.

Row 9: 1 selvedge stitch, k2tog, k3, yo1; repeat from * to * as in Row 1; end with k1, yo1, k3, skp, 1 selvedge stitch.

Row 11: 1 selvedge stitch, k2tog, k2, yo1, k1; repeat from * to * as in Row 3; end with k2, yo1, k2, skp, 1 selvedge stitch.

Row 13: 1 selvedge stitch, k2tog, k1, yo1, k2; repeat from * to * as in Row 5; end with k3, yo1, k1, skp, 1 selvedge stitch.

Row 15: 1 selvedge stitch, k2tog, yo1, k3; repeat from * to * as in Row 7; end with k4, yo1, skp, 1 selvedge stitch.

Keep repeating these 16 rows.

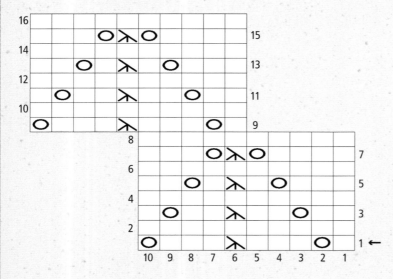

☐ knit stitch on right side or purl stitch on wrong side

O yo: yarn over

⋏ sl 1 kwise, k2tog, psso: slip 1 stitch knitwise, knit the next 2 stitches together, pass the slipped stitch over the stitch obtained and off the needle

k2tog: knit 2 together on right side or purl 2 together on wrong side

Long Leaves

Number of stitches needed for symmetry: multiple of 8 + 9 + 1 selvedge stitch at each end.

Rows 1 (right side of work), 17, and 19: 1 selvedge stitch, *k1, yo1, k2, sl 2 kwise, k1, p2sso, k2, yo1*; repeat from * to *; end with k1, 1 selvedge stitch.

Row 2 and all even numbered rows: all purl (stitches and yarn overs).

Row 3: 1 selvedge stitch, *k2, yo1, k1, sl 2 kwise, k1, p2sso, k1, yo1, k1*; repeat from * to *; end with k1, 1 selvedge stitch.

Row 5: 1 selvedge stitch, *k3, yo1, sl 2 kwise, k1, p2sso, yo1, k2*; repeat from * to *; end with k1, 1 selvedge stitch.

Rows 7, 9, and 11: 1 selvedge stitch, k2tog, k2, yo1; repeat from * to * as in Row 1; end with k1, yo1, k2, skp, 1 selvedge stitch.

Row 13: 1 selvedge stitch, k2tog, k1, yo1, k1; repeat from * to * as in Row 3; end with k2, yo1, k1, skp, 1 selvedge stitch.

Row 15: 1 selvedge stitch, k2tog, yo1, k2; repeat from * to * as in Row 5; end with k3, yo1, skp, 1 selvedge stitch.

Keep repeating these 20 rows.

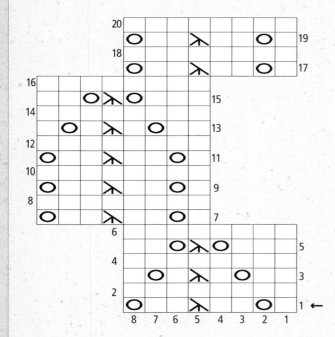

☐ knit stitch on right side or purl stitch on wrong side

O yo: yarn over

⋏ sl 1 kwise, k2tog, psso: slip 1 stitch knitwise, knit the next 2 stitches together, pass the slipped stitch over the stitch obtained and off the needle

sl 2 kwise, k1, p2sso: slip 2 stitches knitwise one after the other, k1, pass the 2 slipped stitches over the knit stitch and off the needle

k2tog: knit 2 together

Apple Tree Leaves

Number of stitches needed for symmetry: multiple of 19 + 2 (except in Rows 15 and 30 + 1) + 1 selvedge stitch at each end.

Rows 1 (right side of work), 3, 5, and 7: 1 selvedge stitch, k1, *skp, k3, yo1, °skp, yo1°; repeat from ° to ° 2 times, k1, °yo1, k2tog°; repeat from ° to ° 2 times, yo1, k3, k2tog*; repeat from * to *; end with k1, 1 selvedge stitch.

Row 2 and all even numbered rows: all purl (stitches and yarn overs).

Row 9: 1 selvedge stitch, k1, *skp, k2, yo1, °k2tog, yo1°; repeat from ° to ° 2 times, k3, °yo1, skp°; repeat from ° to ° 2 times, yo1, k2, k2tog*; repeat from * to *; end with k1, 1 selvedge stitch.

Row 11: 1 selvedge stitch, k1, *skp, k1, yo1, °k2tog, yo1°; repeat from ° to ° 2 times, k5, °yo1, skp°; repeat from ° to ° 2 times, yo1, k1, k2tog*; repeat from * to *; end with k1, 1 selvedge stitch.

Row 13: 1 selvedge stitch, k1, *skp, °yo1, k2tog°; repeat from ° to ° 2 times, yo1, k7, °yo1, skp°; repeat from ° to ° 2 times, yo1, k2tog*; repeat from * to *; end with k1, 1 selvedge stitch.

Row 15: 1 selvedge stitch, skp, *yo1, °k2tog, yo1°; repeat from ° to ° 2 times, k3, k2tog, k4, °yo1, skp°; repeat from ° to ° 3 times*; repeat from * to *; end with yo1 and 1 selvedge stitch.

Rows 17, 19, 21, and 23: 1 selvedge stitch, *k1, °yo1, k2tog°; repeat from ° to ° 2 times, yo1, k3, k2tog, skp, k3, °yo1, skp°; repeat from ° to ° 2 times, yo1*; repeat from * to *; end with k1, 1 selvedge stitch.

Row 25: 1 selvedge stitch, *k2, yo1, °skp, yo1°; repeat from ° to ° 2 times, k2, k2tog, skp, k2, °yo1, k2tog°; repeat from ° to ° 2 times, yo1, k1*; repeat from * to *; end with k1, 1 selvedge stitch.

Row 27: 1 selvedge stitch, *k3, yo1, °skp, yo1°; repeat from ° to ° 2 times, k1, k2tog, skp, k1, °yo1, k2tog°; repeat from ° to ° 2 times, yo1, k2*; repeat from * to *; end with k1, 1 selvedge stitch.

Row 29: 1 selvedge stitch, *k4, yo1, °skp, yo1°; repeat from ° to ° 2 times, k2tog, skp, °yo1, k2tog°; repeat from ° to ° 2 times, yo1, k3*; repeat from * to *; end with k1, 1 selvedge stitch.

Row 31: 1 selvedge stitch, k1, *k4, °yo1, skp°; repeat from ° to ° 3 times, yo1, °k2tog, yo1°; repeat from ° to ° 2 times, k3, k2tog*; repeat from * to *; end with k4, °yo1, skp°; repeat from ° to ° 3 times, yo1, °k2tog, yo1°; repeat from ° to ° 2 times, k5, 1 selvedge stitch.

Keep repeating these 32 rows.

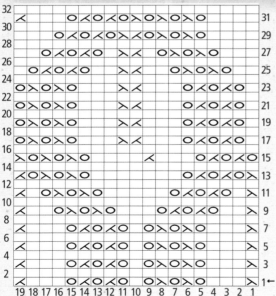

"V" Eyelet Pattern

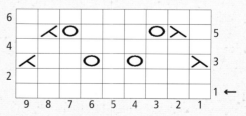

knit stitch on right side or purl stitch on wrong side

⟨ k2tog: knit 2 together on right side or purl 2 together on wrong side

⟩ skp: slip 1 stitch knitwise, knit the next stitch, then pass the slipped stitch over the knit stitch and off the needle

O yo: yarn over

Number of stitches needed for symmetry: multiple of 9 + 1 selvedge stitch at each end.

Row 1 (right side of work): all knit.

Row 2 and all even numbered rows: all purl

Row 3: 1 selvedge stitch, *skp, k2, yo1, k1, yo1, k2, k2tog*; repeat from * to *; end with 1 selvedge stitch.

Row 5: 1 selvedge stitch, *k1, skp, yo1, k3, yo1, k2tog, k1*; repeat from * to *; end with 1 selvedge stitch.

Keep repeating these 6 rows.

knit stitch on right side or purl stitch on wrong side

⟨ k2tog: knit 2 together on right side or purl 2 together on wrong side

⟩ skp: slip 1 stitch knitwise, knit the next stitch, then pass the slipped stitch over the knit stitch and off the needle

O yo: yarn over

Lace and Eyelet Stitches

Eyelet Mosaic

Number of stitches needed for symmetry: multiple of 10 + 11 + 1 selvedge stitch at each end.

Row 1 (right side of work): 1 selvedge stitch, *k3, k2tog, yo1, k1, yo1, skp, k2*; repeat from * to *; end with k1, 1 selvedge stitch.

Row 2 and all even numbered rows: all purl (stitches and yarn overs).

Row 3: 1 selvedge stitch, *k2, k2tog, yo1, k3, yo1, skp, k1*; repeat from * to *; end with k1, 1 selvedge stitch.

Row 5: 1 selvedge stitch, *k1, k2tog, yo1, k5, yo1, skp*; repeat from * to *; end with k1, 1 selvedge stitch.

Rows 7, 9, 11, 13, and 15: 1 selvedge stitch, *k2, yo1, k2, sl 1 kwise, k2tog, psso, k2, yo1, k1*; repeat from * to *; end with k1, 1 selvedge stitch.

Row 17: 1 selvedge stitch, *k1, yo1, skp, k5, k2tog, yo1*; repeat from * to *; end with k1, 1 selvedge stitch.

Row 19: 1 selvedge stitch, *k2, yo1, skp, k3, k2tog, yo1, k1*; repeat from * to *; end with k1, 1 selvedge stitch.

Row 21: 1 selvedge stitch, *k3, yo1, skp, k1, k2tog, yo1, k2*; repeat from * to *; end with k1, 1 selvedge stitch.

Waves

Number of stitches needed for symmetry: multiple of 18 + 1 selvedge stitch at each end.

Rows 1 (right side of work) and 3: all knit.

Row 2 and all even rows: all purl (stitches and yarn overs).

Row 5: 1 selvedge stitch, p2tog (3 times), °k1, yo1°; repeat from ° to ° 6 times, p2tog (3 times)*; repeat from * to *; end with 1 selvedge stitch.

Keep repeating these 6 rows.

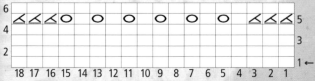

☐ knit stitch on right side or purl stitch on wrong side

◺ p2tog: purl 2 together on right side or knit 2 together on wrong side

O yo: yarn over

Rows 23, 25, 27, 29, and 31: 1 selvedge stitch, k2tog, k2, yo1, k1; repeat from * to * as in Row 7; end with k2, yo1, k2, skp, 1 selvedge stitch.

Keep repeating these 32 rows.

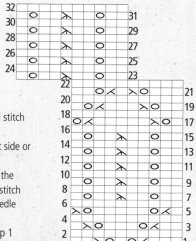

☐ knit stitch on right side or purl stitch on wrong side

⟋ k2tog: knit 2 together on right side or purl 2 together on wrong side

⟍ skp: slip 1 stitch knitwise, knit the next stitch, then pass the slipped stitch over the knit stitch and off the needle

○ yo: yarn over

⅄ slip 1 knitwise, k2tog, psso: slip 1 stitch knitwise, knit the next 2 stitches together, pass the slipped stitch over the stitch obtained and off the needle

Little Waves

Number of stitches needed for symmetry and joining: multiple of 11 + 1 selvedge stitch at each end.

Row 1 (right side of work): 1 selvedge stitch, *k2tog (2 times), yo1, k1, yo1, k1, yo1, k1, yo1, k2tog*; repeat from * to *; end with 1 selvedge stitch.

Rows 2 and 4: all purl (stitches and yarn overs).

Row 3: all knit.

Keep repeating these 4 rows.

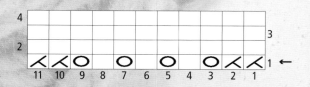

☐ knit stitch on right side or purl stitch on wrong side

⟋ k2tog: knit 2 together on right side or purl 2 together on wrong side

○ yo: yarn over

Lace and Eyelet Stitches

Angled Eyelets (1)

Number of stitches needed for symmetry: multiple of 10 + 1 + 1 selvedge stitch at each end.

Row 1 (right side of work): 1 selvedge stitch, *k1, yo1, k3, sl 1 kwise, k2tog, psso, k3, yo1*; repeat from * to *; end with k1, 1 selvedge stitch.

Row 2 and all even numbered rows: all purl (stitches and yarn overs).

Row 3: 1 selvedge stitch, *k2, yo1, k2, sl 1 kwise, k2tog, psso, k2, yo1, k1*; repeat from * to *; end with k1, 1 selvedge stitch.

Row 5: 1 selvedge stitch, k2tog, yo1, *k1, yo1, k1, sl 1 kwise, k2tog, psso, k1, yo1, k1, yo1, sl 1 kwise, k2tog, psso, yo1*; repeat from * to *; end with k1, yo1, k1, sl 1 kwise, k2tog, psso, k1, yo1, k1, yo1, skp, 1 selvedge stitch.

Keep repeating these 6 rows.

☐ knit stitch on right side or purl stitch on wrong side

O yo: yarn over

⋋ sl 1 kwise, k2tog, psso: slip 1 stitch knitwise, knit the next 2 stitches together, pass the slipped stitch over the stitch obtained and off the needle

skp: slip 1 stitch knitwise, knit the next stitch, then pass the slipped stitch over the knit stitch and off the needle

Houses

Number of stitches needed for symmetry: multiple of 10 + 1 + 1 selvedge stitch at each end.

Note: This stitch begins on the wrong side of the work.

Row 1 (wrong side of work) and all odd rows: all purl.

Rows 2, 4, and 6: 1 selvedge stitch, *k1, yo1, skp, k2tog, yo1, k1, yo1, skp, k2tog, yo1*; repeat from * to *; end with k1, 1 selvedge stitch.

Row 8: 1 selvedge stitch, *k1, yo1, skp, k5, k2tog, yo1*; repeat from * to *; end with k1, 1 selvedge stitch.

Row 10: 1 selvedge stitch, *k2, yo1, skp, k3, k2tog, yo1, k1*; repeat from * to *; end with k1, 1 selvedge stitch.

Row 12: 1 selvedge stitch, *k3, yo1, skp, k1, k2tog, yo1, k2*; repeat from * to *; end with k1, 1 selvedge stitch.

Row 14: 1 selvedge stitch, *k4, yo1, sl 1 kwise, k2tog, psso, yo1, k3*; repeat from * to *; end with k1, 1 selvedge stitch.

Keep repeating Rows 2 through 15.

Inserted Eyelets

Number of stitches needed for symmetry: multiple of 6 + 7 + 1 selvedge stitch at each end.

Rows 1 (right side of work), 3, 5, and 7: 1 selvedge stitch, *k2, yo1, sl 1 kwise, k2tog, psso, yo1, k1*; repeat from * to *; end with k1, 1 selvedge stitch.

Row 2 and all even rows: all purl (stitches and yarn overs).

Rows 9, 11, 13, and 15: 1 selvedge stitch, k2tog, yo1, k1; repeat from * to * as in Row 1; end with k2, yo1, skp, 1 selvedge stitch.

Keep repeating these 16 rows.

☐ knit stitch on right side or purl stitch on wrong side

O yo: yarn over

⋏ sl 1 kwise, k2tog, psso: slip 1 stitch knitwise, knit the next 2 stitches together, pass the slipped stitch over the stitch obtained and off the needle
k2tog: knit 2 together on right side or purl 2 together on wrong side

---

☐ knit stitch on right side or purl stitch on wrong side

O yo: yarn over

⋏ k2tog: knit 2 together on right side or purl 2 together on wrong side

⋋ skp: slip 1 stitch knitwise, knit the next stitch, then pass the slipped stitch over the knit stitch and off the needle

⋏ sl 1 kwise, k2tog, psso: slip 1 stitch knitwise, knit the next 2 stitches together, pass the slipped stitch over the stitch obtained and off the needle

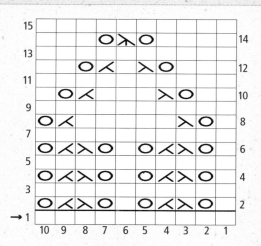

Arches

Number of stitches needed for symmetry: multiple of 10 + 1 + 1 selvedge stitch at each end.

Rows 1 (right side of work), 3, and 5: 1 selvedge stitch, *k1, yo1, k2tog, k5, skp, yo1*; repeat from * to *; end with k1, 1 selvedge stitch.

Row 2 and all even numbered rows: all purl (stitches and yarn overs).

Row 7: 1 selvedge stitch, *k1, yo1, k3, sl 1 kwise, k2tog, psso, k3, yo1*; repeat from * to *; end with k1, 1 selvedge stitch.

Row 9: 1 selvedge stitch, *k2, yo1, k2, sl 1 kwise, k2tog, psso, k2, yo1, k1*; repeat from * to *; end with k1, 1 selvedge stitch.

Row 11: 1 selvedge stitch, *k3, yo1, k1, sl 1 kwise, k2tog, psso, k1, yo1, k2*; repeat from * to *; end with k1, 1 selvedge stitch.

Row 13: 1 selvedge stitch, *k4, yo1, sl 1 kwise, k2tog, psso, yo1, k3*; repeat from * to *; end with k1, 1 selvedge stitch.

Keep repeating these 14 rows.

☐ knit stitch on right side or purl stitch on wrong side
O yo: yarn over
╲ skp: slip 1 stitch knitwise, knit the next stitch, then pass the slipped stitch over the knit stitch and off the needle
╱ k2tog: knit 2 together on right side or purl 2 together on wrong side
⅄ sl 1 kwise, k2tog, psso: slip 1 stitch knitwise, knit the next 2 stitches together, pass the slipped stitch over the stitch obtained and off the needle

Garland of Leaves

Number of stitches needed for symmetry: multiple of 11 + 1 + 1 selvedge stitch at each end.

Note: This stitch requires a minimum of 25 stitches.

Row 1 (right side of work): 1 selvedge stitch, k2tog, *k5, yo1, k1, yo1, k2, sl 1 kwise, k2tog, psso*; repeat from * to *; end with skp in place of the double decrease, 1 selvedge stitch.

Row 2 and all even numbered rows: all purl (stitches and yarn overs).

Row 3: 1 selvedge stitch, k2tog, *k4, yo1, k3, yo1, k1, sl 1 kwise, k2tog, psso*; repeat from * to *; end with skp in place of the double decrease, 1 selvedge stitch.

Row 5: 1 selvedge stitch, k2tog, *k3, yo1, k5, yo1, sl 1 kwise, k2tog, psso*; repeat from * to *; end with skp in place of the double decrease, 1 selvedge stitch.

Row 7: 1 selvedge stitch, k2tog, *k2, yo1, k1, yo1, k5, sl 1 kwise, k2tog, psso*; repeat from * to *; end with skp in place of the double decrease, 1 selvedge stitch.

Row 9: 1 selvedge stitch, k2tog, *k1, yo1, k3, yo1, k4, sl 1 kwise, k2tog, psso*; repeat from * to *; end with skp in place of the double decrease, 1 selvedge stitch.

Row 11: 1 selvedge stitch, k2tog, *yo1, k5, yo1, k3, sl 1 kwise, k2tog, psso*; repeat from * to *; end with skp in place of the double decrease, 1 selvedge stitch.

Keep repeating these 12 rows.

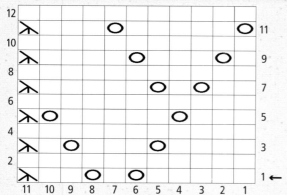

knit stitch on right side or purl stitch on wrong side

O yo: yarn over

⋏ sl 1 kwise, k2tog, psso: slip 1 stitch knitwise, knit the next 2 stitches together, pass the slipped stitch over the stitch obtained and off the needle

skp: slip 1 stitch knitwise, knit the next stitch, then pass the slipped stitch over the knit stitch and off the needle

Lace and Eyelet Stitches

Overlapping Waves

Number of stitches needed for symmetry: multiple of 10 + 3 + 1 selvedge stitch at each end.

Rows 1 (right side of work), 3, 9, and 11: 1 selvedge stitch, *p3, k7*; repeat from * to *; end with p3, 1 selvedge stitch.

Rows 2, 4, 8, 10, 12, and 16: knit each stitch as it appears in previous row (i.e., knit a knit stitch, purl a purl stitch) and purl the yarn overs.

Row 5: 1 selvedge stitch, *p3, k2, k2tog, k3, yo1*; repeat from * to *; end with p3, 1 selvedge stitch.

Row 6: 1 selvedge stitch, k3, *p1, yo1, p3, p2tog, p1, k3*; repeat from * to *; end with 1 selvedge stitch.

Row 7: 1 selvedge stitch, *p3, k2tog, k3, yo1, k2*; repeat from * to *; end with p3, 1 selvedge stitch.

Row 13: 1 selvedge stitch, *p3, yo1, k3, skp, k2*; repeat from * to *; end with p3, 1 selvedge stitch.

Row 14: 1 selvedge stitch, k3, *p1, ssp, p3, yo1, p1, k3*; repeat from * to *; end with 1 selvedge stitch.

Row 15: 1 selvedge stitch, *p3, k2, yo1, k3, skp*; repeat from * to *; end with p3, 1 selvedge stitch.

Keep repeating these 16 rows.

Angled Eyelets (2)

Number of stitches needed for joining: multiple of 10 + 1 + 1 selvedge stitch at each end.

Row 1 (right side of work): 1 selvedge stitch, *k1, yo1, k3, sl 1 kwise, k2tog, psso, k3, yo1*; repeat from * to *; end with k1, 1 selvedge stitch.

Row 2 and all even numbered rows: all purl (stitches and yarn overs).

Row 3: 1 selvedge stitch, *k2, yo1, k2, sl 1 kwise, k2tog, psso, k2, yo1, k1*; repeat from * to *; end with k1, 1 selvedge stitch.

Row 5: 1 selvedge stitch, *k3, yo1, k1, sl 1 kwise, k2tog, psso, k1, yo1, k2*; repeat from * to *; end with k1; 1 selvedge stitch.

Row 7: 1 selvedge stitch, *k4, yo1, sl 1 kwise, k2tog, psso, yo1, k3*; repeat from * to *; end with k1, 1 selvedge stitch.

Keep repeating these 8 rows.

knit stitch on right side or purl stitch on wrong side

− purl stitch on right side or knit stitch on wrong side

O yo: yarn over

⟋ k2tog: knit 2 together on right side or purl 2 together on wrong side

⟍ skp: slip 1 stitch knitwise, knit the next stitch, then pass the slipped stitch over the knit stitch and off the needle (ssp on wrong side)

p2tog: purl 2 together
ssp: slip 2 stitches knitwise, place them back on the left needle, and purl them together through the back loops

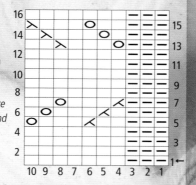

knit stitch on right side or purl stitch on wrong side

O yo: yarn over

⋏ sl 1 kwise, k2tog, psso: slip 1 stitch knitwise, knit the next 2 stitches together, pass the slipped stitch over the stitch obtained and off the needle

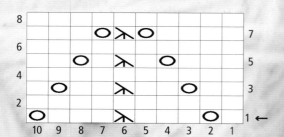

Eyelet Chevrons (3)

Number of stitches needed for symmetry: multiple of 16 + 1 + 1 selvedge stitch at each end.

Row 1 (right side of work): 1 selvedge stitch, *p1, yo1, k2, k2tog, k7, skp, k2, yo1*; repeat from * to *; end with p1, 1 selvedge stitch.

Row 2 and all even numbered rows: knit each stitch as it appears in previous row (i.e., knit a knit stitch, purl a purl stitch) and purl the yarn overs.

Row 3: 1 selvedge stitch, *p1, k1, yo1, k2, k2tog, k5, skp, k2, yo1, k1*; repeat from * to *; end with p1, 1 selvedge stitch.

Row 5: 1 selvedge stitch, *p1, k2, yo1, k2, k2tog, k3, skp, k2, yo1, k2*; repeat from * to *; end with p1, 1 selvedge stitch.

Row 7: 1 selvedge stitch, *p1, k3, yo1, k2, k2tog, k1, skp, k2, yo1, k3*; repeat from * to *; end with p1, 1 selvedge stitch.

Row 9: 1 selvedge stitch, *p1, k4, yo1, k2, sl2 kwise, k1, p2sso, k2, yo1, k4*; repeat from * to *; end with p1, 1 selvedge stitch.

Keep repeating these 10 rows.

Legend:
- knit stitch on right side or purl stitch on wrong side
- **O** yo: yarn over
- **–** purl stitch on right side or knit stitch on wrong side
- **skp:** slip 1 stitch knitwise, knit the next stitch, then pass the slipped stitch over the knit stitch and off the needle
- **k2tog:** knit 2 together on right side or purl 2 together on wrong side
- **sl2 kwise, k1, p2sso:** slip 2 stitches knitwise, knit the next stitch, pass 2 slipped stitches over the knit stitch and off the needle

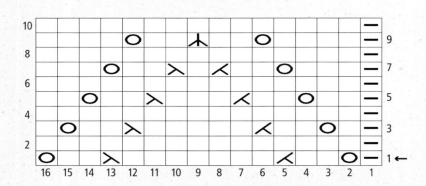

Row	16	15	14	13	12	11	10	9	8	7	6	5	4	3	2	1
10																–
9					O			sl2-k1-p2sso			O					–
8																–
7				O			skp		k2tog			O				–
6																–
5			O			skp				k2tog			O			–
4																–
3		O			skp						k2tog			O		–
2																–
1	O			skp								k2tog			O	–

Lily of the Valley

Number of stitches needed for symmetry and joining: multiple of 18 + 1 selvedge stitch at each end.

Row 1 (right side of work): 1 selvedge stitch, *k4, p2tog, k2, yo1, k5, yo1, k2, p2tog, k1*; repeat from * to *; end with 1 selvedge stitch.

Row 2 and all even numbered rows: all purl (stitches and yarn overs).

Row 3: 1 selvedge stitch, *k3, p2tog, k2, yo1, k1, yo1, k2, p2tog, k6*; repeat from * to *; end with 1 selvedge stitch.

Row 5: 1 selvedge stitch, *k2, p2tog, k2, yo1, k3, yo1, k2, p2tog, k5*; repeat from * to *; end with 1 selvedge stitch.

Row 7: 1 selvedge stitch, *k1, p2tog, k2, yo1, k5, yo1, k2, p2tog, k4*; repeat from * to *; end with 1 selvedge stitch.

Row 9: 1 selvedge stitch, *k6, p2tog, k2, yo1, k1, yo1, k2, p2tog, k3*; repeat from * to *; end with 1 selvedge stitch.

Row 11: 1 selvedge stitch, *k5, p2tog, k2, yo1, k3, yo1, k2, p2tog, k2*; repeat from * to *; end with 1 selvedge stitch.

Keep repeating these 12 rows.

☐ knit stitch on right side or purl stitch on wrong side

O yo: yarn over

⊿ p2tog: purl 2 together on right side or knit 2 together on wrong side

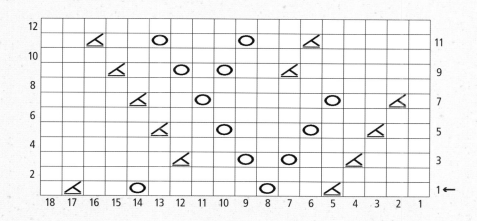

Lace and Eyelet Stitches

Eyelet Leaves

The directions for this pattern consist of 25 stitches. **Note:** the number of stitches is not consistent in all rows. There will be 25 stitches in Rows 1, 2, 11, and 12, and 23 in the others.

Row 1 (right side of work): k1, yo1, k3, k2tog, p1, skp, k3, yo1, k1, yo1, k3, k2tog, p1, skp, k3, yo1, k1.

Row 2 and all even numbered rows: knit each stitch as it appears in previous row (i.e., knit a knit stitch, purl a purl stitch) and purl the yarn overs.

Row 3: k1, yo1, k1, yo1, k2, k2tog, p1, skp, k1, k2tog, p1, skp, k1, k2tog, p1, skp, k2, yo1, k1, yo1, k1.

Row 5: k1, yo1, k3, yo1, k1, k2tog, p1, skp, k1, p1, k1, k2tog, p1, skp, k1, yo1, k3, yo1, k1.

Row 7: k1, yo1, k5, yo1, k2tog, p1, skp, p1, k2tog, p1, skp, yo1, k5, yo1, k1.

Row 9: k1, yo1, k7, yo1, sl 1 kwise, k2tog, psso, p1, k3tog, yo1, k7, yo1, k1.

Row 11: k1, yo1, k9, yo1, sl 1 kwise, k2tog, psso, yo1, k9, yo1, k1.

Keep repeating these 12 rows.

"V" Eyelet Pattern in Relief

Number of stitches needed for symmetry and joining: multiple of 13 + 1 selvedge stitch at each end.

Row 1 (right side of work): 1 selvedge stitch, *p4, k5, p4*; repeat from * to *; end with 1 selvedge stitch.

Row 2 and all even numbered rows: knit each stitch as it appears in previous row (i.e., knit a knit stitch, purl a purl stitch) and purl the yarn overs.

Row 3: 1 selvedge stitch, *p3, k2tog, k1, yo1, k1, yo1, k1, skp, p3*; repeat from * to *; end with 1 selvedge stitch.

Row 5: 1 selvedge stitch, *p2, k2tog, k1, yo1, k3, yo1, k1, skp, p2*; repeat from * to *; end with 1 selvedge stitch.

Row 7: 1 selvedge stitch, *p1, k2tog, k1, yo1, k5, yo1, k1, skp, p1*; repeat from * to *; end with 1 selvedge stitch.

Row 9: 1 selvedge stitch, *k2tog, k1, yo1, k7, yo1, k1, skp*; repeat from * to *; end with 1 selvedge stitch.

Keep repeating these 10 rows.

knit stitch on right side or purl stitch on wrong side

− purl stitch on right side or knit stitch on wrong side

O yo: yarn over

× stitch that does not exist

⋋ skp: slip 1 stitch knitwise, knit the next stitch, then pass the slipped stitch over the knit stitch and off the needle

⋏ k2tog: knit 2 together on right side or purl 2 together on wrong side

⋏ k3tog: knit 3 together on right side or purl 3 together on wrong side

⋏ sl 1 kwise, k2tog, psso: slip 1 stitch knitwise, knit the next 2 stitches together, pass the slipped stitch over the stitch obtained and off the needle

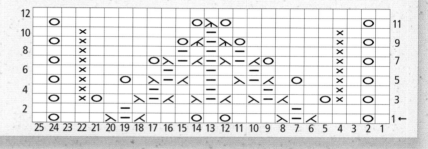

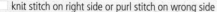

knit stitch on right side or purl stitch on wrong side

− purl stitch on right side or knit stitch on wrong side

O yo: yarn over

⋏ k2tog: knit 2 together on right side or purl 2 together on wrong side

⋋ skp: slip 1 stitch knitwise, knit the next stitch, pass the slipped stitch over the stitch obtained

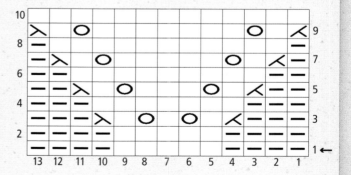

Lace and Eyelet Stitches

Fern Stitch

The directions for this pattern consist of 28 stitches, on background of knit stockinette stitch or purled stockinette stitch.

Row 1 (right side of work): sl 1 kwise, k2tog, psso, k9, yo1, k1, yo1, p2, yo1, k1, yo1, k9, sl 1 kwise, k2tog, psso.

Row 2 and all even numbered rows: knit each stitch as it appears in previous row (i.e., knit a knit stitch, purl a purl stitch) and purl the yarn overs.

Row 3: sl 1 kwise, k2tog, psso, k8, yo1, k1, yo1, k1, p2, k1, yo1, k1, yo1, k8, sl 1 kwise, k2tog, psso.

Row 5: sl 1 kwise, k2tog, psso, k7, yo1, k1, yo1, k2, p2, k2, yo1, k1, yo1, k7, sl 1 kwise, k2tog, psso.

Row 7: sl 1 kwise, k2tog, psso, k6, yo1, k1, yo1, k3, p2, k3, yo1, k1, yo1, k6, sl 1 kwise, k2tog, psso.

Row 9: sl 1 kwise, k2tog, psso, k5, yo1, k1, yo1, k4, p2, k4, yo1, k1, yo1, k5, sl 1 kwise, k2tog, psso.

Keep repeating these 10 rows.

☐ knit stitch on right side or purl stitch on wrong side

– purl stitch on right side or knit stitch on wrong side

O yo: yarn over

⅄ sl 1 kwise, k2tog, psso: slip 1 stitch knitwise, knit the next 2 stitches together, pass the slipped stitch over the stitch obtained and off the needle

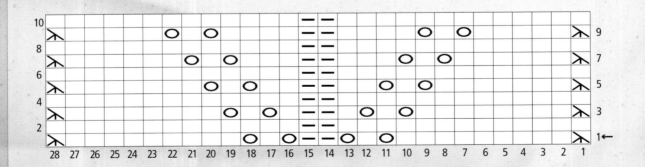

Ginkgo Leaf Stitch

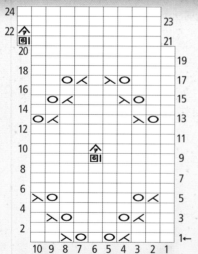

Number of stitches needed for symmetry: multiple of 10 + 1 + 1 selvedge stitch at each end.

Row 1 (right side of work): 1 selvedge stitch, *k3, k2tog, yo1, k1, yo1, skp, k2*; repeat from * to *; end with k1, 1 selvedge stitch.

Rows 2, 4, 6, 8, 12, 14, 16, 18, 20, and 24: all purl.

Row 3: 1 selvedge stitch, *k2, k2tog, yo1, k3, yo1, skp, k1*; repeat from * to *; end with k1, 1 selvedge stitch.

Row 5: 1 selvedge stitch, *k1, k2tog, yo1, k5, yo1, skp*; repeat from * to *; end with k1, 1 selvedge stitch.

Rows 7, 11, 19, and 23: all knit.

Row 9: 1 selvedge stitch, *k6, make 1 long loop in each of 6 eyelets (slide right needle into first eyelet in Row 5 from front to back, yo1, bring a long loop back through, and keeping it on the needle, repeat for each of the following 5 eyelets), k4*; repeat from * to *; end with k1, 1 selvedge stitch.

Row 10: 1 selvedge stitch, p1, *p4, purl together the 6 long loops and the following stitch, p5*; repeat from * to *; end with 1 selvedge stitch.

Row 13: 1 selvedge stitch, *k1, yo1, skp, k5, k2tog, yo1*; repeat from * to *; end with k1, 1 selvedge stitch.

Row 15: 1 selvedge stitch, *k2, yo1, skp, k3, k2tog, yo1, k1*; repeat from * to *; end with k1, 1 selvedge stitch.

Row 17: 1 selvedge stitch, *k3, yo1, skp, k1, k2tog, yo1, k2*; repeat from * to *; end with k1, 1 selvedge stitch.

Row 21: 1 selvedge stitch, k1, make 1 long loop in each of the 3 eyelets (slide the right needle into the first eyelet in Row 7, yo1, bring a long loop back through, and keeping it on the needle, repeat for the following 2 eyelets), *k10, make 1 long loop in each of the 6 eyelets as in Row 9*; repeat from * to *; end with k10, make 1 long loop in each of the 3 eyelets, 1 selvedge stitch.

Row 22: 1 selvedge stitch, purl together the 3 long loops and the next stitch, p9, *purl together the 6 long loops and the following stitch, p9*; repeat from * to *; end by purling together the 3 long loops and the next stitch, 1 selvedge stitch.

Keep repeating these 24 rows.

☐ knit stitch on right side or purl stitch on wrong side

O yo: yarn over

⟍ skp: slip 1 stitch knitwise, knit the next stitch, then pass the slipped stitch over the knit stitch and off the needle

⟋ k2tog: knit 2 together on right side or purl 2 together on wrong side

▣ on right side of work, make 1 long loop in each eyelet: slide the right needle into the first eyelet in Row 5 from front to back, yo1, bring a long loop back through, and keeping it on the needle, repeat for each of the following 5 eyelets

⋀ purl 7 stitches together on wrong side

Bear Paws

Number of stitches needed for symmetry: multiple of 23 + 1 selvedge stitch at each end.

Row 1 (right side of work): 1 selvedge stitch, *k2, p4, k1, p4, k1, p4, k1, p4, k2*; repeat from * to *; end with 1 selvedge stitch.

Row 2 and all even numbered rows: knit each stitch as it appears in previous row (i.e., knit a knit stitch, purl a purl stitch) and purl the yarn overs.

Row 3: 1 selvedge stitch, *k1, yo1, k1, p2, p2tog, k1, p4, k1, p4, k1, p2tog, p2, k1, yo1, k1*; repeat from * to *; end with 1 selvedge stitch.

Row 5: 1 selvedge stitch, *k2, yo1, k1, p3, k1, p2, p2tog, k1, p2tog, p2, k1, p3, k1, yo1, k2*; repeat from * to *; end with 1 selvedge stitch.

Row 7: 1 selvedge stitch, *k3, yo1, k1, p1, p2tog, k1, p3, k1, p3, k1, p2tog, p1, k1, yo1, k3*; repeat from * to *; end with 1 selvedge stitch.

Row 9: 1 selvedge stitch, *k4, yo1, k1, p2, k1, p1, p2tog, k1, p2tog, p1, k1, p2, k1, yo1, k4*; repeat from * to *; end with 1 selvedge stitch.

Row 11: 1 selvedge stitch, *k5, yo1, k1, p2tog, k1, p2, k1, p2, k1, p2tog, k1, yo1, k5*; repeat from * to *; end with 1 selvedge stitch.

Row 13: 1 selvedge stitch, *k6, yo1, k1, p1, k1, p2tog, k1, p2tog, k1, p1, k1, yo1, k6*; repeat from * to *; end with 1 selvedge stitch.

Keep repeating these 14 rows.

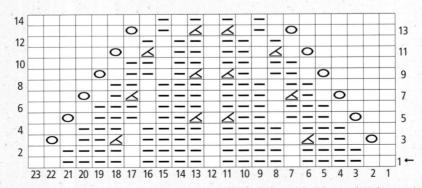

knit stitch on right side or purl stitch on wrong side

− purl stitch on right side or knit stitch on wrong side

O yo: yarn over

⊿ p2tog: purl 2 together on right side or knit 2 together on wrong side

Tulips

Number of stitches needed for symmetry: multiple of 13 + 1 selvedge stitch at each end.

Row 1 (right side of work): all purl.

Row 2: all knit.

Row 3: 1 selvedge stitch, *p6, inc 6 in 1 st (k1, p1, k1, p1, k1, p1), p6*; repeat from * to *; end with 1 selvedge stitch.

Rows 4 and 6: 1 selvedge stitch, *k6, p6, k6*; repeat from * to *; end with 1 selvedge stitch.

Row 5: 1 selvedge stitch, *p6, k6, p6*; repeat from * to *, end with 1 selvedge stitch.

Row 7: 1 selvedge stitch, *p2tog, p2tog, p2, k2, yo1, k2, yo1, k2, p2, p2tog, p2tog; repeat from * to *; end with 1 selvedge stitch.

Row 8: 1 selvedge stitch, *k4, p8, k4*; repeat from * to *; end with 1 selvedge stitch.

Row 9: 1 selvedge stitch, *p2tog, p2tog, k2tog, yo1, k1, yo1, k2tog, yo1, k1, yo1, k2tog, p2tog, p2tog; repeat from * to *; end with 1 selvedge stitch.

Row 10: 1 selvedge stitch, *k2, p9, k2*; repeat from * to *; end with 1 selvedge stitch.

Keep repeating these 10 rows.

 knit stitch on right side or purl stitch on wrong side

− purl stitch on right side or knit stitch on wrong side

O yo: yarn over

⊿ p2tog: purl 2 together on right side or knit 2 together on wrong side

⊾ k2tog: knit 2 together on right side or purl 2 together on wrong side

⑥ inc 6 in 1 st (k1, p1, k1, p1, k1, p1): make 6 stitches in 1 stitch, alternating knit, purl

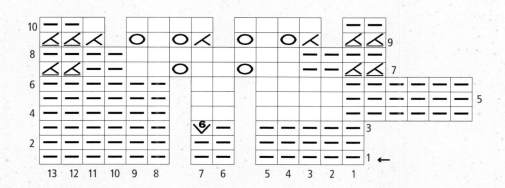

Lace and Eyelet Stitches

Obstacles

Number of stitches needed for symmetry: multiple of 14 + 1 + 1 selvedge stitch at each end.

Row 1 (right side of work): 1 selvedge stitch, *p2, k2tog, k3, yo1, k1, yo1, k3, skp, p1*; repeat from * to *; end with p1, 1 selvedge stitch.

Row 2 and all even numbered rows: knit each stitch as it appears in previous row (i.e., knit a knit stitch, purl a purl stitch).

Row 3: 1 selvedge stitch, *p2, k2tog, k2, yo1, k3, yo1, k2, skp, p1*; repeat from * to *; end with p1, 1 selvedge stitch.

Row 5: 1 selvedge stitch, *p2, k2tog, k1, yo1, k5, yo1, k1, skp, p1*; repeat from * to *; end with p1, 1 selvedge stitch.

Row 7: 1 selvedge stitch, *p2, k2tog, yo1, k7, yo1, skp, p1*; repeat from * to *; end with p1, 1 selvedge stitch.

Row 9: 1 selvedge stitch, *k1, yo1, k3, skp, p3, k2tog, k3, yo1*; repeat from * to *; end with k1, 1 selvedge stitch.

Row 11: 1 selvedge stitch, *k2, yo1, k2, skp, p3, k2tog, k2, yo1, k1*; repeat from * to *; end with k1, 1 selvedge stitch.

Row 13: 1 selvedge stitch, *k3, yo1, k1, skp, p3, k2tog, k1, yo1, k2*; repeat from * to *; end with k1, 1 selvedge stitch.

Alternating Ribs

Number of stitches needed for symmetry: multiple of 6 + 3 + 1 selvedge stitch at each end.

Row 1 (right side of work): 1 selvedge stitch, *k3, p3*; repeat from * to *; end with k3, 1 selvedge stitch.

Rows 2, 3, and 4: knit each stitch as it appears in previous row (i.e., knit a knit stitch, purl a purl stitch).

Row 5: 1 selvedge stitch, *sl 1 kwise, k2tog, psso, p3*; repeat from * to *; end with sl 1 kwise, k2tog, psso, 1 selvedge stitch.

Row 6: 1 selvedge stitch, inc 3 in 1 st (k1, p1, k1), *sl 1 kwise, k2tog, psso, inc 3 in 1 st (k1, p1, k1)*; repeat from * to *; end with 1 selvedge stitch.

Row 7: 1 selvedge stitch, *p3, inc 3 in 1 st (k1, p1, k1)*; repeat from * to *; end with p3, 1 selvedge stitch.

Row 8: 1 selvedge stitch, k3, *p3, k3*; repeat from * to *; end with 1 selvedge stitch.

Rows 9 to 16: knit each stitch as it appears in previous row (i.e., knit a knit stitch, purl a purl stitch).

Row 17: 1 selvedge stitch, *p3, sl 1 kwise, k2tog, psso*; repeat from * to *; end with p3, 1 selvedge stitch.

Row 15: 1 selvedge stitch, *k4, yo1, skp, p3, k2tog, yo1, k3*; repeat from * to *; end with k1, 1 selvedge stitch.
Keep repeating these 16 rows.

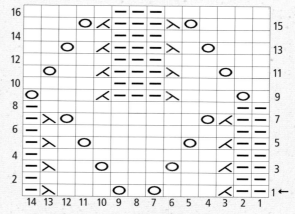

☐ knit stitch on right side or purl stitch on wrong side

– purl stitch on right side or knit stitch on wrong side

O yo: yarn over

╱ k2tog: knit 2 together on right side or purl 2 together on wrong side

╲ skp: slip 1 stitch knitwise, knit the next stitch, then pass the slipped stitch over the knit stitch and off the needle

Row 18: 1 selvedge stitch, sl 1 kwise, k2tog, psso, *inc 3 in 1 st (k1, p1, k1), sl 1 kwise, k2tog, psso*; repeat from * to *; end with 1 selvedge stitch.
Row 19: 1 selvedge stitch, *inc 3 in 1 st (k1, p1, k1), p3*; repeat from * to *; end with inc 3 in 1 st (k1, p1, k1), 1 selvedge stitch.
Row 20: 1 selvedge stitch, p3, *k3, p3*; repeat from * to *; end with 1 selvedge stitch.
Rows 21, 22, 23, and 24: knit each stitch as it appears in previous row (i.e., knit a knit stitch, purl a purl stitch).
Keep repeating these 24 rows.

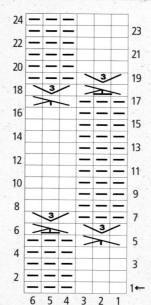

☐ knit stitch on right side or purl stitch on wrong side

– purl stitch on right side or knit stitch on wrong side

⤳ inc 3 in 1 st (k1, p1, k1): make 3 stitches in 1 stitch, alternating knit, purl

⤳ sl 1 knitwise, k2tog, psso on right side: slip 1 stitch knitwise, knit the next 2 stitches together, pass the slipped stitch over the stitch obtained and off the needle

⤳ sl 1 knitwise, k2tog, psso on wrong side: slip 1 stitch knitwise, knit the next 2 stitches together, pass the slipped stitch over the stitch obtained

Lace and Eyelet Stitches

Cross-Stitch Eyelets

Number of stitches needed for symmetry: multiple of 6 + 1 selvedge stitch at each end.

Rows 1 (right side of work) and 3: all knit.

Rows 2 and 4: all purl.

Row 5: 1 selvedge stitch, *1 long purl stitch (slide the right needle into the stitch as if to purl, yo3, purl as usual)*; repeat from * to *; end with 1 selvedge stitch.

Row 6: 1 selvedge stitch, *knit 6 left cross stitches (3 and 3: sl 3 on a cable needle in front of work, k3 from left needle, then k3 from cable needle)*; repeat from * to *; end with 1 selvedge stitch.

Keep repeating these 6 rows.

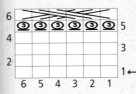

☐ knit stitch on right side or purl stitch on wrong side

℗ long purl stitch: slide the right needle into the stitch as if to purl, yo3, purl as usual

⤬⤬ 6 left cross stitches: sl 3 on a cable needle in front of work, k3 from left needle, then k3 from cable needle

sl: slip stitch from one needle to another without knitting it

Bluebells

Number of stitches needed for symmetry: multiple of 6 + 2 + 1 selvedge stitch at each end.

Row 1 (right side of work): all knit.

Row 2: 1 selvedge stitch, k1, *p5tog, inc 5 in 1 st (k1, p1, k1, p1, k1)*; repeat from * to *; end with k1, 1 selvedge stitch.

Rows 3 and 5: all purl.

Row 4: 1 selvedge stitch, k1, *inc 5 in 1 st (k1, p1, k1, p1, k1), p5tog*; repeat from * to *; end with k1, 1 selvedge stitch.

Row 6: all long knit stitches (slide right needle into stitch as if to knit, yo3, knit as usual).

Row 7: knit all, letting yarn overs slip off the needle.

Keep repeating Rows 2 through 7.

Long-Stitch Eyelets

Number of stitches needed for joining: multiple of 6 + 1 selvedge stitch at each end.

Row 1 (right side of work): all knit.

Row 2: 1 selvedge stitch, *k1, yo3*; repeat from * to *; end with 1 selvedge stitch.

Row 3: 1 selvedge stitch, *6 right cross stitches (sl 6 on the right needle, letting the 3 yarn overs between each stitch slide off, slip stitches back to the left needle, bring the last 3 over the first 3 but leave them on the left needle, k6)*; repeat from * to *; end with 1 selvedge stitch.

Row 4: all knit.

Keep repeating these 4 rows.

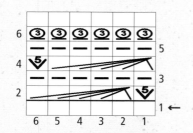

☐ knit stitch on right side or purl stitch on wrong side

– purl stitch on right side or knit stitch on wrong side

② long knit stitch: slide right needle into stitch as if to knit, yo3, knit as usual

Ⅴ inc 5 in 1 st (k1, p1, k1, p1, k1): make 5 stitches in 1 alternating knit, purl (2 times) and ending with a knit stitch

⟍ p5tog: purl 5 together

Knit Below Stitches

Combined with stitches knitted as usual, they are the basis for many patterns in relief.

Knit Below Stitches

Beaded Rib

Number of stitches needed for symmetry: multiple of 2 + 1 + 1 selvedge stitch at each end.

Row 1 (right side of work): all knit.

Row 2: 1 selvedge stitch, p1, *k1b, p1*; repeat from * to *; end with 1 selvedge stitch.

Keep repeating these 2 rows.

On wrong side of work, you will obtain a Fisherman's Rib.

☐ knit stitch on right side or purl stitch on wrong side

⌒ p1b on right side or k1b on wrong side: purl 1 on right side or knit 1 on wrong side by inserting the right needle not into the next stitch on the left needle but into the stitch immediately below it. Let the stitch above slide off the left needle; it will drop down 1 row

Knit Fisherman's Rib

Number of stitches needed for symmetry: multiple of 2 + 1 + 1 selvedge stitch at each end.

Row 1 (right side of work): all knit.

Row 2: 1 selvedge stitch, k1, *k1b, k1*; repeat from * to *; end with 1 selvedge stitch.

Row 3: 1 selvedge stitch, *k1b, k1*; repeat from * to *; end with k1b, 1 selvedge stitch.

Keep repeating Rows 2 and 3.

☐ knit stitch on right side or purl stitch on wrong side

– purl stitch on right side or knit stitch on wrong side

⋂ k1b on right side or p1b on wrong side: knit 1 on right side or purl 1 on wrong side by inserting the right needle not into the next stitch on the left needle but into the stitch immediately below it. Let the stitch above slide off the left needle; it will drop down 1 row

⌒ p1b on right side or k1b on wrong side: purl 1 on right side or knit 1 on wrong side by inserting the right needle not into the next stitch on the left needle but into the stitch immediately below it. Let the stitch above slide off the left needle; it will drop down 1 row

Purled Fisherman's Rib

Knitters who prefer purling to knitting can work Fisherman's Rib in the following fashion.

Number of stitches needed for symmetry: multiple of 2 + 1 + 1 selvedge stitch at each end.

Row 1 (right side of work): all purl.

Row 2: 1 selvedge stitch, p1, *p1b, p1*; repeat from * to *; end with 1 selvedge stitch.

Row 3: 1 selvedge stitch, *p1b, p1*; repeat from * to *; end with p1b, 1 selvedge stitch.

Keep repeating Rows 2 and 3.

☐ knit stitch on right side or purl stitch on wrong side

− purl stitch on right side or knit stitch on wrong side

⋂ k1b on right side or p1b on wrong side: knit 1 on right side or purl 1 on wrong side by inserting the right needle not into the next stitch on the left needle but into the stitch immediately below it. Let the stitch above slide off the left needle; it will drop down 1 row

⌒ p1b on right side or k1b on wrong side: purl 1 on right side or knit 1 on wrong side by inserting the right needle not into the next stitch on the left needle but into the stitch immediately below it. Let the stitch above slide off the left needle; it will drop down 1 row

Mock Rib

Number of stitches needed for symmetry: multiple of 5 + 4 + 1 selvedge stitch at each end.

Row 1 (right side of work): 1 selvedge stitch, *p4, k1*; repeat from * to *; end with p4, 1 selvedge stitch.

Row 2: all knit.

Row 3: 1 selvedge stitch, *p4, k1b*; repeat from * to *; end with p4, 1 selvedge stitch.

Keep repeating Rows 2 and 3.

☐ knit stitch on right side or purl stitch on wrong side

− purl stitch on right side or knit stitch on wrong side

⋂ k1b on right side or p1b on wrong side: knit 1 on right side or purl 1 on wrong side by inserting the right needle not into the next stitch on the left needle but into the stitch immediately below it. Let the stitch above slide off the left needle; it will drop down 1 row

Honeycomb Stitch (1)

Number of stitches needed for symmetry: multiple of 2 + 1 + 1 selvedge stitch at each end.

Rows 1 (right side of work) and 2: all knit.

Row 3: 1 selvedge stitch, *k1, k1b*; repeat from * to *; end with k1 and 1 selvedge stitch.

Row 4: 1 selvedge stitch, k1, *k1 above the k1b (with your right needle, lift the yarn that was slipped in the preceding row and knit it with the stitch sitting on top of it), k1*; repeat from * to *; end with 1 selvedge stitch.

Row 5: 1 selvedge stitch, *k1b, k1*; repeat from * to *; end with k1b, 1 selvedge stitch.

Row 6: 1 selvedge stitch, k1 above the k1b, *k1, k1 above the k1b*; repeat from * to *; end with 1 selvedge stitch.

Keep repeating the 4 rows from Row 3 through Row 6.

knit stitch on right side or purl stitch on wrong side

− purl stitch on right side or knit stitch on wrong side

⋒ k1b on right side or p1b on wrong side: knit 1 on right side or purl 1 on wrong side by inserting the right needle not into the next stitch on the left needle but into the stitch immediately below it. Let the stitch above slide off the left needle; it will drop down 1 row

T k1 on the wrong side above a k1b: with your right needle, lift the yarn that slipped down from the preceding row and knit it together with the stitch sitting on top of it

Honeycomb Stitch (2)

Number of stitches needed for symmetry: multiple of 2 + 1 + 1 selvedge stitch at each end.

Row 1 (right side of work): all purl.

Row 2: all knit.

Row 3: 1 selvedge stitch, *p1, p1b*; repeat from * to *; end with p1, 1 selvedge stitch.

Row 4: 1 selvedge stitch, k1b, *k1, k1b*; repeat from * to *; end with 1 selvedge stitch.

Keep repeating Rows 3 and 4.

knit stitch on right side or purl stitch on wrong side

− purl stitch on right side or knit stitch on wrong side

⋓ p1b on right side or k1b on wrong side: purl 1 on right side or knit 1 on wrong side by inserting the right needle not into the next stitch on the left needle but into the stitch immediately below it. Let the stitch above slide off the left needle; it will drop down 1 row

Ladders / Corded Rib

Number of stitches needed for symmetry: multiple of 6 + 1 + 1 selvedge stitch at each end.

Row 1 (right side of work): 1 selvedge stitch, *p3, k1, p2*; repeat from * to *; end with p1, 1 selvedge stitch.

Row 2: 1 selvedge stitch, k1, *k1, k1b, p1, k1b, k2*; repeat from * to *; end with 1 selvedge stitch.

Row 3: 1 selvedge stitch, *p3, k1b, p2*; repeat from * to *; end with p1, 1 selvedge stitch.

Keep repeating Rows 2 and 3.

knit stitch on right side or purl stitch on wrong side

− purl stitch on right side or knit stitch on wrong side

⋒ k1b on right side or p1b on wrong side: knit 1 on right side or purl 1 on wrong side by inserting the right needle not into the next stitch on the left needle but into the stitch immediately below it. Let the stitch above slide off the left needle; it will drop down 1 row

⋒ p1b on right side or k1b on wrong side: purl 1 on right side or knit 1 on wrong side by inserting the right needle not into the next stitch on the left needle but into the stitch immediately below it. Let the stitch above slide off the left needle; it will drop down 1 row

Knit Below Stitches

Chevron Ribbing

Number of stitches needed for joining: multiple of 2 + 1 selvedge stitch at each end.

Row 1 (right side of work): 1 selvedge stitch, *k1, p1*; repeat from * to *; end with 1 selvedge stitch.

Row 2: 1 selvedge stitch, *k1, p1b*; repeat from * to *; end with 1 selvedge stitch.

Row 3: 1 selvedge stitch, *2 left cross stitches (k1, p1: purl the second stitch on the left needle first, passing the right needle behind the first, then knit the first stitch)*; repeat from * to *; end with 1 selvedge stitch.

Row 4: 1 selvedge stitch, *p1b, k1*; repeat from * to *; end with 1 selvedge stitch.

Row 5: 1 selvedge stitch, *2 right cross stitches (p1, k1: knit the second stitch on the left needle first, passing the right needle in front of the first, then purl the first stitch)*; repeat from * to *; end with 1 selvedge stitch.

Keep repeating Rows 2 through 5.

☐ knit stitch on right side or purl stitch on wrong side

− purl stitch on right side or knit stitch on wrong side

∩ p1b on right side or k1b on wrong side: purl 1 on right side or knit 1 on wrong side by inserting the right needle not into the next stitch on the left needle but into the stitch immediately below it. Let the stitch above slide off the left needle; it will drop down 1 row

✕ 2 left cross stitches: purl the second stitch on the left needle first, passing the right needle behind the first, then knit the first stitch

✕ 2 right cross stitches: knit the second stitch on the left needle first, passing the right needle behind the first, then purl the first stitch

Checkered Fisherman's Rib

Number of stitches needed for symmetry: multiple of 2 + 1 + 1 selvedge stitch at each end.

Note: Each time you reverse the ribbing—in Rows 8, 14, 20, and so on—pick up the extra loop from the previous row when you knit each k1b.

Row 1 (right side of work): all knit.

Rows 2, 4, and 6: 1 selvedge stitch, k1, *k1b, k1*; repeat from * to *; end with 1 selvedge stitch.

Rows 3, 5, and 7: 1 selvedge stitch, *k1b, k1*; repeat from * to *; end with k1b, 1 selvedge stitch.

Rows 8, 10, and 12: 1 selvedge stitch, k1b, *k1, k1b*; repeat from * to *; end with 1 selvedge stitch.

Rows 9, 11, and 13: 1 selvedge stitch, *k1, k1b*; repeat from * to *; end with k1, 1 selvedge stitch.

Keep repeating the 12 rows between Row 2 and Row 13.

Wheat Germ Stitch

Number of stitches needed for symmetry: multiple of 2 + 1 selvedge stitch at each end.

Row 1 (right side of work), 3, 7, and 9: all knit.

Rows 2, 4, 8, and 10: all purl.

Row 5: 1 selvedge stitch, *p1, k1*; repeat from * to *; end with 1 selvedge stitch.

Row 6: 1 selvedge stitch, *p1, k2b*; repeat from * to *; end with 1 selvedge stitch.

Row 11: 1 selvedge stitch, *k1, p1*; repeat from * to *; end with 1 selvedge stitch.

Row 12: 1 selvedge stitch, *k2b, p1*; repeat from * to *; end with 1 selvedge stitch.

Keep repeating these 12 rows.

☐ knit stitch on right side or purl stitch on wrong side

− purl stitch on right side or knit stitch on wrong side

k2b on wrong side: knit 1 by inserting the right needle not into the next stitch on the left needle but into the stitch two rows below it; slip the corresponding stitch off the left needle; it will fall onto the row without being dropped

---

☐ knit stitch on right side or purl stitch on wrong side

− purl stitch on right side or knit stitch on wrong side

⋒ k1b on right side or p1b on wrong side: knit 1 on right side or purl 1 on wrong side by inserting the right needle not into the next stitch on the left needle but into the stitch immediately below it. Let the stitch above slide off the left needle; it will drop down 1 row

∩ p1b on right side or k1b on wrong side: purl 1 on right side or knit 1 on wrong side by inserting the right needle not into the next stitch on the left needle but into the stitch immediately below it. Let the stitch above slide off the left needle; it will drop down 1 row

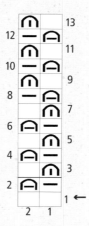

233

Cast-Off Stitches and Fancy Stitches

Cast-off stitches, almost always paired with yarn overs, form unique textures. With fancy stitches, options for patterns are nearly limitless.

Cast-Off Stitches and Fancy Stitches

Bamboo Stitch

Number of stitches needed for symmetry and joining: multiple of 2 + 1 selvedge stitch at each end.
Row 1 (right side of work): 1 selvedge stitch, *yo1, k2, pass yo over k2*; repeat from * to *; end with 1 selvedge stitch.
Row 2: all purl.
Keep repeating these 2 rows.

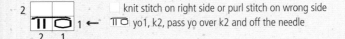

☐ knit stitch on right side or purl stitch on wrong side
yo1, k2, pass yo over k2 and off the needle

Elm Seed Stitch

Number of stitches needed for symmetry: multiple of 4 + 2 + 1 selvedge stitch at each end.
Rows 1 (right side of work) and 3: all knit.
Row 2: 1 selvedge stitch, yo1, p2, pass yo over p2, *p2, yo1, p2, pass yo over p2*; repeat from * to *; end with 1 selvedge stitch.
Row 4: 1 selvedge stitch, p2, *yo1, p2, pass yo over p2, p2*; repeat from * to *; end with 1 selvedge stitch.
Keep repeating these 4 rows.

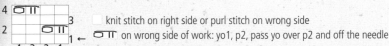

☐ knit stitch on right side or purl stitch on wrong side
on wrong side of work: yo1, p2, pass yo over p2 and off the needle

Stream Stitch

Number of stitches needed for symmetry: multiple of 4 + 1 selvedge stitch at each end.
Row 1 (right side of work): 1 selvedge stitch, *k2tog and without pulling stitches off needle, knit the first stitch again through the back loop, k2*; repeat from * to *; end with 1 selvedge stitch.
Row 2: all purl.
Row 3: 1 selvedge stitch, *k2, k2tog, k2tog and without pulling stitches off needle, knit the first stitch again through the back loop*; repeat from * to *; end with 1 selvedge stitch.
Row 4: all purl.
Keep repeating these 4 rows.

k2tog: knit 2 together

Gathered Bands

Number of stitches needed for joining: multiple of 1 + 1 selvedge stitch at each end.

Note: this stitch uses one small set of needles and one larger set of needles.

Rows 1 (right side of work), 3, and 5, with the smaller needles: all knit.

Rows 2, 4, and 6, with the smaller needles: all knit.

Row 7, with the larger needles: 1 selvedge stitch, *k1 f&b*; repeat from * to *; end with 1 selvedge stitch.

Rows 8, 10, and 12, with the larger needles: all purl.

Rows 9, and 11, with the larger needles: all knit.

Row 13, with the smaller needles: 1 selvedge stitch, *k2tog*; repeat from * to *; end with 1 selvedge stitch.

Keep repeating Rows 2 through 13.

  knit stitch on right side or purl stitch on wrong side

− purl stitch on right side or knit stitch on wrong side

× stitch that does not exist

⅃ k1 f&b: knit 2 stitches in 1 stitch by knitting first into the front of the loop, then into the back

⟋ k2tog: knit 2 together on right side or purl 2 together on wrong side

Mashrabiya

Number of stitches needed for symmetry: multiple of 7 + 5 + 1 selvedge stitch at each end.

Twisted stitch: knit through the back of the loop; purl through the back of the loop.

Row 1 (right side of work): 1 selvedge stitch, *p5, k2 tbl*; repeat from * to *; end with p5, 1 selvedge stitch.

Row 2: 1 selvedge stitch, k5, *p2 tbl, k5*; repeat from * to *; end with 1 selvedge stitch.

Keep repeating these 2 rows.

When your work is finished, use working yarn and a tapestry needle to join the ribs every 10-12 rows, creating a diamond pattern.

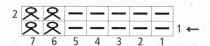

⅄ k tbl: knit 1 through the back of the loop on right side, creating a twisted stitch, or purl 1 through the back of the loop on wrong side

− purl stitch on right side or knit stitch on wrong side

p tbl: purl through the back of the loop

Chain Bracelet Stitch

Number of stitches needed for symmetry: multiple of 8 + 2 + 1 selvedge stitch at each end.

Rows 1 (right side of work), 3, 9, 11, 13, and 15: 1 selvedge stitch, *p2, k2*; repeat from * to *; end with p2, 1 selvedge stitch.

Rows 2, 4, 10, 12, 14, and 16: knit each stitch as it appears in previous row (i.e., knit a knit stitch, purl a purl stitch).

Row 5: 1 selvedge stitch, *p2, sl 2 on a cable needle behind work, sl 2 on a second cable needle in front of work, p2tog from left needle, k2 from second cable needle, k2tog from first cable needle*; repeat from * to *; end with p2, 1 selvedge stitch.

Row 6: 1 selvedge stitch, k2, *p4, k2*; repeat from * to *; end with 1 selvedge stitch.

Row 7: 1 selvedge stitch, *p2, k4*; repeat from * to *; end with p2, 1 selvedge stitch.

Smocked Ribbing

Number of stitches needed for symmetry: multiple of 6 + 4 + 1 selvedge stitch at each end.

Rows 1 (right side of work), 3, and 5: 1 selvedge stitch, *k4, p2*; repeat from * to *; end with k4, 1 selvedge stitch.

Row 2 and all even numbered rows: knit each stitch as it appears in previous row (i.e., knit a knit stitch, purl a purl stitch).

Row 7: 1 selvedge stitch, *insert right needle into space after fourth knit stitch on left needle, yo1 and pull loop through, place loop on left needle, k2tog tbl loop and next stitch, k3, p2*; repeat from * to *; end by inserting right needle into space after fourth knit stitch on left needle, yo1 and pull loop through, place loop on left needle, k2tog tbl loop and next stitch, 1 selvedge stitch.

Rows 9, 11, and 13: 1 selvedge stitch, k1, p2, *k4, p2*; repeat from * to *; end with k1, 1 selvedge stitch.

Row 8: 1 selvedge stitch, k2, *sl 1 on a cable needle in front of work, sl 2 on a cable needle behind work, (k1, p1) in next stitch on left needle, k2 from second cable needle, (k1, p1) in stitch on first cable needle, k2*; repeat from * to *; end with 1 selvedge stitch.
Keep repeating these 16 rows.

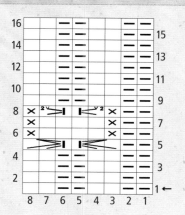

knit stitch on right side or purl stitch on wrong side
× stitch that does not exist
— purl stitch on right side or knit stitch on wrong side
╱ k2tog: knit 2 together on right side or purl 2 together on wrong side
⤜⤛ sl 2 on a cable needle behind work, sl 2 on a second cable needle in front of work, p2tog from left needle, k2 from second cable needle, k2tog from first cable needle

'⤜ ⤛' sl 1 on a cable needle in front of work, sl 2 on a cable needle behind work, (k1, p1) in next stitch on left needle, k2 from second cable needle, (k1, p1) in stitch on first cable needle
sl: slip stitch from one needle to another without knitting it
p2tog: purl 2 together

Row 15: 1 selvedge stitch, k1, p2, *insert right needle into space after fourth knit stitch on left needle, yo1 and pull loop through, place loop on left needle, k2tog tbl loop and next stitch, k3, p2*; repeat from * to *; end with k1, 1 selvedge stitch.
Keep repeating Rows 1 through 16.

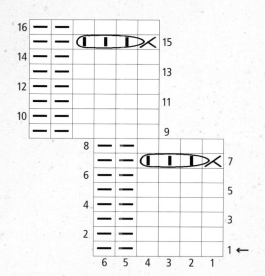

knit stitch on right side or purl stitch on wrong side
— purl stitch on right side or knit stitch on wrong side
⬯╳ insert right needle into space after fourth knit stitch on left needle, yo1 and pull loop through, place loop on left needle, k2tog tbl loop and next stitch, k3
k2tog tbl: knit 2 together through the backs of the loops

Trefoil

Number of stitches needed for joining: multiple of 12 + 1 + 1 selvedge stitch at each end.

Row 1 (right side of work): 1 selvedge stitch, *k1, yo1, k4, sl 1 kwise, k2tog, psso, k4, yo1*; repeat from * to *; end with k1, 1 selvedge stitch.

Row 2 and all even numbered rows: all purl (stitches and yarn overs).

Row 3: 1 selvedge stitch, *k2, yo1, k3, sl 1 kwise, k2tog, psso, k3, yo1, k1*; repeat from * to *; end with k1, 1 selvedge stitch.

Row 5: 1 selvedge stitch, *k3, yo1, insert right needle between seventh and eighth stitches on left needle, yo1 and pull loop through, place it on left needle, k2tog loop and next stitch, k1, sl 1 kwise, k2tog, psso, k2, yo1, k2*; repeat from * to *; end with k1, 1 selvedge stitch.

Row 7: 1 selvedge stitch, k2tog, k4, yo1, *k1, yo1, k4, sl 1 kwise, k2tog, psso, k4, yo1*; repeat from * to *; end with k1, yo1, k4, skp, 1 selvedge stitch.

Row 9: 1 selvedge stitch, k2tog, k3, yo1, k1, *k2, yo1, k3, sl 1 kwise, k2tog, psso, k3, yo1, k1*; repeat from * to *; end with k2, yo1, k3, skp, 1 selvedge stitch.

Row 11: 1 selvedge stitch, k2tog, k2, yo1, k2, *k3, yo1, insert right needle between seventh and eighth stitches on left needle, yo1 and pull loop through, place it on left needle, k2tog loop and next stitch, k1, sl 1 kwise, k2tog, psso, k2, yo1, k2*; repeat from * to *; end with k3, yo1, k2, skp, 1 selvedge stitch.

Keep repeating these 12 rows.

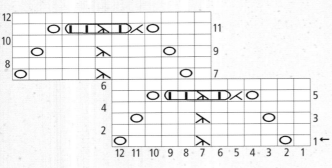

☐ knit stitch on right side or purl stitch on wrong side

O yo: yarn over

⅄ sl 1 kwise, k2tog, psso: slip 1 stitch knitwise, knit the next 2 stitches together, pass the slipped stitch over the stitch obtained and off the needle

⊏⅄⊐╳ on right side of work: insert right needle between seventh and eighth stitches on left needle, yo1 and pull loop through, place it on left needle, k2tog loop and next stitch, k1, sl 1 kwise, k2tog, psso, k2

k2tog: knit 2 together

Acorns

Number of stitches needed for symmetry: multiple of 6 + 1 + 1 selvedge stitch at each end.

Row 1 (right side of work): 1 selvedge stitch, *k4, p2*; repeat from * to *; end with k1, 1 selvedge stitch.

Rows 2, 3, 4, 8, 9, 10, and 14: knit each stitch as it appears in previous row (i.e., knit a knit stitch, purl a purl stitch).

Row 5: 1 selvedge stitch, *insert right needle into space after fourth stitch on left needle, yo1 and pull loop through, place it on left needle, k1, p2, k3*; repeat from * to *; end with k1, 1 selvedge stitch.

Row 6: 1 selvedge stitch, p1, *p3, k2, p2tog*; repeat from * to *; end with 1 selvedge stitch.

Row 7: 1 selvedge stitch, *k1, p2, k3*; repeat from * to *; end with k1, 1 selvedge stitch.

Row 11: 1 selvedge stitch, k1, *k2, insert right needle into space after fourth stitch on left needle, yo1 and pull loop through, place it on left needle, k1, p2, k1*; repeat from * to *; end with 1 selvedge stitch.

Row 12: 1 selvedge stitch, *p1, k2, p2tog, p2*; repeat from * to *; end with p1, 1 selvedge stitch.

Row 13: 1 selvedge stitch, k1, *k3, p2, k1*; repeat from * to *; end with 1 selvedge stitch.

Keep repeating Rows 3 through 14.

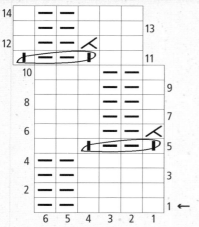

☐ knit stitch on right side or purl stitch on wrong side

− purl stitch on right side or knit stitch on wrong side

⟋ k2tog: knit 2 together on right side or purl 2 together on wrong side

⟞−⟝ on right side of work: insert right needle into space after fourth stitch on left needle, yo1 and pull loop through, place it on left needle, k1, p2, k1

p2tog: purl 2 together

Garland Stitch

Number of stitches needed for symmetry and connections: multiple of 9 + 1 selvedge stitch at each end.

Row 1 (right side of work): 1 selvedge stitch, *p2, k5, p2*; repeat from * to *; end with 1 selvedge stitch.

Rows 2 and 4: 1 selvedge stitch, *k2, p5, k2*; repeat from * to *; end with 1 selvedge stitch.

Row 3: 1 selvedge stitch, *p2, m1, k1, p3tog, k1, m1 tbl, p2 *; repeat from * to *; end with 1 selvedge stitch.

Keep repeating these 4 rows.

knit stitch on right side or purl stitch on wrong side

− purl stitch on right side or knit stitch on wrong side

⩘ p3tog: purl 3 together on right side

◀ m1: using the left needle, pick up the strand between 2 stitches from back to front and knit as usual to increase 1

▶ m1 tbl: using the left needle, pick up the strand between 2 stitches from front to back, and k1 through the back loop to increase 1

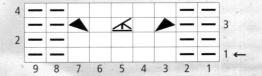

Granite Stitch

Number of stitches needed for symmetry: multiple of 2 + 1 selvedge stitch at each end.

Row 1 (right side of work): all knit.

Row 2: 1 selvedge stitch, *k2tog*; repeat from * to *; end with 1 selvedge stitch.

Row 3: 1 selvedge stitch, *k1 f&b*; repeat from * to *; end with 1 selvedge stitch.

Row 4: all purl.

Keep repeating these 4 rows.

✕ k2tog: knit 2 together on right side or purl 2 together on wrong side

Ⅴ k1 f&b: knit 2 stitches in 1 stitch by knitting first into the front of the loop, then into the back

Daisy Stitch

Number of stitches needed for symmetry: multiple of 4 + 1 selvedge stitch at each end.

Row 1 (right side of work): 1 selvedge stitch, *p1, yo1*; repeat from * to *; end with 1 selvedge stitch.

Row 2: 1 selvedge stitch, *slip 4 stitches onto right needle, dropping the yarn overs, replace the 4 now elongated stitches onto the left needle, then °insert the right needle into these 4 stitches, from left to right, yo1, pull a loop through and put it on the left needle (leave the 4 stitches on the left needle), k1 in this loop°; repeat from ° to ° 3 more times then take the 4 stitches off the left needle*; repeat from * to *; end with 1 selvedge stitch.

Row 3: 1 selvedge stitch; p2, *p1, yo1*; repeat from * to *; end with p2, 1 selvedge stitch.

Row 4: same as Row 2 except because of decreasing by 2 stitches, start with 1 selvedge stitch, k2 and end with k2, 1 selvedge stitch.

Keep repeating these 4 rows.

Cast-Off Stitches and Fancy Stitches

Berry Stitch

Number of stitches needed for symmetry: multiple of 4 + 1 selvedge stitch at each end.

Row 1 (right side of work): all purl.

Row 2: 1 selvedge stitch, *inc 3 in 1 st (k1, p1, k1), k3tog*; repeat from * to *; end with 1 selvedge stitch.

Rows 3 and 5: all purl.

Row 4: 1 selvedge stitch, *k3tog, inc 3 in 1 st (k1, p1, k1)*; repeat from * to *; end with 1 selvedge stitch.

Keep repeating Rows 2 through 5.

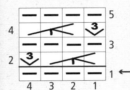

— purl stitch on right side or knit stitch on wrong side

⅊ inc 3 in 1 st (k1, p1, k1): make 3 stitches in 1 stitch, alternating knit, purl

⟋ k3tog: knit 3 together on right side or purl 3 together on wrong side

Popcorn

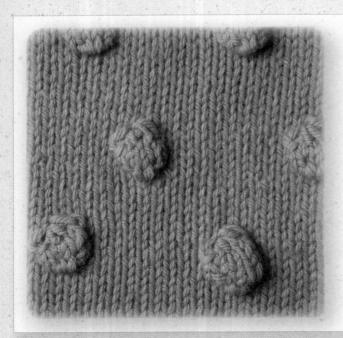

Number of stitches needed for symmetry: multiple of 12 +11 + 1 selvedge stitch at each end.

Rows 1 (right side of work), 3, and 5: all knit.

Row 2 and all even numbered rows: all purl.

Row 7: 1 selvedge stitch, *k5, 1 bobble (inc 5 in 1 st [k1, p1, k1, p1, k1], turn work: p5, turn work: k5, turn work: p5, turn work: k5, then pass the first 4 stitches over the fifth and off the needle, starting with the nearest), k6*; repeat from * to *; end with k5, 1 bobble, k5, 1 selvedge stitch.

Rows 9, 11, 13, 15, and 17: all knit.

Row 19: 1 selvedge stitch, *k11, 1 bobble*; repeat from * to *; end with k11, 1 selvedge stitch.

Rows 21 and 23: all knit.

Keep repeating these 24 rows.

Cells

Number of stitches needed for symmetry: multiple of 2 + 1 + 1 selvedge stitch at each end.

Row 1 (right side of work): 1 selvedge stitch, k1, *k1 by inserting the right needle into the space between the first and second stitches on the left needle, k2*; repeat from * to *; end with 1 selvedge stitch.

Row 2: 1 selvedge stitch, p1, *p1, p2tog*; repeat from * to *; end with 1 selvedge stitch.

Row 3: 1 selvedge stitch, k2, *k1 by inserting the right needle into the space between the first and second stitches on the left needle, k2*; repeat from * to *; end with k1 by inserting the right needle into the space between the first and second stitches on the left needle, k1, 1 selvedge stitch.

Row 4: 1 selvedge stitch, *p1, p2tog*; repeat from * to *; end with p1, 1 selvedge stitch.

Keep repeating these 4 rows.

p2tog: purl 2 together

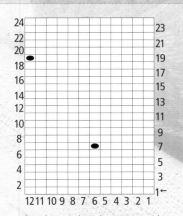

☐ knit stitch on right side or purl stitch on wrong side

● 1 bobble: inc 5 in 1 st [k1, p1, k1, p1, k1], turn work: p5, turn work: k5, turn work: p5, turn work: k5, then pass the first 4 stitches over the fifth and off the needle, starting with the nearest

inc 5 in 1 st (k1, p1, k1, p1, k1): make 5 stitches in 1 stitch, alternating knit, purl

Oblique Pillar Stitch

Number of stitches needed for symmetry: multiple of 6 + 1 selvedge stitch at each end.

Row 1 (right side of work): 1 selvedge stitch, *k2, 1 bobble (inc 6 in 1 st [k1, p1, k1, p1, k1, p1], then pass the first 5 stitches over the sixth and off the needle, starting with the nearest), p3*; repeat from * to *; end with k2, 1 bobble, p3, 1 selvedge stitch.

Row 2 and all even numbered rows: knit each stitch as it appears in previous row (i.e., knit a knit stitch, purl a purl stitch).

Row 3: 1 selvedge stitch, p1, *k2, 1 bobble, p3*; repeat from * to *; end with k2, 1 bobble, p2, 1 selvedge stitch.

Row 5: 1 selvedge stitch, p2, *k2, 1 bobble, p3*; repeat from * to *; end with k2, 1 bobble, p1, 1 selvedge stitch.

Row 7: 1 selvedge stitch, p3, *k2, 1 bobble, p3*; repeat from * to *; end with k2, 1 bobble, 1 selvedge stitch.

Row 9: 1 selvedge stitch, 1 bobble, p3, *k2, 1 bobble, p3*; repeat from * to *; end with k2, 1 selvedge stitch.

Row 11: 1 selvedge stitch, k1, 1 bobble, p3, *k2, 1 bobble, p3*; repeat from * to *; end with k1, 1 selvedge stitch.

Keep repeating these 12 rows.

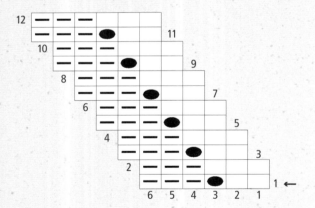

☐ knit stitch on right side or purl stitch on wrong side

— purl stitch on right side or knit stitch on wrong side

● bobble: inc 6 in 1 st [k1, p1, k1, p1, k1, p1], then pass the first 5 stitches over the sixth and off the needle, starting with the nearest

inc 6 in 1 st (k1, p1, k1, p1, k1, p1): make 6 stitches in 1 stitch, alternating knit, purl

Rosebud Stitch

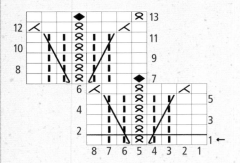

knit stitch on right side or purl stitch on wrong side

ℝ k tbl: knit through the back of the loop on right side (or purl on wrong side)

k2tog: knit 2 together on right side or purl 2 together on wrong side

◆ crochet bobble: insert a crochet hook into a stitch, yo1 on the crochet hook, pull a loop through, yo1, insert the crochet hook into the same stitch, yo1, pull 1 loop through, yo1 and pass it through the 3 loops on the crochet hook, place this stitch on the left needle, purl it

p tbl: purl through the back of the loop

Number of stitches needed for symmetry: multiple of 8 + 1 + 1 selvedge stitch at each end.

Note: This stitch requires a crochet hook.

Rows 1 (right side of work) and 3: 1 selvedge stitch, *k4, k1 tbl, k3*; repeat from * to *; end with k1, 1 selvedge stitch.

Rows 2 and 4: 1 selvedge stitch, p1, *p3, p1 tbl, p4*; repeat from * to *; end with 1 selvedge stitch.

Row 5: 1 selvedge stitch, *k2, insert a crochet hook under the horizontal thread that connects the twisted stitch 4 rows below with the preceding stitch, °yo1 on the crochet hook, pull 1 long loop through, yo1, insert the crochet hook into the same stitch, yo1, pull 1 long loop through, yo1 and pass it through the 3 loops on the crochet hook, place this stitch on the right needle°, k2, k1 tbl, k2, insert a crochet hook under the horizontal thread that connects the twisted stitch 4 rows below with the next stitch, repeat from ° to °, k1*; repeat from * to *; end with k1, 1 selvedge stitch.

Row 6: 1 selvedge stitch, p1, *p2tog, p2, p1 tbl, p2, p2tog, p1*; repeat from * to *; end with 1 selvedge stitch.

Row 7: 1 selvedge stitch, k4, *insert a crochet hook into the next stitch, °yo1 on the crochet hook, pull 1 loop through, yo1, insert the crochet hook into the same stitch, yo1, pull 1 loop through, yo1 and pass it through the 3 loops on the crochet hook, place this stitch on the left needle, purl it°, k3, k1 tbl, k3*; repeat from * to *; end with insert a crochet hook into the next stitch, repeat from ° to °, k4, 1 selvedge stitch.

Rows 8 and 10: 1 selvedge stitch, p5, *p3, p1 tbl, p4*; repeat from * to *; end with p4, 1 selvedge stitch.

Row 9: 1 selvedge stitch, k4, *k4, k1 tbl, k3*; repeat from * to *; end with k5, 1 selvedge stitch.

Row 11: 1 selvedge stitch, k4, *k2, insert a crochet hook under the horizontal thread that connects the twisted stitch 4 rows below with the preceding stitch, °yo1 on the crochet hook, pull a long loop through, yo1, insert the crochet hook into the same stitch, yo1, pull 1 long loop through, yo1 and pass it through the 3 loops on the crochet hook, place this stitch on the right needle°, k2, k1 tbl, k2, insert a crochet hook under the horizontal thread that connects the twisted stitch 4 rows below with the next stitch, repeat from ° to °, k1*; repeat from * to *; end with k5, 1 selvedge stitch.

Row 12: 1 selvedge stitch, p5, *p2tog, p2, p1 tbl, p2, p2tog, p1*; repeat from * to *; end with p4, 1 selvedge stitch.

Row 13: 1 selvedge stitch, k4, *k1 tbl, k3, insert a crochet hook into the next stitch, °yo1 on the crochet hook, pull 1 loop through, yo1, insert the crochet hook into the same stitch, yo1, pull 1 loop through, yo1 and pass it through the 3 loops on the crochet hook, place this stitch on the left needle, and purl it°, k3*; repeat from * to *; end with k1 tbl, k4, 1 selvedge stitch.

Keep repeating Rows 2 through 13.

Fur Stitch

Number of stitches needed for symmetry: multiple of 2 + 1 selvedge stitch at each end.

Row 1 (right side of work): all knit.

Row 2: 1 selvedge stitch, *k1, do not slide stitch off the left needle, bring yarn to front, wind it around your left thumb to form a roughly 1-1/2 inch loop, bring yarn to back, knit the stitch on the left needle again, let it slide off the needle, yo1, pass the 2 stitches on the right needle over the yarn over and off the needle, k1*; repeat from * to *; end with 1 selvedge stitch.

Row 3: all knit.

Row 4: 1 selvedge stitch, *k1, do not slide stitch off the left needle, bring yarn to front, wind it around your left thumb to form a roughly 1-1/2 inch loop, bring yarn to back, knit the stitch on the left needle again, let it slide off the needle, yo1, pass the 2 stitches on the right needle over the yarn over and off the needle*; repeat from * to *; end with 1 selvedge stitch.

Keep repeating these 4 rows.

Pillows made with the stitches in this book...

Ecru Pillow

DIMENSIONS: 14" x 14" (35 cm x 35 cm)

MATERIALS: approx. 288 yd (264 m) worsted weight yarn (4 skeins of 72 yd or 66 m), size 9 (5.5 mm) needles, 14" x 14" (35 cm x 35 cm) pillow to cover or synthetic stuffing

STITCHES UTILIZED: Rib Stitch k1, p1 (p. 19), Knit Stockinette Stitch (p. 18)

DIRECTIONS:
Side 1: Cast on 50 stitches using size 9 needles (5.5 mm), and knit in stockinette (see page 18). At 14" (35 cm) in height, cast off loosely.
Side 2: Cast on 80 stitches using size 9 needles (5.5 mm), and knit in Rib Stitch k1, p1 (see page 19). At 14" (35 cm) in height, cast off loosely.

MAKING UP AND FINISHING TOUCHES: Join the two pieces on three sides. Slide a pillow into the cover or fill it with synthetic stuffing. Close the pillow by sewing up the last side.

Pillows made with the stitches in this book

Navy Blue Pillow

DIMENSIONS: 14" x 14" (35 cm x 35 cm)

MATERIALS: approx. 288 yd (264 m) worsted weight yarn (4 skeins of 72 yd or 66 m), size 9 (5.5 mm) needles, cable needle, 14" x 14" (35 cm x 35 cm) pillow to cover or synthetic stuffing

STITCHES UTILIZED: Knit Stockinette Stitch (p. 18), Lattices (p. 132)

DIRECTIONS:
Side 1: Cast on 50 stitches using size 9 (5.5 mm) needles, and knit in Knit Stockinette Stitch (p. 18). At 14" (35 cm) in height, cast off loosely.
Side 2: Cast on 74 stitches using size 9 (5.5 mm) needles, and knit in Lattices (see p. 132). At 14" (35 cm) in height, cast off loosely.

MAKING UP AND FINISHING TOUCHES:
Join the two pieces on three sides. Slide a pillow into the cover or fill it with synthetic stuffing. Close the pillow by sewing up the last side.

Heather Pillow

DIMENSIONS: 14" x 14" (35 cm x 35 cm)

MATERIALS: approx. 544 yd (500 m) sport weight yarn (4 skeins of 136 yd or 125 m), size 9 (5.5 mm) needles, 14" x 14" (35 cm x 35 cm) pillow to cover or synthetic stuffing

STITCHES UTILIZED: Knit Stockinette Stitch (p. 18), Diamond Blister Stitch (p. 26)

DIRECTIONS:
Side 1: Cast on 50 stitches using double yarn and size 9 (5.5 mm) needles, and knit in Knit Stockinette Stitch (p. 18). At 14" (35 cm) in height, cast off loosely.
Side 2: Cast on 63 stitches using double yarn and size 9 (5.5 mm) needles, and knit in Diamond Blister Stitch (p. 26). At 14" (35 cm) in height, cast off loosely.

MAKING UP AND FINISHING TOUCHES:
Join the two pieces on three sides. Slide a pillow into the cover or fill it with synthetic stuffing. Close the pillow by sewing up the last side.

Pink Pillow

DIMENSIONS: 14" x 14" (35 cm x 35 cm)

MATERIALS: approx. 544 yd (500 m) sport weight yarn (4 skeins of 136 yd or 125 m), size 9 (5.5 mm) needles, 14" x 14" (35 cm x 35 cm) pillow to cover or synthetic stuffing

STITCHES UTILIZED: Knit Stockinette Stitch (p. 18), Ladder Eyelets (p. 185)

DIRECTIONS:
Side 1: Cast on 50 stitches using double yarn and size 9 (5.5 mm) needles, and knit in Knit Stockinette Stitch (p. 18). At 14" (35 cm) in height, cast off loosely.
Side 2: Cast on 63 stitches using double yarn and size 9 (5.5 mm) needles, and knit in Ladder Eyelets (p. 185). At 14" (35 cm) in height, cast off loosely.

MAKING UP AND FINISHING TOUCHES:
Join the two pieces on three sides. Slide a pillow into the cover or fill it with synthetic stuffing. Close the pillow by sewing up the last side.

Sky Blue Pillow

DIMENSIONS: 14" x 14" (35 cm x 35 cm)

MATERIALS: approx. 544 yd (500 m) sport weight yarn (4 skeins of 136 yd or 125 m), Size 9 (5.5 mm) needles, 14" x 14" (35 cm x 35 cm) pillow to cover or synthetic stuffing

STITCHES UTILIZED: Knit Stockinette Stitch (p. 18), Beaded Rib (p. 228)

DIRECTIONS:
Side 1: Cast on 50 stitches using double yarn and size 9 (5.5 mm) needles, and knit in Knit Stockinette Stitch (p. 18). At 14" (35 cm) in height, cast off loosely.
Side 2: Cast on 63 stitches using double yarn and size 9 (5.5 mm) needles, and knit in Beaded Rib (p. 228). At 14" (35 cm) in height, cast off loosely.

MAKING UP AND FINISHING TOUCHES:
Join the two pieces on three sides. Slide a pillow into the cover or fill it with synthetic stuffing. Close the pillow by sewing up the last side.

Pillows made with the stitches in this book

Grey Pillow

DIMENSIONS: 14" x 14" (35 cm x 35 cm)

MATERIALS: 288 yd (264 m) worsted weight yarn (4 skeins of 72 yd or 66 m), size 9 needles (5.5 mm), 14" x 14" (35 cm x 35 cm) pillow to cover or synthetic stuffing

STITCHES UTILIZED: Knit Stockinette Stitch (p. 18), Mop Ribbing (p. 177)

DIRECTIONS:
Side 1: Cast on 50 stitches using size 9 needles (5.5 mm), and knit in Knit Stockinette Stitch (p. 18). At 14" (35 cm) in height, cast off loosely.
Side 2: Cast on 63 stitches using size 9 needles (5.5 mm), and knit in Mop Ribbing (p. 177). At 14" (35 cm) in height, cast off loosely.

MAKING UP AND FINISHING TOUCHES: Join the two pieces on three sides. Slide a pillow into the cover or fill it with synthetic stuffing. Close the pillow by sewing up the last side.

Sienna Pillow

DIMENSIONS: 14" x 14" (35 cm x 35 cm)

MATERIALS: 288 yd (264 m) worsted weight yarn (4 skeins of 72 yd or 66 m), size 9 needles (5.5 mm), 14" x 14" (35 cm x 35 cm) pillow to cover or synthetic stuffing

STITCHES UTILIZED: Knit Stockinette Stitch (p. 18), Waves (p. 206)

DIRECTIONS:
Side 1: Cast on 50 stitches using size 9 needles (5.5 mm), and knit in Knit Stockinette Stitch (p. 18). At 14" (35 cm) in height, cast off loosely.
Side 2: Cast on 63 stitches using size 9 needles (5.5 mm), and knit in Waves (p. 206). At 14" (35 cm) in height, cast off loosely.

MAKING UP AND FINISHING TOUCHES: Join the two pieces on three sides. Slide a pillow into the cover or fill it with synthetic stuffing. Close the pillow by sewing up the last side.

Camel Pillow

DIMENSIONS: 14" x 14" (35 cm x 35 cm)

MATERIALS: 288 yd (264 m) worsted weight yarn (4 skeins of 72 yd or 66 m), size 9 needles (5.5 mm), 14" x 14" (35 cm x 35 cm) pillow to cover or synthetic stuffing

STITCHES UTILIZED: Knit Stockinette Stitch (p. 18), Fur Stitch (p. 248)

DIRECTIONS:
Side 1: Cast on 50 stitches using size 9 needles (5.5 mm), and knit in Knit Stockinette Stitch (p. 18). At 14" (35 cm) in height, cast off loosely.
Side 2: Cast on 63 stitches using size 9 needles (5.5 mm), and knit in Fur Stitch (p. 248). At 14" (35 cm) in height, cast off loosely.

MAKING UP AND FINISHING TOUCHES: Join the two pieces on three sides. Slide a pillow into the cover or fill it with synthetic stuffing. Close the pillow by sewing up the last side.

Ecru Pillow

DIMENSIONS: 14" x 14" (35 cm x 35 cm)

MATERIALS: 288 yd (264 m) worsted weight yarn (4 skeins of 72 yd or 66 m), size 9 needles (5.5 mm), cable needle, 14" x 14" (35 cm x 35 cm) pillow to cover or synthetic stuffing

STITCHES UTILIZED: Knit Stockinette Stitch (p. 18), 4-Stitch Cables (right cross) (p. 59)

DIRECTIONS:
Side 1: Cast on 50 stitches using size 9 needles (5.5 mm), and knit in Knit Stockinette Stitch (p. 18). At 14" (35 cm) in height, cast off loosely.
Side 2: Cast on 86 stitches using size 9 needles (5.5 mm), and knit in 4-Stitch Cables (right cross) (p. 59). At 14" (35 cm) in height, cast off loosely.

MAKING UP AND FINISHING TOUCHES: Join the two pieces on three sides. Slide a pillow into the cover or fill it with synthetic stuffing. Close the pillow by sewing up the last side.

Acknowledgments

Thank you to:

BUTONS DU MONDE: www.butonsdumonde.com
COMPTOIR DE FAMILLE: www.comptoir-de-famille.com
ENTRÉE DES FOURNISSEURS: www.lamercerieparisienne.com/en
FLEUX: www.fleux.com

Printed hatboxes: Comptoir de Famille
Wicker heart and linen tablecloth: Butons du Monde
Scissors: Entrée des Fournisseurs

Mini-basket and blue cloth: Butons du Monde
Heart basket: Comptoir de Famille
Wood and bark bird: Fleux

Small picnic basket: Comptoir de Famille

2-basket dish and mauve linen voile tablecloth: Comptoir de Famille
Yarn and scissors: Entrée des Fournisseurs

Square metal box: Comptoir de famille
Flowered cloth: Butons du Monde

Gray-mauve pure linen embroidered place mats:
Comptoir de Famille

Mini-basket: Butons du Monde
Violet linen voile tablecloth: Comptoir de Famille
Scissors: Entrée des Fournisseurs

Polka-dotted linen curtain: Butons du Monde
Heart-shaped basket: Comptoir de Famille

Square metal box: Comptoir de Famille
Blue cloth: Butons du Monde
Measuring tape: Entrée des Fournisseurs

Printed hatbox: Comptoir de Famille
Embroidered table runner: Butons du Monde

Lace cushion cover: Butons du Monde

Oval box: Comptoir de Famille

English adaptation © 2016 Peter Pauper Press, Inc.

Peter Pauper Press would like to thank Vesna Neskow, Miriam Roberts, and Micah Sizemore for their contributions to the English translation.

Published in the United States by Peter Pauper Press, Inc.
202 Mamaroneck Avenue
White Plains, New York 10601
U.S.A.

Published in the United Kingdom and Europe by Peter Pauper Press, Inc.
c/o White Pebble International
Unit 2, Plot 11 Terminus Road
Chichester, West Sussex PO19 8TX, UK

Original title: La Bible du Tricot © 2012 by Éditions Marie Claire—Societé d'Information et de Créations (SIC)
www.editionsmarieclaire.com
Executive Editor: Thierry Lamarre
Concept and production: Charlotte Rion
Photographs: Pierre Nicou
Stylist: Aurélie Tamin
Design: Phildar
Retouching/Digitalization: Jean Michel Boillot
Explanations, grids, knitting, and diagrams: Yolaine Fournie
Graphic design, layout: Either Studio
Cover: Either Studio
Proofs/revisions: Véronique Blanc
Editorial assistant: Marie Lecocq
Phildar coordinator: Myriam Prez

Library of Congress Cataloging-In-Publication Data Available

ISBN 978-1-4413-1971-5
Printed in Hong Kong
7 6 5 4 3 2 1

Visit us at www.peterpauper.com